opy

THE COMPENDIUM
OF NOSH

THE COMPENDIUM OF NOSH

Jack McLean

JOHN MURRAY

© Jack McLean 2006
Illustrations by Jack McLean

First published in Great Britain in 2006 by John Murray (Publishers)
A division of Hodder Headline

1

A CIP catalogue record for this book is available from the British
Library.

ISBN 0 7195 6825 0

Typeset in 10.25/14pt Trump Mediaeval by Servis Filmsetting Ltd,
Manchester

Printed and bound by Clays Ltd, St Ives plc

Hodder Headline policy is to use papers that are natural, renewable
and recyclable products and made from wood grown in sustainable
forests. The logging and manufacturing processes are expected to
conform to the environmental regulations of the country of origin.

John Murray (Publishers)
338 Euston Road
London NW1 3BH

For John and Madeleine

PREFACE

This book came about as a result of a conference on Scottish food in the famous Gleneagles Hotel during a question-and-answer session, when the people who had paid through the nose to be patronized by celebrities tried to get their money's worth from the experts engaged to patronize them. Though I had indeed written on food and cookery, and had been a columnist on the subject, it was as a so-called authority on Scotch whisky that I had been invited.

It was when I discovered that my knowledge of whisky was equalled and indeed outdone by my fellow panellists that I also found that I possessed a huge store of irrelevant arcana on an array of foods and cuisines, and was persuaded to write this book. It was also when I found that I had a huge ignorance of many other aspects of eating, and that I maintained perhaps too flippant an attitude to the subject, that I decided to embark upon this volume. It was meant to be as flippant and frivolous in approach, and certainly short and reasonably concise. Two years later it was no longer short or concise, but I hope I kept the frivolity.

Perhaps the greatest problem that many, today probably most, people have when they confront cooking is the lack of knowledge of the principles of cookery. Despite the plethora of TV cookery shows and countless glossy books, many would-be cooks – particularly and sadly many young women – are anxious and lacking in confidence in the kitchen. The decline of Domestic Science in the school curriculum in the last twenty years or so has meant that many young women no longer know how to cook at all. And certainly have no concept of even the simplest principles of food provision. There was even a time when radical feminists seem to have scorned cookery skills for girls, seeing such things as an aspect of male domination. The situation was not helped when, in the mistaken notion that sex equality meant boys and girls should be considered as somehow the same sex entirely, boys were introduced into the Home Economics classes and brought their frustrations, immaturity and disruptiveness into what was once a haven for many a schoolgirl, and certainly for her cookery teachers.

But I learned about cooking from the toddler stage onwards, 'helping' my mother and grandma in the kitchen. It didn't strike my family as odd behaviour on my part, any more than my obsession with drawing, and reading books. In the working-class community in which I partly grew up the above would indeed have seemed eccentric, but my family was part working-class and part bourgeois. Furthermore my father was a school janitor, then, in Scotland, a job that signified some status and regarded as bestowing a certain labour aristocracy.

It helped that he had been a regular soldier for nearly twenty years and had travelled in China, Egypt and India, as well as in most of the European theatres of war, where he had picked up exotic (and often quixotic) tastes. Add the fact that my grandmother was Cornish, and had been, for an Edwardian girl, well educated. And that my grandfather was a Hungarian whose culinary tastes included much French cuisine. Then again, in the aftermath of the Second World War my native Glasgow possessed large immigrant communities from Italy and Poland and Jewish communities from the Balkans and the Ukraine, many of them stemming from even before the Great War and well integrated, though not so overwhelmingly assimilated as to lose their cuisines. And bear in mind that delicatessens abounded throughout this grittiest of north European cities.

As you will have read many times elsewhere, the war years

and their aftermath of post-war austerity left much British cookery floundering. It has, despite once again all these telly chef shows, never really recovered. You will find a great many references to the Second World War, and indeed to the world conflict before that, in this book. British cookery – and I am British – has been so influenced, in a way less known to any other country, by both conflicts that it is hardly surprising that such references should course through this volume. Britain has a long history and in its glory years of Empire was the most important and influential country in the world, but I suspect that when the same histories are considered in retrospect it will be the years during and just after the Second World War that will display what Britain was in reality, and what it had done to shape the latter half of the twentieth century and the present one as well. This is as yet a little too prescient perhaps, but I think you will find eventually that I Am Right.

In the early 1960s the allure of London – soon to become, in hindsight all too briefly, 'Swinging London' – brought myself along with thousands of other young provincials to the Great Wen, and there I discovered more and different types of food, and more and different nationalities and cultures. I also discovered the arts – theatre, film, literature, painting – and blues bands. For some years in London I worked as a cook, waiter and barman (I was barman in the famous World's End pub at the far end of the King's Road). I worked in pubs, restaurants, cafés and hotels. Then I became a commercial artist, went off to art college in Edinburgh, taught art for a while, became a writer and broadcaster, and, though I do not much like travelling, travelled a lot in the nature of my journalistic career. All these play a major part in my attitude to food and, well, of course, everything else.

Here's a confession too. I don't actually eat very much myself, though I love to eat out: I just don't consume much. It is cooking I love. Friends like me to come round and cook for them, which I gladly do. They pay for the materials and, of course, the drink that I, like all decent cooks, shove down my throat throughout the process. But then, I have been cooking for others much of my life, first in my own parental home, later as a young man living in bedsits and then as a student, a time in which my culinary skills were highly prized as most of my young (and younger: I was a mature student) coevals were straight from school and home, where their fond mamas had prepared all their meals.

There may very well have been a time when it was considered 'cissy' for a man to cook the meal in the average domestic home, but I have never encountered the allegation of effeminacy towards my love of cooking. Indeed in my circle of friends it is astounding how many of my male chums do the cooking, and not only the fancy dinner-party stuff but also the day-to-day routine of mealtimes.

And talking of fancy. Too much British restaurant cookery today is bloody ludicrous in its attempts at absurd experimentation. Cooking is, or should be, generally simple. You will find very complicated dishes indeed in some aspects of *haute cuisine*. Few domestic cooks can, or should, attempt such elevated cuisine. Usually you should leave it to the very highly qualified chefs who have trained long and hard to achieve their magnificent dishes. As Elizabeth David wrote, quoting Escoffier and Carême, the secret of cookery is to keep it simple. The secret of *enjoying* cookery lies with that watchword.

But this is not a cookery book – it is perhaps a little too idiosyncratic for that. It is a book about food – *nosh* – about the quirkiness of it sometimes, about the strange and wonderful things we put into our mouths. I hope it informs a little, but most of all I hope it amuses. Well, writing it amused me.

Jack McLean
Glasgow, 2005

A

À la

While this a perfectly sensible phrase in French, and in France if it comes to that, it is a high-falutin', positively poncey, phrase when used on a menu anywhere else, especially in Britain. It means 'in the style of' and can be useful when it describes dishes from a variety of regions. Thus *à la bourguignonne* (meat cooked in red burgundy wine, usually with shallots and mushrooms and often bacon) or *à la bretonne* (referring to a hearty lamb stew with haricot beans from the Brittany area, though it is also sometimes used as a term for a fish accompaniment involving leeks and mushrooms with celery in a velouté sauce). Breton food is very rich, and onions are a staple. The 'onion johnnies' seen so often in the UK in the immediate post-war years on their bicycles, with their strings of onions draped over the handlebars, came from Brittany.

But *à la* is a term used so often in French cuisine that you will find the phrase right throughout this book. It is still fine in France. It is pretentious drivel in Britain.

I

A l'ardennaise

A French term denoting the inclusion of juniper berries in stews and *daubes*, common in the Ardennes area of Belgium. Juniper originally came from Scotland but was later transported to the Low Countries and is the origin of whatever flavour **gin** consists of.

À la carte

Literally 'on the card', this term means choosing from the menu rather than from the sort of special offers that restaurants often advertise on their menu cards (especially lunch or pre-theatre meals). In France there is also the *carte du jour* (the menu of the day), and this has often led to misunderstandings by those unfamiliar with the French language but with aspirations to smart dining.

Abattoir

A public slaughterhouse. There are several ways of slaughtering animals (see **kosher** and **halal**), but one thing is certain: most people who ever see the inside of an abattoir may well be persuaded to vegetarianism or even worse. I can think of two novels set in slaughterhouses: *The Jungle*, by Upton Sinclair, and *The Dear Green Place*, by Scottish writer Archie Hind. Hind had been a slaughterman and once told me that one of the delights of the job was drinking hot fresh blood during a coffee break.

Abernethy biscuit

A 'light' shortbread biscuit with less fat, this is named not after, as some would have it, the town of Abernethy in Tayside, Scotland, but after Dr John Abernethy (1764–1831), a Scots surgeon who got his local baker to make them as 'health' biscuits for his patients just as Dr Oliver had done with his eponymous biscuits in the eighteenth century.

Abernethy biscuits are flavoured with caraway seeds, often ground. Charles Dickens in his *Pickwick Papers* has a Mr Solomon Pell regaling himself with 'a cold collation of an Abernethy biscuit and a **saveloy**'.

Incidentally, P.G. Wodehouse features a Scotch terrier called Abernethy in one of his Jeeves novels. He describes him as looking like a particularly stern Church of Scotland Elder about to make a sermon from the pulpit. James Thurber also named one of his 'Scotties' by the appellation.

Absinthe

This liqueur, invented in the eighteenth century, is made from a spirit flavoured with oil of wormwood, which is, in fact, a poison. (The Italian **vermouth** contains this also: the name derives from *Wermut*, the German for wormwood.) As a result of a celebrated murder trial in France in the 1890s in which the accused successfully argued that his responsibility had been diminished by drinking absinthe, the liqueur is now illegal in France and some other European countries. Substitutes were later invented, such as the aniseed drinks Pernod and Ricard. The famous painting by Degas titled *The Absinthe Drinker*, in which two apparently debauched drinkers are seated at a table in some Montmartre drinking den, was in fact a portrait of a well-known actress called Ellen Andrée and the distinguished engraver and artist Marcellin Desboutin. After the lurid trial France promptly banned the painting from public display along with absinthe itself.

Absinthe – without the essential wormwood – has recently been marketed again and has proved popular in the UK and the USA. It may seem odd that it has become fashionable among young urban Greeks but surely not: remember **retsina**.

Acadian blueberry grunt

I broke one of my intended rules soon after embarking on this book. I had intended that no obscure dishes would be included, but this name was just too good. So, as you will see, are many others.

This dessert, a speciality of Nova Scotia in Canada, is made from blueberries topped with a scone mixture and served with cream. (Incidentally a 'grunt' is the Irish name for a small immature perch, and a famous soup is made using this in the Emerald Isle.)

There was a famous Scottish court case, known as the Rotary Tools Trial, in which a leading protagonist was a Polish–Scots prostitute called Anna Grunt. Many bawdy ballads ensued, mainly because it was dreadfully easy to rhyme the lassie's name with 'stunt'. As well as other words.

Acids

Important in pickling and preserving, vinegar and, for instance, lemon juice are acids. So is, in powdered form, cream of tartar. When acids are being used, all utensils should be non-ferrous as acid reacts with metals. The popular boiled sweets – that is until boiled sweets disappeared – called Acid Drops did indeed contain acid; that is to say, citric acid.

Afternoon tea

No longer the English institution that once it was, this is a light repast involving, of course, tea, in dainty teacups with, traditionally, scones and jam and, if Oscar Wilde is to be believed, cucumber sandwiches (and meat or fish paste: many a murder mystery involved poisoned fish paste sandwiches).

Actually afternoon tea was a major feature of British social life for over a century. It is said to have been invented as a refreshing break by Anna, wife of the Duke of Bedford, while the men went out to kill stags or whatever. One of the greatest short-story writers of all time, Saki, has a wonderful piece on this dreary phenomenon of the Edwardian era. It is simply titled 'Tea'. Edwardian? It lasted long: I can remember as a child in the early 1950s handing round the sandwiches and fairy cakes from – what else? – a cake stand, on tea plates with paper doilies, to ladies of any years from nineteen to irascible old age. Afternoon tea is sadly gone forever. So could tea itself soon be, as instant coffee has taken over, and many levels of the splendid formality enjoyed by past generations have disappeared. See also **sandwich**, **tea** and **high tea**.

Afters

Second helpings, much used by schoolchildren, especially after the Second World War, when Austerity became not only a byword but a Word as well. Much later it was used by rather *bijou* Chelsea hostesses to describe desserts, in much the same way that they use the word, invariably erroneously, 'puddings'. I am inclined to Chelsea hostesses myself and think of 'pudding' with a less edible, so to speak, sense. See also **ladle**.

Aioli

A mayonnaise sauce flavoured with garlic and used for fish and meat. Nothing can smell more Mediterranean than this sauce, which occurs throughout southern Europe but most famously in Provence, where it is often thickened with breadcrumbs. The Italians have a version of it but add anchovies. If the aioli is perfect, you should reek of garlic for months. If it is not, you smell of timidity.

Al dente

This is the way that Italians prefer to serve their **pasta**, which is to say, 'to the tooth': in short, rather undercooked. The Brits tend to overcook pasta, as they do everything else, but all pasta dishes should be *al dente*.

Al fresco

Italian for 'in the open air'. Dining *al fresco* is rarely possible in Britain, owing to the climate. Despite this, the British have an absurd penchant for the **picnic**. See also **salami**.

Alcohol

This is a chemical compound, a powder often infused with water, which is a fermentation of sugars. It is likely that Arab chemists were the first to develop its properties, which is a touch ironic in that the non-medical use of it is now banned by the Islamic religion today embraced by most Arab countries. The original Arab word was *alcool*. There would appear to be no culture in which a basic *alcool* does not occur. The chemical is of enormous importance in medicine: paradoxically it is often the cause of considerable health problems. Alcoholism – the addiction to the substance – is not uncommon, though not as much as many people suggest, despite concerns frequently raised in many, especially European, cultures. Addiction to opium-based chemicals is more widespread but leads to less of an anxiety, or did once: the astounding upsurge throughout the Western world of addiction to heroin and other such opiates, and the attendant social problems in the last twenty years, is now seen as among the greatest social problems facing us all. Incidentally alcohol is part of the natural body fluid and is an essential chemical.

Ale

See **beer**.

Almonds

See **bitter almonds** and **marzipan**.

Amaretti

These are small macaroon biscuits made with almonds and almond oil and can last for years. The most famous are from Salsomaggiore, in Parma; in Britain the imported biscuits made by Lazzaroni and Co. come in splendid tin caskets: the biscuits themselves arrive in twisted paper scrolls. There is a lovely trick with the papers in which you put a flame under them and watch them rise to the ceiling. This delights children and Italian waiters alike. For some reason it worries adult diners, who suspect you have already drunk too much.

Amaretto

This is an almond-based liqueur and is very sweet and delicious. Ideal for very young girls at the end of a meal. For very old girls try **grappa**.

Anchovy

Found in warm seawater, this round-bodied fish can grow up to 20cm in length (though most of us find them preserved in oil and very small, rather like **whitebait**) and is caught in the Mediterranean and the Bay of Biscay. It has a very distinctive flavour. So much so that it has become an important element in a variety of dishes, among them the famous sauce of Piedmont, **bagna cauda**, which combines anchovies with garlic and oil. The real Neapolitan **pizza** has got to have a garnish of anchovies.

This salty little delicacy is also the base for **Gentleman's Relish**, much beloved of very posh Oxbridge students who wish to revisit the Brideshead of Evelyn Waugh. I have always pondered why Evelyn Waugh married his first wife, who was also called Evelyn. Something fishy there, I think.

Angelica

The leaves of this herb are most often seen as decorations for cakes, especially in the remarkably ornate confectionery of Sicily (see also **marzipan**). They are crystallized and candied for this purpose. Legend has it that the plant was so named because an angel came to earth and supplied it as a cure for plague.

Angels on horseback

Often served as a cocktail snack or occasionally a savoury at a formal meal, these are smoked oysters wrapped in streaky bacon and then grilled. An inspired combination.

Angels' share

In the distillation of whisky this is the considerable amount of alcohol that is evaporated when in the cask. It is also a term used by bar staff to describe the small amount left at the end of a bottle which cannot make a legal measure (sometimes known as 'the barman's dram').

Angostura bitters

This proprietary essence was first produced by Dr J.G.B. Siegert in the town of Angostura in Venezuela as a medical compound. Today it is mainly made in Trinidad. It is the mixer for the famous pink gin, much beloved by naval chaps and, well, chaps. Where would any would-be Noel Coward be without a pink gin?

Aniseed

The seeds of a plant grown in North Africa (though today Turkey is the main producer) are the basis of many alcoholic liqueurs through their liquorice-flavoured oils. Anisettes such as the brands Pernod and Ricard are hugely popular in northern France and Belgium and appear in Italy in the form of **strega**. The seeds are also used in breads and confectionery.

Annatto
These are hard seeds from an oriental tree (*Bixa oreliano*) and are used for colouring, chiefly for producing that disgusting red colour which some Cheddar cheese manufacturers go in for.

Antipasti
Italian term for **hors d'œuvres**. See also **salami**.

Aphrodisiac foods
There are a number of foods that are claimed to possess the property of exciting sexual desire. Some are thought to be so because they have a physical resemblance to sexual organs (**oysters** are an example) or have aromatic qualities (such as the **truffle**) that are said to be erotic. (Though the writer and gourmet Brillat-Savarin said of the last that though they were not a true aphrodisiac, they did tend to make 'women more affectionate and men more attentive'.)

Other foods are clearly sexually related because of their financial value (such as **champagne** or **caviar**). And some doubtless do elicit a sexual response. The Japanese seem to believe that most foods have the ability to elicit priapic responses as well as desire from their partners. Almost all such claims come from males: sensibly, women seem to think of food as . . . well, food.

Appetite
It was of course Rabelais who wrote that 'appetite comes with eating', but in his day the word meant excessive desire, as can be evinced in the dictionary meaning, and referred not just to food and wine but also to sexual interest. Shakespeare also

found the word important in that sense when he wrote that there were those of us who 'cloy the hungry edge of appetite by bare imagination of a feast'. The cliché of the last century, or more of a phrase, 'a healthy appetite' has lost the sense of excess, and indeed a healthy appetite is of course healthy. And the injunction by French waiters as they serve your food is '*bon appetit*': they mean it.

Apple

The fruit of a tree related to the rose family and, though probably originating in Persia, now grown in any temperate part of the world. It comes in three basic varieties: the wild 'crab' apple, the cultivated dessert apple and the cooking apple. Alexander the Great believed that apples brought long life. In this he was much mistaken: he died aged thirty-three. (Incidentally I recollect that a chap from the small town of Dungloe in Donegal, Ireland, was known as Alexander the Grate. He sold fireplaces.) Though the apple is today regarded as quintessentially English, most Brits are now presented with the ubiquitous Golden Delicious from perfidious France.

There are over 500 varieties of apple grown in the UK, however, among which are the famed Cox's Orange Pippin and the less well-known Ribston Pippin, about which the sardonic Hilaire Belloc, no less, once wrote a poem. There is a literary reference to a cooking apple too – the Codlin cooking apple. Dickens named a character in *The Old Curiosity Shop* Thomas Codlin, a surname probably deriving from a song titled 'Hot Codlins', often performed by the clown Grimaldi (whose biography Dickens wrote).

For some reason the apple is seen as a symbol of bucolic innocence, as English as the sound of leather on willow, or in America as American as apple pie. There is also the cliché that a rotten apple will spoil the whole barrel, and a 'bad apple' is a term for a cad anywhere. In fact I find this fruit one of the most tedious of all, though it is, when puréed, quite necessary as an accompaniment to roast pork.

Against that is the disgusting pudding apple crumble. When I was a child, my mum used to make apple crumble for me, without the apple. The crumble was splendid: it was the apple that ruined it. See also **strudel**.

For culinary purposes the apple is used widely in the rich dishes of Normandy, and their famous **cider**, the fermentation made from apples, is justly acclaimed, as are some ciders from England's West Country. The Normans also produce a fabulous brandy called Calvados, made from apples. If an apple a day keeps the doctor away, frequent applications of Calvados will ensure his equally frequent visits: Calvados is wonderfully strong. (Commercially 40% abv, home-distilled it can reach astronomical levels.)

Apricots

If I am not much impressed by peaches (see **peach**), I can state that I dislike apricots. This is doubtless because they were always dried apricots when I was a child, as just after the war it was difficult to obtain fresh fruit. This was and remains a problem with apricots because they, more than most fruits, need to be very fresh. As boys we got them reconstituted with water and served invariably with the horrid **rice pudding**.

Apricot jam was another disaster because such jams and jellies as the wonderful raspberry and strawberry conserves were both expensive and hard to come by after the war. It has to said, however, that apricot jam and a glaze made from it are much used by pastry cooks. It is widely used by French *patissiers*. Despite my contempt for this fruit of Chinese origin, I certainly concede that the liqueur made from it, *eau de noyaux*, is very good indeed.

Arborio

A round, short-grain Italian rice essential for the making of **risotto**. Another version of it is carnaroli, which is grown lower down in the Po valley.

Arbroath smokies

Scottish smoked haddock fillets. Today these are, like many so-called smoked items, simply painted with an essence and dyed, so it is rare to come up against a real Arbroath smokie, but when you do it is worth it.

Aristology

A splendid word, meaning the art and science of dining. (The US scholar and lexicologist Norman Schur claims this is from the Greek *aristos*, 'breakfast' or 'lunch', and *logos*, 'discourse', though it should be pointed out that *aristos* also means 'the best' in Greek; thus the *aristocracy* means the rule of the best.)

Early writers on aristology were Petronius and Lucullus in the Classical world. Brillat-Savarin, the French epicure, wrote a witty treatise on the art of dining, *La physiologie du goût* (*The Physiology of Taste*, 1801), and has been followed by other gourmets ever since. Norman Douglas, much quoted by Elizabeth David in her groundbreaking *Mediterranean Food* (1950), is a perfect example of an enthusiastic epicure who could hardly boil an egg.

But a few chefs were also fine writers – Auguste Escoffier (1847–1935), who rose to become head chef at the Savoy in London, is perhaps the best known of writer–chefs. Certainly few restaurant critics can cook, and most know nothing of the art: their knowledge is of *aristology*. And then there is the book of essays *The Autocrat of the Breakfast Table*, by the American author Oliver Wendell Holmes, who eventually croaked it in 1894, which gave rise to the legend on every jar of the Chivers company's **marmalade**, 'The aristocrat of the breakfast table'. My grandma gave us children this marmalade, while preserving (*sic*) the more expensive Frank Cooper's conserve for herself. 'You won't like it', she said. We didn't find out if we did or not until much later.

Aroma

The sense of smell is extremely important to food – possibly as much as the sense of taste – as the olfactory nerve endings are so allied to the functions of flavour, and most of us are more acute to the scent of food than we imagine. Smell is much in the forefront of our memories, and thus certain odours invoke in us our childhood to the extent that supermarket bakeries, for instance, use scented sprays to ensure that their bread and baking areas are impregnated with artificial aromas of newly baked bread. The aroma of **coffee** is an example. See also **bacon**.

Few of us are impervious to the scent of fish and chips from outlets, and the astounding perfume of a really good curry is enough to have you salivating. And then there are foodstuffs in which the scent is more important than the taste. See **truffle**.

Artichoke

Though there exists a potato-like tuber called a Jerusalem artichoke, the proper artichoke is a thistle-like vegetable popular in many regions of the Mediterranean countries. Artichokes are of the thistle family and, though the leaves of the young vegetable are edible, it is the heart of this vegetable that is prized. Damon Runyon wrote of 'some young Italian guy by the name of Marco Sciarra, or some such, who is in the artichoke business with his old man. I will not give you ten cents for all the artichokes you can pack in the Hudson tubes, as I consider them a very foolish fruit any way you look at them.' One tends to agree with Mr Runyon, but it is indeed true that artichoke hearts are greatly liked by southern Italians.

Asafoetida

An important spice in Indian cuisine, this is used in small quantities and imparts an onion flavour. It comes from a resinous sap from a perennial plant grown widely in Afghanistan. I once encountered this weed in Iran and it smells like dog turds. Not for the first time did I wonder how or why anybody ever thought of such unlikely vegetation as a source of food.

Asparagus

This perennial plant is grown in northern Europe and is also known as 'sparrow grass', which is quite lovely. It is a member of the lily family and is slender, with a unique and evocative flavour. It is also very expensive.

Asparagus spears can be used as an accompaniment, though to my mind this is a shocking waste of its delicate flavour. Asparagus tips should be eaten as a separate dish, with a hot butter sauce. G.K. Chesterton, a famous meat-eater and foe to the fad of vegetarianism, once remarked that he could fall prey to vegetables if asparagus only was provided. And it was Saki who stated that a man who doesn't love asparagus, oysters or good wine doesn't have a soul or a stomach either. 'He simply got the instinct for being unhappy highly developed.' In this I concur with the great man.

Attar

This oil, from roses cultivated in some areas of the Middle East (such as Iran), is chiefly made in Bulgaria, in areas where the damask rose is commonplace. It is highly aromatic and is an essential oil for the perfumery industry. It is also used, however, in many Arab countries and in India as flavouring in sweetmeats, such as *loukoumi* (**Turkish delight**).

Aubergine

I first discovered this in a West Indian store in London's Notting Hill Gate. It would be about 1962 and, as a young Scottish immigrant who knew that vegetables were carrots, swedes and cabbages and that was about it, I was much intrigued by the lovely glossy purple skin, so bought two of these things, which were called in fact 'eggplants' by the store owner. Neither my brother nor myself, both recent Londoners, had the slightest idea of how to cook these exotic objects, so we boiled them. For hours. The result was dreadful.

Years later I discovered the delight of aubergines, not least in the Greek dish known as **moussaka**, in which, of course, this splendid member of the tomato family is first degorged (i.e. sliced and salted to bring out most of its water content) and then sautéed in oil or butter. Aubergines are also eaten with a stuffing, like pimentos, and are a major ingredient of the Mediterranean accompaniment **ratatouille**, a vegetable ragoût involving tomatoes, courgettes, peppers, onions, olive oil and garlic. And, yes, you can boil aubergines.

Avgolemono

An egg and lemon sauce known throughout the Balkans, but essentially Greek. It is embodied in meat and fish dishes and the Greek national soup, *avgolemono soupa*, is made from a variant. The soup contains chicken stock, rice, lemons and eggs, and is heavily seasoned with peppercorns. Most Brits find it difficult because it is very sweet. Most Brits miss a lot.

Avocado

I first ate this in a casino in Manchester in 1964, as a starter. I had never seen this pear-shaped exotic, and it came with a sort of prawn cocktail mixture in the part where the nut had been hollowed out. I thought it then wonderfully sophisticated, and I still do. (Its name is not sophisticated, however: it is said to derive from the Portugese word for a testicle. If any mammal has a testicle the size and colour of an avocado, it will not be very well at that.) It has a buttery and slight flavour and texture. If not absolutely ripe it is woody and difficult to masticate. But when perfect it is perfect.

B

Bacon

This is cured pork meat, using salt, sugar and spices as preservatives, and is often smoked to boot. Unsmoked bacon is often known as 'green' bacon; in Italy it is called *coppa*, though Italian bacon is sometimes smoked as well. Unsmoked bacon is to be preferred for cooking in such stews as **boeuf bourguignon**, as it doesn't have as strong a flavour.

Bacon, smoked or otherwise, seems to have an almost addictive taste, as anybody with Jewish friends can testify. If there is one item of food that can tempt Jewish people to apostasy over kosher laws, it is a bacon sandwich. This also holds true for even the most dedicated vegetarian. I once discovered a god-daughter who had spent months proselytizing her new-found faith to us all standing in the kitchen with the aroma of grilled streaky throughout the entire house and her standing with the bacon butty in her very mitts. (Mind you, a friend of mine, the publican and restaurateur Gay Graham, maintains that the smell of fried bacon, like good coffee, far surpasses the taste and that it is the olfactory nature of both which produces the addiction.)

Bacon is a staple of the admired-over-the-world English breakfast. Elizabeth David once claimed, indeed, that even the French thought the British eggs and bacon a splendid dish, a notion I was inclined to view with scepticism until I discovered it was true when friends from Paris insisted on what they referred to as *oeufs sur le plat avec le jambon* for breakfast in my house.

Bagels

Bread rolls, which, though Jewish in origin, are now a staple of the New Yorker's diet, often eaten with lox, a Jewish version of smoked salmon. They are boiled before finally being baked in an oven. When I was a boy, my father used to take me across to the south side of my city to the Jewish quarter, then situated in the infamous Gorbals, to eat hot buttered bagels and poppy bread. In those days only Jewish storekeepers (and the ubiquitous Scottish **dairy**) could open on the Sabbath in Scotland. Thus bagels for breakfast, and dashed good they were.

Bagna cauda

This is a dip originating in Piedmont and much loved by Italians. It is made with olive oil, butter, anchovies and a great deal of garlic, and is consumed with raw vegetables such as celery or cardoons (see **cardoon**) and pimentos. A snack, it is best washed down with rough red wine. I once lost a girlfriend because of my delight in this ambrosia: it does make your breath fairly reek.

Baked Alaska

This dessert, like Black Forest gateau, is now seen as impossibly 1960s and is surely, like the gateau, due for a well-deserved comeback. It consists of a sponge cake topped with ice cream and jam, covered completely with meringue and browned quickly in a very hot oven. Surprisingly the ice cream remains solid, or should at any rate. Many a neophyte young wife has come to tears attempting this glorious sweet. If you want to be very *chic*, a flambé with cognac or a liqueur such as Cointreau is rather spectacular.

Baked beans

In these I am an expert. Since I first discovered them at the age of four, shortly after the war, I have been addicted to them and consume at least six large tins of them each week. I doubt if anybody, save bean freaks like myself, ever makes this delectable dish him/herself, though it is well worth the effort because none of the proprietary brands is anything like as good as it used to be. Today's taste is for a less sweet and spicy tomato sauce, and blandness has taken over.

Haricot beans baked and in a spicy tomato sauce (though not always: in Steinbeck's *Of Mice and Men*, Lenny, the giant with learning difficulties, is heard to wish that his beans had come in tomato ketchup instead of being plain fried) are probably the most famous canned food ever. Though now seen as quintessentially English, they are in fact American, based on a New England recipe, a variant of the famous Boston baked beans, and came to the UK as a delicacy sold originally only in Fortnum and Mason. In the beginning they were horribly expensive. In 1911 a 16oz can cost 9 old pence, then about 3% of the average weekly wage. There was always a piece of salt pork in them to add flavour and, though this was discontinued during the Second World War, the little cube of pork returned in the early 1950s, only to be left out once again when the manufacturers discovered that vegetarians saw tinned baked beans as a bit of a savoury saviour. In recent years health fiends have decreed that there is less sugar content (and indeed some baked bean companies advertise them as 'sugar-free'), and the taste for blandness has reduced the spice content.

Heinz are the brand leaders, though they are nothing like as good as HP in my view. The best were Crosse & Blackwell, with a very spicy sauce, but I haven't seen that brand in years. (Many supermarket brands are quite good too.) I now supplement tinned beans with the Indian spice mixture known as **garam masala** and, what is more, I fry them in bacon fat, rather as the Mexicans do with their *frijoles refritos* (refried beans to you).

Today's Britons put away more tins of beans than any other nation on earth (13lb per person per year), and, despite their unjustified reputation for flatulence, baked beans continue to be the most popular tinned foodstuff in the world. Perhaps a reason for this is that the best and easiest snack ever is Beans on Toast. There is no perhaps about it.

Baking

The practice of cooking in an oven. There was a time when few domestic residences could sport such a thing, and thus it was common for housewives to take their stews or casseroles or whatever to the local baker, who would place the dishes in the oven as it cooled down from his early morning bread-making.

In the early twentieth century commercial bakeries became cheap enough for many housewives to discontinue the age-old practice of baking for themselves, and today there are few people who bake at home at all. When I was a child in Scotland, I recollect that 'shop-bought' cakes were held in some contempt (though it did not stop my mother's generation from large-scale cheating in the matter), and home-baking skills were much admired. The tradition of Scots baking is legendary and, by now, largely mythical. There are exceptions. The Scottish master baker James Burgess, late of the once prestigious One Devonshire Gardens hotel in Glasgow, achieved an international reputation for his bakery products for the Amaryllis restaurant of the hotel. Among his fans, as well as celebrities such as Billy Connolly, Celine Dion and Madonna, can be numbered cookery writers Delia Smith, Catherine Brown and others, and chefs such as Michel Roux of The Waterside Inn, Bray, Gordon Ramsay and Anton Mossiman. Burgess not only produced traditional bakery items to recipes that had almost been lost; he also pioneered new confections. The great baking tradition of Scotland may be returning. Certainly it would seem to be true that, considering the appalling cuisine indulged in by most Scots, past and present, the baking tradition was once a beacon in the night: hopefully it will continue.

Balsamic vinegar

In recent times this has become almost ubiquitous in many smart restaurant dishes, certainly much used in *nouvelle cuisine*. It has been produced for centuries, especially in Italy and France, but some of the more expensive balsamic vinegars are aged in wood casks for many years and command prices that an old brandy will fetch. A unique feature of the liquid is that it can be used for savoury dishes and also for desserts. Try a few drops on fresh strawberries, for instance, and you will find its sweet and sour presence unusual but delightful.

Banana

The banana has a place in the folklore of those born during, and just after, the Second World War: it was the touchstone of the unavailability of pre-war foods. I can testify to the astounding mythology of this fruit (its cousin the plantain is officially a vegetable). I can recollect, when I was a child, a fellow pupil bringing to my primary school some bananas that his merchant-seaman uncle had brought from a recent voyage in the Caribbean. Every child was given a slice of this, then exotic, fruit to taste. I know this sounds unlikely, but it is true. The headmistress showed off one of the bananas in a glass case in the school hall. The best-known importer to the UK, and other European countries, is the firm of Fyffes.

Perhaps because the curving shape looks quite so phallic, there is always something rather risible about the banana, something not unnoticed by comedian Billy Connolly, who on stage frequently sports boots fashioned like them.

Actually bananas are a very flexible food. They can be eaten raw or cooked. Fried bananas are an essential accompaniment to Maryland chicken and, as fritters, are a common dessert in Chinese restaurants. They can also be dried and ground into flour. And something you didn't know. Diced cucumber, when cooked with a few cloves, will produce the taste of banana. Though not genetically related, the banana and the cucumber are both shaped like phalluses. It is hardly surprising therefore that in the Hindu religion both are regarded as symbols of fertility. (So are onions: the female version of the banana.)

And here's a nice wee tip. Peel a ripe banana, thread it onto a lollipop stick, and freeze it in the ice-making cabinet of your refrigerator. It makes a cheap, cheerful and intriguing treat for children.

Banquet

Though this now simply means a feast, usually formal and in celebration of some perceived achievement such as winning a pointless sports contest, it was originally a drinking party at which Ancient Greeks got well and truly rubbered while discussing politics, philosophy and the other burning issues that accompany decent drunkenness and which was called a *symposium*. Today this latter word is used in English to describe extraordinarily dreary meetings for brown-nosing corporate executives wishful in their ambitions. A far cry from Plato's *symposia*, in which the Greek god of wine,

Dionysus (to Romans, Bacchus), was toasted, followed by speeches and wit.

I occasionally hold a Sunday afternoon symposium myself, which I call a *conversazione*. This is not as pretentious as it sounds. Though such gatherings are dying out, they were once quite a common feature of Scottish middle-class life on Sundays, owing to the closure of licensed premises on the Sabbath. At my gatherings actual drunkenness is frowned upon. So is actual sobriety.

Barbecue

To my mind an especially disgusting ritual enjoyed by Australians (whose national rite this is) and smug middle-class male suburbanites. The word itself derives from the Portuguese and meant the rough wool beard at the tail of a sheep which Portuguese shepherds in Brazil would flourish after roasting a whole sheep in open-air fire-pits. Yet if you take away the ritual aspects of the barbecue, it has to be said that cooking steaks, or sausages, hamburgers or even fish over a charcoal grill produces mouth-watering food. It is just a pity that the barbecue attracts nerds, antipodean or otherwise.

Barley

Probably the oldest cultivated crop, this cereal is fundamental to the alcohol business. Beer is based on malted barley (see **malt**), and so, of course is **whisky** (or, in Ireland and America, whiskey). Another drink – barley water – is made from the water in which barley is boiled. The best-known manufacturer of this thirst-quenching soft drink is Robinson's.

But barley is also widely used as a thickener in stews and ragoûts. It is the necessary ingredient of **Scotch broth**, a soup of infinite variety except one thing: there must be barley.

There is also barley sugar, a brittle boiled sweet made from the decoction of barley in a water and sugar syrup. The sweets are usually formed into a twist shape, and thus the four pillars of the Bernini-designed bronze baldacchino over the high altar in St Peter's in Rome are described by architects as 'barley-sugar twists'.

Basil
Related to the mint family, this pungent herb (also known as sweet basil) has its origins in India and Iran but is now grown all over Europe. The Hindu religion fosters it as a source of happiness, the French call it the 'royal herb', and the word itself means 'kingly' in Ancient Greek. But the greatest proponents of its use are the Italians, who use it liberally in almost all their tomato-based sauces. They have even produced a most magnificent sauce – **pesto** – which uses basil.

Basil is easy to grow in the British climate and can be cultivated in the house (kitchen odours are much enhanced by basil plants), but even dried basil is splendidly effective. And the smallest pinch of basil in any dish summons up a terrace in Italy on a hot day.

Basmati
Though the patna variety is commonly used in many parts of India, in my view no other rice but basmati is quite right for Indian food and curries. Certainly it is unwise to attempt a **biriyani** with anything other than this small but long-grained rice, which originally was grown in the cool foothills of the Himalayas. But beware when buying this: many packet brands are diluted with other, inferior, rices. Best to purchase from a reputable Indian store.

Basting
Spooning pan juices over roast meats and poultry while cooking, to keep them moist and reduce shrinkage. It is especially necessary in pot-roasting.

Bath Oliver

An unsweetened plain biscuit invented by a Dr Oliver of Bath some time in the eighteenth century, ostensibly as a health food to go with the waters from the spas of that city. Perfect with cheese, of course, there is also a luxury chocolate-covered Bath Oliver, but it is very difficult to come by. As a young chap in the Swinging London of the 1960s I used to order them in a tearoom owned by Bentinck's of Mayfair. Both Bentinck's and Bath Olivers cost more than I could really afford, but it made me feel a toff for an afternoon.

Battenberg

A cake once very popular but rarely seen today, it consists of pink and natural-coloured sponge mixtures covered in **marzipan**. When cut, it has a chequered appearance. It was boycotted during the First World War (Lord Louis Mountbatten was originally a Battenberg and the Royals changed their German names to Windsor); another fine example of this Great War outbreak of animosity towards the horrid Hun was the case of what are now called Empire Biscuits, which were originally called German Biscuits. Such sensitivity in food matters was not confined to the UK: during the same conflict **hamburgers** were renamed 'Liberty Sandwiches' in the USA, and **sauerkraut** became, equally ludicrously, 'Liberty Cabbage'. Americans can sometimes appear stupendously absurd in their culinary patriotism: during the Iraq crisis, when France refused to take part in the USA's warmongering, the Yanks renamed French fries 'Freedom potatoes'.

Bay leaves

Laurel leaves. They were the leaves that made up the wreaths with which the Greeks and Romans crowned their heroes. In my opinion it is all they are fit for. I have never discerned any possible flavour from them and omit the dashed things from the ubiquitous **bouquet garni**.

Beans

Seeds or pods of the legume family which are not peas or lentils. They can be easily dried, in which use one should be careful. Many beans possess toxins which can be harmful to humans and the beans must be soaked before use. The water in which they lay should not be poured down the sink as the resulting aroma is unpleasant. Haricot beans make good eating (see **cassoulet**), as does the variety known in Italy as borlotti. The latter must be boiled for at least fifteen minutes, as the toxins in the outer skins are very poisonous indeed. One cannot help but wonder how many people in ancient times croaked it before they discovered the boiling-beans-to-death method. See also **baked beans**.

Béarnaise sauce

A classic sauce from the Béarn region of south-west France, this is basically a **Hollandaise sauce** with onions, shallots, vinegar, white wine, tarragon and parsley. French chefs make so much noise about sauces. The Brits tend to imagine they do so because they are masking inferior ingredients. This is, of course, mince, but one does wish that French cooks would shut up for a minute or two and cease their condescension towards the rest of the world.

Béchamel sauce

Another classic of French *haute cuisine*, this sauce is said to be named after Louis de Béchamel when he was *maître d'* at the court of the Sun King. Basically a white sauce, it is flavoured with onion, carrots, parsley and celery. It can also contain mace or nutmeg, but some modern chefs omit these, feeling them to be too strong for the, usually, delicate flavours of the fish for which this sauce is designed. This is not the case in Italy, where their *besciamella* is heavily laced with **nutmeg**.

Beef

This is the flesh of mature cattle and is very much the preferred meat of the British. And Americans in both continents. That said, beef was once enjoyed almost exclusively by the middle and upper classes. The notion of the Sunday joint and the roast beef of Olde England was confined, until comparatively recently, to those who could afford it. Thus if meat was eaten at all, it would be pig meat in areas such as the West Country and mutton in the north of England.

The Americas saw the growth of cattle-rearing, and the entire economy of Argentina is based on the beef industry. Argentinian beef cattle were bred from imported Aberdeen Angus breeds, and Aberdeen Angus beef is still a byword for the top-quality meat. (Scotland has also produced much praised beef from the Galloway breed and the shorthorn. For a good many years the supermarket chains were inclined to prefer continental breeds such as the French Charolais, which produced a leaner meat, with less marbled fat. But though the development of pedigree Scottish breeds has been going on for only a little over two hundred years, Scotland is now regarded as producing the finest beef in the world, along with its famed wild **salmon** and of course its **whisky**. The quality of this small country's products far outweighs its cooking.)

Beef has taken a knock since the much-publicized outbreak of Creutzfeldt-Jakob disease (the human form of so-called Mad Cow Disease), but it remains the most highly prized of animal flesh. It can be grilled, roasted, fried, boiled and stewed. It can even be eaten raw (as in steak tartare). There are simply too many beef dishes to be described here, as no other meat has so many recipes attached to it. But one recipe must be mentioned. The late Jock Stein, manager of the first British football club to win the European Cup (Glasgow Celtic), was wont to order a pre-match repast of minced fillet steak, fried and topped with a poached egg. One day the renowned Irish chef William McKimmey added a few anchovies (a kind of steak Holstein), and the football legend demanded this addition ever afterwards. Jock never knew what the anchovies were, but insisted on them. He thought they were strips of salty bacon.

Incidentally one of the great myths about beef is that it should be bright red if fresh. In fact some supermarkets inject their beef with saltpetre to make it look juicily pillar-box red. Properly hung beef should be a dark red colour and have a slightly gamey bouquet. And a great deal of the quality of beef has to do with the skill of the **butcher**.

Beef Stroganoff
A Russian dish, created for Count Stroganoff in the middle of the nineteenth century, it consists of strips of fillet steak with onions and mushrooms and then simmered with soured cream. A small glass of sherry is often added. Coarsely ground pepper must be there too. A Hungarian variant includes hot **paprika** and caraway seeds. A perfect dinner party dish: though expensive in its ingredients, it is virtually impossible to ruin. It is served with rice and my advice is to use the **basmati** type, though this Indian variety is virtually unknown in Hungary.

Beer
I do not like beer, In fact the only time I have drunk a pint of this bitter and gaseous liquid, in over thirty years was when I was writing a feature on a much-lauded real ale in a brewery in the Yorkshire dales. The next morning I experienced the worst diarrhoea of my life.

But beer is probably the most popular alcoholic drink in the world, and beer nerds have a great deal of clout even within an industry that created, via the beer barons of the early nineteenth century, enormous political power. Possibly the most effective consumer pressure group ever has been Camra (the Campaign for Real Ale), and for that I applaud them. But see also **stout**.

Beestings
A thick and creamy milk which is the first milk cows give after calving. In the West Country of England, and especially Devon, it is used for their version of **junket**, producing an incredibly rich dessert.

Beetroot
A root vegetable and member of the beet family, it owes its characteristic red colour to its purplish skin: when peeled and boiled, it loses much of its colour. Beetroot is used mainly as a pickle and for no reason I can see was once a staple of school dinners. It was also invariably a component of what most Brits called a salad.

Betel
Both the leaves and the nuts of this climbing plant are used as breath-fresheners and aids to digestion by South-East Asians. Their use is much frowned upon in Malaysia, however, as adherents to them often spit, a practice that is illegal in that part of the world. (Draconian as that sounds, it is quite sensible in that the most common means of transmitting the disease that once devastated the region, tuberculosis, is the deposit of human saliva.)

Bird's nest soup

For many years this was regarded as a fantasy by most of the Western world. Richmal Crompton features the idea of it in one of her William stories, in which the rascally young Mr Brown is scathing on the notion.

But it is real enough and is made from nests of swifts, using the saliva and seaweed with which these birds build their nests. It imparts a subtle flavour and is rather gelatinous. The substance is, of course, incredibly expensive even in China, where it is a luxury item. Eastern cookery abounds in unlikely foodstuffs, from fatally poisonous blowfish (it is said that over 200 deaths a year in Japan are due to the consumption of this so-called delicacy) to soups made from the poisonous sacs of cobras in East Africa, to the lymph glands of monkeys. This tendency to *omnivare* is one of the reasons why humans can survive in circumstances of every kind of deprivation. Humans, especially Japanese ones, can and will eat anything. Contrast that with pandas, which are becoming extinct because they will only eat a particular type of leaf from only one tree, the stupid buggers.

Biriyani

A rice dish brought to India by the Moghuls some time in the sixteenth century. It is almost a staple as the daily meal all over the Punjab. Ingredients of this dish of the North-West Frontier are usually meat – often lamb or mutton or poultry, though seafood sometimes appears – and the rice is cooked along with them. Aromatics are used, though it is not normally a hot dish. The result is dry, so a curry gravy is usually served with it. It is of course very filling and as a student it was a favourite: you could do without food for days after a large portion of this splendid dish.

Biscuit

In the USA this is the generic name for a kind of scone, eaten fried, with ham and eggs, at **breakfast**. But in Britain biscuits are generally crispy flour-based sweetmeats and are highly sugared (see **gingernut** and **digestive biscuit**). North Americans call biscuits 'cookies'; in Scotland this is a term for a bun. Also in Scotland a term for a sweetheart. In that same country a biscuit is an old-fashioned word for a loose woman. The English phrase 'that takes the biscuit' is lost in the mists of time. Perhaps it derives from Scottish vernacular speech. Whatever the etymology, like most English aphorisms the phrase makes no sense whatsoever.

Bistro

Though a common slang name for a small tavern in France, it was not until the Swinging Sixties that the word became used in Britain for a cheap and cheerful licensed trattoria (see **trattorias**). I will bet you didn't know this though. The word itself is from the Russian language, in which *bistro* simply means 'fast' or, colloquially, 'hurry up'. There.

Bitter almonds

A relation to sweet almonds, these are bitter because of the presence of a toxin called benzaldehyde, which is an ingredient of Benzedrine, a drug also known, to its fans, as 'speed'. (The late Sir Anthony Eden was, incidentally, addicted to this amphetamine, which possibly explains his extraordinary behaviour during the Suez crisis of 1956.) It is a useful flavouring, however, and is often found in Asian food, and of course in confectionery and many French desserts. Bitter almonds also contain a small amount of prussic acid, a poison. For this reason most confectioners utilize almond oil extract. See **marzipan**.

Blachan

Also known as *trasi*, this is a basic flavouring in cookery all over South-East Asia. It is made from prawns or shrimps, which are salted, dried, pounded and rotted. The many who now enjoy Thai food in the UK do not seem to know, or wouldn't care if they did, that this paste is in fact putrefied shellfish. There are a number of such saprogenic food items in world cuisine, and many are highly prized. See **fresh**.

Black bun

This is not a bun, but an astoundingly rich sort of cake, packed so closely with currants and raisins – bound with an astounding range of spices including ground **ginger**, **caraway seeds**, **nutmeg**, **cloves**, black pepper and more – that it is hard to recognize it as a cake at all. **Sugar** and **treacle** also go into it, as does a large amount of brandy. The mixture is enclosed in a thin and rich pastry. This exotic sweetmeat is entirely Scottish and has become known and admired throughout the world, undoubtedly because it is traditionally made for New Year's Eve, in Scotland known as Hogmanay, and every Scottish expat community has introduced the natives to this remarkable concoction. See also **clootie dumpling** and **Scottish food**.

Black Forest gateau

A chocolate layer cake filled with cherries and cream which was extremely popular in the 1960s and '70s, as a result of which it has become as naff as being called Tracy or Kevin. But, just as some Kevins are splendid fellows, and a considerable number of Tracys are absolutely lovely, Black Forest gateau is still a grand cake and its rediscovery is long overdue.

Black pepper

See **pepper**.

Black pudding

My old friend the writer Godfrey Smith (of the *Sunday Times*) once wrote that black pudding was in fact white and was dyed black. He had been told this by the then amusing northerner Michael Parkinson and, like all South Britons, was gullible enough to believe this farrago. It is a blood sausage made from the blood of sheep, pigs or sometimes ox, heavily spiced and thickened with cereal and onions.

It is indeed true that this wonderful item is mainly confined to the northern palate in the British Isles, but it is highly regarded in northern Europe too, where it is known in Germany as *blutwurst* and in France as *boudin noir*. Both countries serve potato purée and apple sauce with black pudding, a practice much to be recommended.

Disgusting as black pudding sounds to sensitive Home Counties ears, it is certainly a fact that no heart attack fried **breakfast** should fail to include it. See also **white pudding**.

Blackcurrant

Virtually inedible when raw, this berry makes perhaps one of the best jams ever. It is also the basis for the drink that every toddler knows as Ribena. An alcoholic version, so to speak, is cassis, home-made for generations by peasants in Dijon, consisting of the berries, sugar and brandy. It is a damned sight more palatable than Ribena at that.

Blancmange

Made from sweetened cornflour and flavoured and coloured, this is possibly the most disgusting milk pudding ever inflicted on children. It was a staple of mothers in the 1950s, as I know well myself. Nothing can excuse mothers, even my own, from the application of this repellent dish to their unsuspecting progeny.

Blintzes

Jewish pancakes filled with cream cheese and fried in butter. They are sprinkled with cinnamon and served with sour cream. All I can say is that Jewish mothers are sadists, as is well reflected in the food they provide. (See mothers above.) The Russian blini is related, though this is a different matter and is often filled with caviar.

Boar

Still eaten in Europe, especially in the Balkans, the total absence of boars in the UK has tended to render this animal impossible to encounter in that country. The famous boar's head has been replaced in banquets by that of a pig. In this form it is still pretty grisly.

Boeuf bourguignon

Actually I first encountered this in Burgundy and was astonished to discover that French people keep some wines for cooking and others for drinking. (The British have been brought up to believe that the French would use a wine of noble vintage for cooking: as if.)

This is a hearty beef stew, more of an **estouffade** really, and consists of good rump steak, bacon strips, carrots, stock and onions cooked in red wine. Small pickling onions and lightly fried mushrooms are added at the end. This is a slow-cooked stew and ideally should be made the day before and allowed to sweat overnight. The traditional accompaniment is boiled potatoes. My friend in Burgundy (Esther lives in the town of Beaune and was the god-daughter of the writer Colette) added croutons and told me that in her late age her godmother insisted on having the fried bread served separately and only embarked on the boeuf bourguignon after consuming a bloody great plateful of the *fritos*.

Boiled sweets

These sweetmeats (the old-fashioned name for them is 'sugar-plums'), made from boiled and coloured sugar, were once highly prized by British children everywhere and are the stuff of legend. Black-striped balls and cinnamon balls, sherbet lemons and acid drops, soor plooms and the much-desired bull's-eyes. These 'boilings' are hardly known or seen these days, though there is a small market for them, drawn almost entirely from the children of pre-, during and post-war days.

It is difficult to explain to people under forty about the heyday of the sweets, dating from the time when sweets were on the ration. They did not come off until 1954, though every child in the nation was gifted a tin of toffees to commemorate the coronation of the present Queen Elizabeth on 2 June 1953.

Bollito

This is one of the great winter dishes of the rich northern Italy, a selection chosen from the trolley of beef, calves' heads and feet, chickens and turkeys, and the rich spiced pork sausage known as *cotechino*, all of them boiled – thus the name. A *salsa verde* is served with it. I must be honest here: I do not much like it, especially as I do not care to eat as much at one sitting as Italians do, but the people of northern Italy regard their *bollito* as a great treat.

Bolognese sauce

This world famous sauce is known in Italy as *ragù* and is so often misused by cooks throughout the planet that here I must give you the bare bones of the basic recipe. It is a meat sauce (in Italian *sugo* is the term for any meat sauce) and uses minced prime beef cuts such as rump, together with onions and grated carrot, strips of *coppa* (see **bacon**), celery or celery seeds, garlic, stock cubes (use if possible either Maggi or a kosher stock cube called Kosher Telma, both of which are unsalted), red wine, olive oil and butter, tomato purée and a goodly scraping of nutmeg. (Do not despise, as so many British would-be-cooks do, tomato purée: it is, like tinned Italian plum tomatoes, a necessary wonder to us all.) Mushrooms can be, and in my view should be, added. Use flavourful mushrooms such as the oyster variety or *shitake* (see **mushroom**). A last addition is cream and something else, though these days it is difficult to get: the unlaid eggs called, in Italian, *ovarine*, which produce a richness otherwise missed by most recipes. Some insist on chicken livers but I would disagree. But I have missed out perhaps the most important ingredient: you must have **basil**.

This is the sauce vouchsafed to me (and surprisingly similar it is to that Elizabeth David found in Bologna) by Sergio Torelli, head chef of the famous Ristorante Savini in Milan's Galleria Vittorio Emmanuele, a shopping mall on which all other arcades are, or should be, based. Savini's is the Italian version of Maxim's in Paris and is as expensive to boot. But Bolognese sauce with perfectly cooked **spaghetti** cooked **al dente** is cheap at any price.

Bombay duck
A dried and salted fish called a *bummalo* (not a duck at all), this goes with Indian dishes and is an acquired taste. I have acquired it.

Bonne femme, à la
A French term (meaning 'in the manner of a good wife'), this refers to any dish involving bacon, mushrooms and potatoes – especially potatoes. Chicken is often braised with these ingredients, and very good it is too when done in clarified butter. An old-fashioned favourite of French mums is the soup known as *potage bonne femme*, made with potatoes, leeks,

water, seasoning and butter, which is very, very simple to make. It is also the basis of the well-known gourmet soup known as vichyssoise. The latter was devised by a Frenchman, Louis Diat, who was the head chef at the Ritz–Carlton in New York for over forty years. It is simply the same potato and leek soup with lots of thick cream but served iced. I once complained in a very hoity-toity restaurant, as a callow youth, that the soup was cold. In fact, I think I said it was freezing. The *maître d'*, seeing a half-wit, sent it back to the kitchen and had it heated up. I'll bet the boys in the back-room had a laugh.

Bouillabaisse
A fish soup with potatoes and **saffron** from the Mediterranean, this classic French soup is the stuff of legend. And like most legends, it is less than heroic. I first discovered the existence of this potage in a children's book titled *Street Fair*, written, I think, by a lady called Marjory Fischer back in the 1930s. It was a very celebrated children's book, and was the *Harry Potter* of its day. Bouillabaisse figured largely, for some reason, in this enchanting novel. I have never discovered how to pronounce this bouillabaisse.

Bouquet garni
This is a bunch of herbs usually tied together in a muslin bag and consisting more often than not of bay leaves, thyme, parsley and sometimes marjoram or oregano. I cannot see the reason for the idea and instead prefer to put the herbs directly into whatever dish I am cooking.

Bovril
A beef tea created by a Scots-Canadian butcher called John Lawson Johnston in 1874. Its name was derived from the Latin for 'ox' – *bovis* – and the word for 'life' – *vitalis*, a Latin

corruption being *vrilya* meaning 'life force'. (See also **extracts**, **Marmite**.) This most proletarian of drinks, consumed at Association Football matches by countless British footy fans, has thus a surprising Classical background.

Boxty

An Irish potato recipe which calls for cooked mashed potatoes and grated raw potatoes, mixed with flour to make a kind of potato bread. It is, as the *grande dame* of Irish cookery, Florence Irwin, noted, the dish for Hallowe'en and is particularly associated with County Tyrone. There are many variations of it, and it has now become a highly fashionable dish in stylish restaurants. Actually there are similar recipes in Germany and the Balkans, but the Irish claim it as their own.

Brandy

See **cognac**.

Brandy snap

A biscuit mixture using flour, butter, golden syrup, caster sugar and ground ginger. The biscuits are wrapped round the buttered handle of a wooden spoon to make brittle, lacy-looking, hollow tubes which are then filled with stiffly whipped cream. They are luxury items, made all the more so by master baker James Burgess, who actually adds brandy to the mixture.

Bread

This staple of so many countries has had more quotes attached to it than any other foodstuff ever, and it is enough to make you think of it as very, very boring indeed. Man being unable to live by bread alone comes to mind, and so does bread being cast for some reason upon the waters. The Bible is an everlasting source of quotes about bread. But in Old Testament days bread would have been unleavened, as many breads to this day remain.

It was the Egyptians who first introduced yeast to make bread. Today any Ancient Egyptian would be most distressed, however, to see what commercial bread has become: largely tasteless and with a texture often described as similar to cotton wool. The reason for this is what is now known throughout the world as the Chorleywood Bread-Making Process, after the Flour Milling and Baking Research Association at Chorleywood in Hertfordshire in England, which in the 1960s discovered a cheaper method of making bread in which sixteen times as much yeast is used and higher temperatures are involved in the baking.

Wheat is the most common cereal from which bread is made and the much-refined 'white' flour is mainly used. So-called 'brown' bread is popular, but the bulk of commercial bread is white. Few people bake their own bread, though the late John Lennon of the Beatles was famous for spending many of his later days baking bread. My own mother made bread regularly, and the aroma of freshly baked bread permeated the house. Today some bakeries, especially in supermarkets, employ an artificial chemically produced essence to make their products smell more appealing to customers.

During the Second World War bread was one of the few foods that remained unrationed: the post-war austerity saw it rationed and was perhaps one of the reasons why the then Labour government found itself defeated in 1951. It was then, literally, a bread and butter issue.

Bread and butter pudding
An old-fashioned British pudding made from bread and butter with currants and sultanas, eggs and sugar, this has become a favourite with expensive and exclusive London restaurants in London, much to the bemusement of anyone

who has never been subjected to meals in English public schools.

There is, however, a quite acceptable variant of this, called *scheiterhaufen*, which I once had in a mountain-top restaurant in Innsbruck in the Tirol. It included rum, schnapps, apples, raisins, almonds and lemon zest. It was by no means bland.

Bread sauce
Another English nonsense, this boring sauce, traditionally an accompaniment to roast poultry, is made with breadcrumbs, onions, spices (specifically cloves) and milk. Only the English could think this up.

Breakfast
The English breakfast is the stuff of legend (though Scots and Irish people object to being asked for an English breakfast, as they have their own variants) and is a lot rarer today than is imagined. Few people now eat a cooked breakfast unless they have a visit to a hotel, in which case they indulge themselves horribly. The best breakfast I ever experienced was in a guest house in the Cotswolds, where myself and chums, the morning after a rather exotic wedding, encountered the following: fried eggs, bacon rashers, grilled kidneys, tomatoes, refried beans, black pudding, hash browns (potatoes), **bubble and squeak**, with alternatives (which we also ate) of kippers and **kedgeree**. Included were breakfast cereals such as **cornflakes**, fresh orange juice, toast and **marmalade**, **tea** and **coffee**. We washed it down with **whisky**. The other guests, from France, looked on with awe at our ingestuous labours.

Continentals have their own breakfast, which consists of bread rolls and ham and cheese, and is the reason, so Brits imagine, why Europeans lack the spirit of true Britons. This may be the basis for the UK belief that Europeans are not quite sound and do so badly in such things as world wars: they do not have a proper breakfast. But I once worked on an American army base in Germany and discovered that the Yanks eat **hominy grits**, biscuits (see **biscuit**), maple syrup and T-bone steaks for breakfast.

An Irish breakfast comes with fried **soda bread** and **colcannon** (similar to bubble and squeak, with added spring onions). And whisky. Evelyn Waugh always had his Bright Young Things quaffing champagne for brekkers, either with orange juice or Guinness **stout** (Black Velvet). The most amazing breakfast I have heard of was described in *The Gourmet's Guide to Europe* (1903), in which there were eight courses and enough alcohol to stay the desires of bloody Dylan Thomas and Brendan Behan in New York, the last days.

Brie

A soft and velvety French cheese made all over Europe but originally from the Normandy region of France, it has a highly piquant taste and, though experts maintain that it should be firm, it has to be said that some of us prefer it when well over-ripe and almost runny, smelling of ammonia, which is the way most of us get it from chums returning from holidays in France.

Broiler

An old hen chicken in Britain (in the USA it means a *young* one), this is also an insulting term for a lady a bit past her sell-by date and is regarded as somewhat offensive, and quite right too.

Brunch

A hybrid word (a contraction of breakfast/lunch). Americans invented it. Only Americans should use it. When Europeans do, it means that a collection of well-heeled capitalists have decided that eating should involve talking about money.

Brussels sprout

Why this marvellous member of the cabbage family is so derided today I do not know. Though grown in what is now Belgium from the thirteenth century onwards, it was first introduced to Britain in the middle of the nineteenth century and was regarded as the very height of ton at dinner parties. These mini-cabbages are more flavoursome than their elder sister and, when heavily buttered, are delicious. It has become fashionable to despise them and children are taught not to eat them. It is surely time to rediscover the noble sprout.

Bubble and squeak

Cold mashed potatoes mixed with cooked chopped cabbage and fried in lard, dripping, butter or, perhaps best of all, bacon fat. This delectable dish has many variations throughout the world. The Irish add spring onions (also known as 'scallions' in Ireland, 'syboes' in Scotland) and sometimes just ordinary onions to make the dish known as **colcannon**. (The other great Irish potato dish, **champ**, is often mixed with chives and sometimes nettle leaves.)

The Hungarians (who have some of the most exquisite potato dishes in the world) have a version made with cauli-flower and sour cream, and their *burgonyahab* – creamed mashed potatoes – is often mixed with spinach and onions. In Sri Lanka there is a similar dish which also includes green chillies. Southern India has a version (*methi aloo*), using spinach and potatoes, fenugreek leaves, garlic, ginger and other assorted spices.

There is probably no nation on earth that does not have a potato dish, which, considering potatoes were unknown any-where outside the southern continent of America until their introduction in the sixteenth century, is more than remark-able. See also **Hungarian cookery** and **potato**.

Buffalo

Visiting a farmer friend who lived near the small town of Giugliano, near Naples, I witnessed the most frightening animals I have ever seen in the flesh. They were massive, black, hugely horned and very frightening indeed. Much to the amusement of my friend Aurelio, I was absolutely terrified, but rooted to the spot. He led one of the great black-horned beasts up to me. 'This is my little girl, Beatrice', he announced, presenting this lumbering horror, which then nuzzled me gently with its wet nose. It was a buffalo.

Originating, it is said, in India, the buffalo is reared in Italy entirely for its milk, which makes the famous **mozzarella** cheese. Despite their fearsome appearance, buffaloes are shy and gentle. So could the cheese be thus described.

There is also the animal known as buffalo in North America, which is, of course not a buffalo but a bison. This is now a very scarce meat, but a speciality in Canada is a curious pie made with bison meat and spices and beer, called sweet-grass pie. I have never encountered it, but my Canadian chum Steve says it is delicious.

Buffet

An informal meal usually run on a self-service basis. Hot and cold foods are generally served, and this ranges all the way through to the very elaborate. The so-called 'finger buffet' is popular at household parties and such occasions as receptions. The term 'buffet' is still used to describe the snack counter on railway carriages. Now that the once splendid British railway restaurant cars have all but disappeared, this is about all you can get.

It is said that the name of the Beefeaters of the Tower of London is derived from the word 'buffeteers'; i.e. waiters at banquets.

Butcher

The craft of the butcher requires considerable skill and knowledge, thus the apprenticeship is fairly long. To quote Elizabeth David: 'A skilful, experienced butcher treats his meat almost as a tailor does his cloth.' Sadly this has changed as the supermarket and packaging industry has swamped the small family high street butchers. Yet there are still master butchers, who have to be yearly qualified and inspected by their respective guilds, and who know how to make the different cuts and how to hang their carcasses. Unfortunately many butchers now are forced to sell other products, and some are almost mini-markets. Still, if you want good meat and products such as real sausages and so on, go to a real butcher.

Incidentally the butcher gets a bad press generally, either thought of as a, well, beefy sort of chap or as a sinister figure such as the psychopath depicted in Claude Chabrol's splendid film *Le Boucher*, in which the eponymous protagonist butchers more than domesticated animals. I have, however, always found butchers to be very cheery fellows.

Butter

Rich and creamy, and held to be a serious element in problems of high **cholesterol**, butter is a churned fat from milk products and is today often replaced by other fat products. No other substance can be used for many cooked or baked dishes, and it is folly to try. Sadly butter is more often than not highly salted, and the result is ruinous. As a child I remember great kegs of fresh white butter from which the grocer would take a scoop; he would then pat it with wooden implements designed for the purpose and often end with giving it a decorative flourish by means of a butter-pat mould.

The most commonly used fat for cooking in India is clarified butter, called ghee, which can be produced by gently heating ordinary butter and removing the surplus creamy foam. Most Indians, however, buy their ghee in large canisters, and I am surprised so few Westerners have not adopted this splendid fat. It can be preserved far longer than ordinary untreated butter, and another bonus: as it heats to a higher temperature than unclarified butter, its use avoids the greatest danger of cooking with normal butter – burning it.

Buttermilk

Making a comeback in the UK in recent years, this is the liquid left after butter-making. It is still popular in Ireland and is also used for making soda scones or **soda bread**. As a cold drink it is very refreshing. It is said that the Asian drink **lassi**, often made today from iced water and yoghurt, was popularized by Irish soldiers serving in the subcontinent who missed their native buttermilk.

C

Cabbage

Though highly prized throughout the continent of Europe, where it is often served with elaborate stuffings, as in the Hungarian Christmas speciality *toltost kapostzta* and the French *chou farci*, in Britain this vegetable is associated with the hated school dinners, and such institutions figure largely in its British perceptions (prisons, workhouses, bedsits and hospitals are often mentioned in the same breath as cabbage). This is of course due to the fact that the British have only one recipe for it (save the magnificent **bubble and squeak**): that is to say, boiling it till about all it is fit for is perhaps paper-making.

It is also widely used in pickled dishes such as **sauerkraut**, beloved throughout Germany and Central Europe. But for possibly the most elegant dishes involving cabbage you have to go to the Alsace-Lorraine region near the border between France and Germany, where you will discover exquisite stuffed cabbages cooked in wines and herbs and which are often the centrepiece of an entire meal. There is also the Jewish delicacy of cabbage leaves enclosing a mixture of rice and meat simmered in a sweet tomato sauce, called *holishkes*. Chinese cooking also possesses an elaborate stuffed cabbage dish called *kai choy*, which uses the Chinese bitter cabbage often known as 'mustard greens'. Not be confused with the sweet and softer *pak choy*.

Cabbage has medicinal purposes, owing to the rich amount of vitamin C that it contains. Because of this it became an important vegetable in the prevention of the ever prevalent scurvy which coursed for so long throughout mariners' working lives (see **guinea pig**). During Captain Cook's first expedition in 1769 some forty members of the crew of *The Adventurer* were injured during a violent storm. The ship's doctor saved them from gangrene by applying poultices made from cabbage leaves. The ship's log testifies that the doctor got the idea after eating a meal of cabbage and bacon. Presumably he dismissed the idea of bacon compresses.

Perhaps the reason why the British so despise the cabbage is that so few varieties are available. And that traditionally it was regarded as cattle food. Yet this vegetable is the subject of one of the most famous lines in poetry, 'Of ships and seals and sealing wax, and cabbages and kings' by Lewis Carroll, and indeed *Cabbages and Kings* is the title of the only novel by the great short story writer O. Henry.

Café

There are coffee houses throughout the world, of course, and in the Arab world they act much as pubs do in the UK, but the café is a different matter. Two countries in particular have cultures in which the café has become synonymous with, well, their cultures – Italy and France. In Italy you will find sandwiches or pastries, perhaps ice cream – *gelati* – wines, beers, spirits and coffee. They are not ristorantes or **trattorias**. They are not bars either. They are places to talk and exchange information, to meet informally. Unlike Britain and its public houses (though these institutions are rapidly changing), women and men meet in them without any sense of intimidation. And some of the cafés of the far north of Piedmont, for instance, are extraordinarily ornate. (I cite for example the Rococo interior of the famous Mulassano café in Turin: it would pass for a mini Palace of Versailles.)

But for the country which has perfected the café, indeed created what is now called 'café society', you have to look to France. There you will find bars and bistros and little eating places for working men called *estaminets*, and the small *tabacs* in which older men will have a drink, but cafés are the social centres of French life. It is impossible to think of France without thinking of cafés. These are not the eating houses of Britain, such as cafeterias. They are fundamental to the life, politics, philosophy, literature and intellectual pursuits of the French, much to the bemusement of the Anglo-American world.

Just why Britain has evolved a culture in which alcohol abuse is the major form of public entertainment rather than the civilized French café is difficult to grasp.

Calves' liver

This, like **veal**, is both expensive and increasingly difficult to obtain unless you are in the restaurant trade. It is creamy and subtle and much favoured by Italians, who cannot do without their veal. Following a considerable campaign by soppy-eyed veggies (especially women, I am afraid), it became virtually impossible to find the flesh of calves in butcher shops. Veal is, it is true, the flesh of the young of a cow, and the animal has never been weaned and is then slaughtered when only a few weeks old. I am a sentimental chap myself, but calves' liver (and veal) finds me crying all the way over the plate in front of me.

Camembert

A cheese from the Normandy village of the same name. A farmer's wife called Madame Marie Harel is said to have invented it in 1791, though, in truth, it was known a century before that. (Housewives made cheese, and all the great *fromages* throughout the world were created by farmers' wives. A little-known fact is that it was the womenfolk who brewed the beer as well. Thus the women-led prohibition laws of the USA seem, to say the least, ironic.)

I prefer it, like its near-sister **brie**, over-ripe and rather runny. This preference is much disapproved of by experts, but to hell with them.

Camp coffee

This coffee and chicory concentrate was popular in the late nineteenth century and during the first half of the twentieth, before the development of instant coffee. It was made by R. Paterson and Sons of Glasgow and was recognizable by the illustrated label showing a British officer being served by a turbaned Indian servant. The moustachioed soldier was not, as many assumed, Lord Kitchener. He was in fact General Sir Hector Macdonald, known as 'Scotland's Pride', hero of the first Boer War. Some of the pride was dissipated when Sir Hector shot himself in a Paris hotel following allegations of homosexuality. Many years later Lord Kitchener himself was accused of a similar taste for young men. By this time it hardly mattered: he was long in his watery grave. But another interesting fact. The Indian servant depicted on the label actually existed too. His name was Gurjeet Singh and, far from being a servant, he was a wealthy Indian nabob.

Candy

What Americans call, ludicrously, chocolate. ('Candy is dandy/But liquor is quicker', as Dorothy Parker has it.) In

Britain candy is a sweetmeat made with boiled sugar. Candy floss is a highly whipped sugar and water mixture sold at fairgrounds and the like and is virtually tasteless.

But the word itself goes back to about AD 1000, when the Arabs first constructed sugar refineries on the island of Candia – what we now call Crete – and called the result of their labours *quandi*, which came to mean 'crystallized sugar'.

Cannabis

A resin obtained from the hemp plant, also known as bhang, marijuana or hashish (from which the word 'assassin' is derived: the members of a Persian sect of the twelfth and thirteenth centuries were said to lull their victims to sleep by use of this drug before murdering them). It is an illegal narcotic in most parts of the world, though much used for all that. It is said to be of medical use as a painkiller and relaxant, especially for those suffering from chronic arthritis or muscular dystrophy, and considerable research is currently being undertaken to substantiate this claim. Most medical opinion seems to be in favour of its use by such patients. But its only culinary use seems to be in sponge cakes, as an alternative to smoking it.

Cannibalism

Humans are perhaps alone in their revulsion at eating the flesh of their own species, at least physically: they commonly enjoy it psychologically. *In extremis* the practice is not unknown: some have been forced by circumstances – lost at sea, aeroplane crashes etc. – to resort to this. The last person to have been convicted in Britain was the celebrated Scottish cannibal Sawney Bean. Germany had the rather dreadful Joachim Kroll, who ate his victims, not it seems from any other sense of gratification than that it was cheaper than meat. The Polynesian islands seem to have practised cannibalism as a ritual rather than for sustenance. It appears that they claimed European flesh was 'disgusting'. The best-known example of human cannibalism, much practised, and indeed extolled, would appear to be the feeding of human infants on mothers' milk. A graceful literary note from Baudelaire: bored by his would-be sophisticated lady companion at dinner, he delicately inquired if she didn't think that 'the brains of new-born babies have a slight after-taste of nuts?'.

This remark, however, did not cause as much offence as the entry in Diderot's *Encyclopédie* in which, at the conclusion of a long and learned description of cannibalism, he inserted 'See also: Holy Communion'. For such and other provocations he was, of course, excommunicated and his *Encyclopédie* remained on the Catholic Church's *Index* long after it had become virtually unread by anybody.

Canning

This process of preservation of foods by sterilizing at a high temperature and canning in cylinders of thin tin plate (today steel) dates from fairly late, around the mid-nineteenth century, and constituted a godsend for many. Though you will find consume-by dates on tins, actually the food is likely to be perfectly healthy beyond the usual two years or so which they claim. In fact, in low temperatures tinned products are safe for many years. When one of Captain Scott's polar camps was discovered eighty years later, the tins of bully beef were found to be perfectly edible.

Yet there has always been a certain stigma attached to canned foods, at least in Europe, in much the same way that ladies who provided 'shop-bought' cakes were despised. One reason was and is that many canned foods started out with inferior recipes. There are, however, many luxury products. And it was the great Escoffier himself who invested in canning, in conjunction with the firm of Crosse & Blackwell.

Capercaillie

This large member of the grouse family (it is the size of a **turkey**) is found only in areas of Scotland and Sweden. In both countries the bird is an endangered species and is thus rarely encountered, let alone eaten.

Capers

Pickled buds from a shrub grown in the Mediterranean and often used as an ingredient of **tartare sauce**.

Capon

Rarely seen these days, this used to be popular as a more flavoursome substitute for **turkey**. It is a neutered cockerel, which as a result becomes larger and plumper than other chickens. If this seems cruel, you must bear in mind that when hens' chicks, the nice fluffy little things that they are, are sexed, almost all the little male birds are immediately thrown into a bin and incinerated. The females, after all, lay eggs. The practice of assassinating male animals is widespread. Sheep, pigs, goats: virtually all male domestic animals grown for food are often destroyed at birth. There are feminists who feel the same about humans. There are times when I am sympathetic to this view.

Capsicums

Also known as sweet peppers or pimentos. Originating in tropical climes of the Americas, they are green when young and turn yellow or red as they ripen. I never saw them in my childhood and first tasted them in my early twenties, when I was very intrigued by the sharp, fresh, unique flavour of the green pepper. I have, over the years, come to dislike the green variety: I find their sharper flavour too obtrusive. The famous black bean sauce, much used in Cantonese cookery, especially in their beef dishes, is much improved, in my view, by using the mellower, warmer, yellow or red peppers rather than green. Similarly I disapprove of the increasing use of green peppers in curry *massala*: to my mind they add a dissonant note. **Hungarian cookery** agrees with my preference.

Caramel

Browned sugar or glucose, sometimes used more as a colour than a flavour. It was early observed, one could say invented, by the Arabs when they first started an industrial sugar-making process and discovered a thick, brown, sticky product from the decantation of their sugar. The Arabs called it *kurat al milh*, 'ball of sweet salt'. Among its first uses, unlikely as this sounds, was as a depilatory for the ladies of the harem. The very thought of this gives you something to chew on.

Caraway seeds

Though grown mainly in the Netherlands, these are used in a variety of foods, especially in breads and biscuits, but for some reason are widespread in savoury dishes in **Hungarian cookery**. The dish that Hungary has given to the world – goulash (properly spelt *gulyas* and pronounced 'goolyash') – should contain a fair amount of caraway seeds.

Carbonnade

A Belgian **daube** or stew using beer instead of wine. Belgium has a reputation for being boring, but in fact the restaurants of Brussels are perhaps the finest in the world and that city's Grande Place contains eateries representing virtually every known national cuisine.

Though Belgian cookery is largely similar to that of northern France, there are national dishes, among which can be numbered the famous **waterzooi**, a sort of chicken *pot au feu*; the very smart Brussels restaurants serve the chicken whole and carve it in front of you with splendid showmanship. Old-fashioned Belgians eat the soup separately.

The other great Belgian delicacy takes the humble British chips or American French fries to a gourmet's delight unimaginable to either of these peoples. They come in a cone-shaped container, are regarded as a meal in themselves and are, or should be, accompanied by real **mayonnaise**. They are very expensive. They are worth it.

Yet another Belgian achievement is **chocolate**. Why Belgium should have become so expert in the manufacture of this highly addictive sweetmeat is difficult to understand but it is so. And like their *frites*, Belgian chocolates are extraordinarily expensive. Boxes of them are stupendously bound and wrapped in ribbons, and it is then that you cannot grasp why anybody should think the Belgians boring.

Cardoon
A vegetable similar to the globe artichoke, and a member of the thistle family. Used in Italy and France and unusual in Britain. Clarissa Dickson Wright, one of the Two Fat Ladies of TV fame, is very keen on them, one suspects because of her Scottish connections and the novelty value.

Carob
This is a pod grown as a fruit of a Mediterranean shrub and is sometimes known as the 'locust bean'. It is often used as a substitute for **chocolate** and **cocoa** powder.

Carpetbag steak
A North American speciality (also found in Australasia), in which thick steaks have little pockets cut and raw oysters placed in them. Whoever thought this up was as lacking in taste as the cannibals before mentioned.

Carrot

A root vegetable which is now characteristically a vivid orange colour (the first carrots were pale yellow). It is very sweet and can be made into a sugar substitute. There is a sweetened carrot cake much admired by health freaks. The cake is, needless to say, absolutely disgusting. During the Second World War, when there was a surfeit of carrots, it was proclaimed capable of enabling night-fighter pilots to see in the dark. This was drivel, of course, but it did make little boys eat up their carrots. The real reason why this nonsense was put about was because the top-secret radar had been put into operation by the British and the Krauts were daft enough to believe the carrot story.

Incidentally, in the reign of the early Stuart kings the leaves were used for decorations for hats.

Casserole

A cooking method by which meat or poultry and vegetables and liquids are slowly stewed in the oven in a dish with a tightly fitting lid. The argument which many people, especially women, today often of a fundamentalist feminist ideology, make against cooking is that it takes a long time. This is rarely true at all, and in the case of a casserole it takes barely ten minutes to prepare the ingredients. Not only does the oven do all the work thereafter, but if you have a timer on your oven you can set the cooking for a specific time when it begins the cooking process but also the time when it is completed. This means that you can swan about all day or go to work and come home to a hot and satisfying dish. It is so easy that I have no time for female whining about cooking, or ignorance on the part of men in the matter.

Cassoulet

You would think that this is bloody ambrosia according to French writers: it is in fact a stew with beans. A hotpot really, with inferior ingredients, this is a speciality of south-west France, an area noted for its industrial peasantry. Toulouse insists that this hearty bean-based stew must have preserved goose. That is hardly surprising in a region that specializes in **pâté de fois gras**.

There are those who insist that the dish originates in the town of Castelnaudary. It contains pork, sausages and beans. Truth to tell, it is essentially a filler, for poor folk. It also takes for bloody ever to assemble. My father, who had first encountered this when stabled with a family in Paris while he helped to liberate the city in the last war, had a relish for cassoulet and used to make it with black pudding.

Cauliflower

This delicate vegetable, a member of the cabbage family, is most commonly seen in the UK as cauliflower cheese, a dish that is to my mind usually insufferably bland. There are similar dishes in France using mornay sauce (**béchamel sauce** with cheese), in which **cayenne** pepper helps to add heat and flavour, and an excellent Hungarian cauliflower dish made with Hungarian soured cream, hot paprika, potatoes and finely diced ham. The vegetable also makes a wonderful cream soup, and paradoxically, like lettuce, is strong-tasting when puréed for this soup.

But as a simple boiled vegetable a cauliflower is rather boring, a point made by Mark Twain's Pudd'nhead Wilson, who stated that a 'cauliflower is nothing but a cabbage with a college education'.

Caviar

Though beluga caviar is the most famous and expensive variety, there are two other types of this roe, eggs of the sturgeon fish found in the Caspian Sea. (There are sturgeons in estuaries in other countries such as France, Canada, the

USA and Romania, but they are very inferior to those of the Caspian.)

Besides beluga, which is the rarest sturgeon, there are also *osetr*, which is smaller-grained, and the *sevruga*. The only country besides Russia that can produce these magnificent roes is Iran. Islamic dietary laws, which are rather similar to those in Leviticus which give rise to kosher instructions, forbid the eating of any fish without scales or its eggs, and for many years there was no Iranian industry until the father of the last Shah, Rezah Pahlevi, recreated it as part of his modernization of the country. It disappeared for a decade or so when the ayatollahs were at their fanatical height. Needless to say, such a fabulously lucrative trade has since been reintroduced. (It never really went away, and a massive illegal trade went on all through the ayatollah years.)

The caviar business takes great skill and this, combined with the rarity of the fish itself, results in one of the most expensive foodstuffs of all. Caviar is best eaten – and so thought Rabelais, a devotee of this food – with thin slices of toast, without the lemon juice so many seem to think necessary. The drink to go with it should be a good Russian vodka such as Moskovskaya or Stolichnaya. Both are expensive and difficult to come by. So is caviar.

Cayenne

This ground pepper, made from very hot members of the capsicum family and grown in North America and West Africa (see **capsicums**) must be used sparingly. Actually I would suggest using one of the Hungarian hot paprikas or a hot chilli powder instead: they add flavour and not merely heat.

Cellulose

A carbohydrate found in cereals and other vegetable matter. It has virtually no nutritional value but is a component in fruits and vegetables that aids bowel regularity.

Cephalopod

This is the term for marine animals such as octopus, squid and cuttlefish, much used in Mediterranean cookery. I have never found them edible myself. They are also visually abhorrent and the very stuff of nightmares. Naturally the Japanese love them.

Cereal

Most people merely think of this as **breakfast** cereals such as **cornflakes** and **shredded wheat**, and other god-awful brekkie-wekkies, but the word applies to edible grains such as **rice**, **barley**, **maize**, **oats** and **wheat**. The study of paleolithic middens shows that humans consumed cereals from the beginning of time. One way or another, they are the oldest cultivated foods and are still the staples of most of the people of the planet. Ten thousand years ago the city of Jericho was famed for its production of cereals and thus, to protect its grain stores, built walls around the city. To no avail, as it turned out.

Challah

Made with eggs in the yeasted dough and usually braided, then sprinkled with poppy seeds, this delicious bread is for the Jewish *Shabbat* but can be eaten by anybody, on any day of the week, and if you are fortunate to live anywhere near a Jewish bakery, enjoy, enjoy, *goyim* or not.

Champ

This dish is common in Ireland, where it used to be the main food for the fast day of Fridays during Lent. It consists of mashed potatoes mixed with such vegetables or herbs as parsley or nettles, and most often with scallions (spring onions). Good fresh butter is its sauce. See **bubble and squeak**.

Champagne

A naturally sparkling wine from the area around Rheims, this is dry to sweet, and is usually white, though there is a pink champagne. Only champagne from this district is permitted to be titled this in Europe and according to the strict *appellation contrôlée* rules it must be produced by the méthode champenoise, in which the bottles are regularly turned in their racks.

There are champagne-style wines made elsewhere, of course, and most of them are very much cheaper than the exorbitant cost of the French ones. There is even a very acceptable Indian champagne called Omar Khayyam. (The Indian Urdu term – simkin – is a corruption of **champagne**.)

No one quite knows why, but the French ship more bubbly to the UK than anywhere else, even America. It is still expensive but was even more so, relatively speaking, until 1861, when Gladstone reduced the duty on it. It was still a drink for toffs, though, and sold at five bob a bottle. That was then the average weekly wage of a tradesman. In 1869 the most popular music-hall song was George Leybourne's 'Champagne Charlie'. Famous Champagne Charlies range from the swindler Horace Bottomley (whose tipple was Pommery) to Winston Churchill (Pol Roger). On the Great Commoner's death Madame Pol Roger decreed that a black border be put round the edge of the label, where it remains to this day.

There is also the term 'Champagne Socialist', denoting the sort of radical whose lofty ideals for the working class do not get in the way of his taste for the high life, cuff links, evening dress and high-minded dinner party conversations in Chelsea or Hampstead Garden Suburb.

As it happens, I can easily resist this brand of alcoholic pop: for some reason I think it smells of over-hung meat. Incidentally this bubbly is pronounced 'shampanyie'. The Lower Orders insist it is 'shampane'. The Lower Orders, no matter how they pronounce this dreadful fizz, are welcome to it.

Chapati

This is an unleavened bread made from wholemeal flour. Chapatis are cooked daily throughout India and are most common in the north-west of the subcontinent, where other breads such as *naan* and *puri*, also unleavened, predominate over rice.

What pushes chapatis into the history books, however, is that the thin little roundels of bread were used as a code for those fomenting what Indians call the First Indian War of Independence, and what the West calls the Indian Mutiny. This tragedy, for such it was, started in Meerut in 1857, but legend has it that runners went from village to village, carrying with them a chapati and demanding that the receiver cook ten more and distribute them to other recipients – a kind of chain letter.

There is some truth in the legend, and much has been made of this by novelists. John Masters repeats the story in his novel *The Nightrunners of Bengal*, and it also emerges in J.G. Farrell's magnificent *The Siege of Krishnapur* (one of the few readable novels to have won the Booker Prize). But mutiny aside, the next time you eat curry try using chapatis as a utensil and eat with your hands, as Indians do.

Char

Though this is indeed an oily fish found in northern waters, the term usually employed in the UK means something else. Derived from the soldiers of the East India Company's word for **tea**, it was originally a Japanese word, *tcha*, brought to India by the company merchants. 'A cup of char' was synonymous with the cheerful British Tommy, who had brought the corruption back from India, and it was what sustained the British soldier throughout the Second World War, from Dunkirk to Tobruk. To be a proper cup of char it should be heavily sweetened, liberally laced with milk, and the tea should be stewed till it is near fermentation.

Charcuterie
A specialist shop in France for pork produce: the product itself is also known by this name. In my childhood there were similar shops in Britain, and pork butchers abounded. Their wares were of a high quality, but the pork butcher is alas no more in our high streets.

Cheddar
A cheese originally hailing from the Cheddar Gorge area in Somerset, this is now perhaps the most famous, and certainly the most worldwide, cheese of all. Today mild cheddar seems to be preferred and is mind-numbingly bland. When truly mature (from eighteen months upwards), it is a wonder. For a taste sensation try it with a **digestive biscuit**.

Cheese
A condensed and solid form of milk, around since pre-biblical times, probably by nomadic tribes who used it as a form of preserved lactic nutrition.

There are thousands of cheeses, from rich soft cheeses such as **brie** and **camembert**, both manufactured from cow's milk, to heavy, salty, crumbly cheeses made from goat's milk, yak's milk, buffalo milk – in fact, cheese can be and is made from any lactating mammal, though I doubt if humans have attempted it with their own.

Britain has some exceptionally sumptuous cheeses and no blue-veined variety – not the roquefort of France, the gorgonzola of Italy or the Danish blue of Scandinavia – can compare with the kingly **stilton**. But France is the kingdom of cheeses. General de Gaulle once deplored the difficulty of governing a country with more than 300 varieties of cheese. Winston Churchill, though, once memorably said of France during the second World War that a country with so many cheeses could never perish. Both chaps were right.

British cheeses, among which can be numbered Caerphilly, Derby, the crumbly Lancashire, Wensleydale, the splendid Scottish Dunlop and Gloucester (it is a piece of this cheese which is delivered to Bill Sykes by the Artful Dodger in *Oliver Twist*), can be compared favourably with any others in the world, which can rarely be said of most of that island's products.

Cheese is now relatively expensive in Britain – sadly, because it is rich in proteins and ideal for growing children as it is an excellent source of calcium, phosphorous and vitamins A and D (see **vitamins**). Equally sad is that a great many cheeses are today packed full of unpleasant preservatives. Two cheeses I haven't mentioned must be included here. No **pizza** can be made without **mozzarella**, traditionally made from buffalo milk. But though the Italians have a great many splendid versions of their formidable formaggios, one stands out: **parmesan**, a hard cheese from northern Italy, of which the best is *parmigiano reggiano*, from the region of Parma and Bologna, which is protected by labelling laws. It is pleasant as a dessert cheese when young but is best known when grated. This is used in an enormous number of dishes, perhaps the most famous being spaghetti bolognese. Another literary reference: it is a small piece of parmesan that Squire Trelawny presents to the cheese-mad Ben Gunn in *Treasure Island*.

The other cheese that should be mentioned is processed cheese. This commercial muck is so dreadful that the only possible literary reference would be to Dante's *Inferno*.

Cheese pastry
A shortcrust pastry used for savoury dishes and which was the pastry for the wartime **Woolton pie**. It can also be used for the making of the lovely cheese straws, an easily produced treat rarely seen these days.

Cheesecake
Made from cream or cottage cheese, eggs, sugar and butter, often with a crumbed **digestive biscuit** base. And lemon. My brother Richard, on reading this item, wanted to know what happened to the wonderful cheesecake we used to obtain in Glasgow's south-side delicatessens, which had raisins and sultanas and was drenched in **cinnamon**. And something very strange. We used to eat it in Michael Morrison's back shop on *Shabbat* along with vodka. It is generally slightly chilled and, though of Middle European origin, was for many years almost exclusively an American speciality, but it has, justifiably, spread again across Europe. There are few American food imports that can be applauded: in this case we should clap our hands together for Elvis Presley, whose favourite dessert this was. It helped to kill him too, the amount of bloody **cholesterol** that was in it.

Chef
Seriously meaning the senior cook in a kitchen, in restaurants, chefs have now become television personalities throughout the United Kingdom for some reason unknown to the rest of the entire world because virtually none of the British telly chefs is any use.

Starting with the fat and bearded Philip Harben in the early 1950s and then going on to the stately and bathetic Johnny and Fanny Cradock and a succession of idjits, few of the United Kingdom phenomena seem capable of much more than the display of the lack of the syntax available to those educated in a school above the level of what was once known as Secondary Modern in England (see **English cookery**), chefs in the modern age are either the poor sweated buggers who work in proper kitchens or are TV personalities who are prepared to cook a dog's turd in a saffron sauce with a *jus* of the canine's own urine. And if you think I am exaggerating, I am probably not.

But to chefs. Though much nonsense is expressed in words and TV exegeses on these recent phenomena, chefs are indeed chiefs in their own domain of the **restaurant**, and though we have a great deal of drivel about the prominence of such largely spurious personalities, it is certainly true that the last centuries of the development of cooking could not have been achieved without the extraordinary efforts and, if I may say so, genius of those professional cooks.

France has, for instance, a long history of celebrity chefs, and still has them, part of a veritable Pantheon – from *littérateurs* such as the jurist Brillat-Savarin to Escoffier to present day chefs such as Michel Roux and Michel Guérard. (Mention must be made here of Marcel Boulestin, who did so much to promote both French and British cookery during the two world wars – he was incidentally the first chef in the world to demonstrate cookery on television.)

It was in the aftermath of the French Revolution that the chefs of the great *aristo* households were forced by necessity to open up restaurants, as against the former inns and taverns of ordinary people's lives. Beauvilliers, former steward to the Count of Provence, opened what was probably the first modern restaurant as we know it, in Paris, having escaped the Terror. He employed a young twenty-year-old chef who was to become one of the most influential cookery writers of the modern age, Marie-Antoine (Antonin) Carême. Carême wrote an enormous amount of words on the subject and his influence on French, and world, *haute cuisine* cannot be understated. His work was carried on by chefs such as Auguste Escoffier, long of the London Savoy and Carlton hotels, and Jules Gouffe of the French Jockey Club, thus laying the astounding reputation of French chefs, many of whom have travelled the world in all the great hotels and restaurants – as they continue to do – seen as great artists in their own right.

French television would see the Jamie Olivers of England as absurd: they are. A French housewife, north or south, from any province, will consider British celebrity chefs as both presumptuous and ridiculous, as well they might. (Since writing this I have discovered that French television is now broadcasting British celebrity chef shows and young French women are as enthralled, apparently, as their young counterparts in the UK, which suggests that young women throughout Europe no longer know how to cook at all.) See also **cooks**.

Cherry

A fruit of the rose family, related to the plum and, though of Middle-Eastern origin, now grown widely in Central Europe. It is the basis of **Black Forest gateau**, also of liqueurs such as kirsch. But glacé cherries, preserved in sugar and syrup, are widely used as ingredients for cakes. As a boy I was wont to eat the tub of cherries before my mother made the cherry cake. I also ate the cake mixture. As William Brown (*Just William*) thought, actually cooking the mixture seemed a bit of a waste.

Chestnuts

Once a staple food in the mountainous areas of the Mediterranean, where cereals were difficult to grow (indeed Corsica still has its *pulenta* – chestnut bread). The French *marron*, a sweet chestnut, is still widely used in the confection industry. Chestnuts are a much-ignored food, but they course through food history. (Curiously, in times of antiquity chestnuts were reserved for consumption by women only.) The main use of chestnuts in British cookery is as a **stuffing** for **turkey**. And there is a magnificent dessert from Italy called Mont Blanc, which consists of puréed chestnuts topped with whipped cream and resembling the famous mountain.

Chewing gum
Made from the milky sap of the sapodilla tree, which itself produces a rich fruit, chewing gum was used by the native Indians of Mexico. The habit of chewing it was transported to the USA in the nineteenth century, where the Wrigley company quickly became the major manufacturer. It has no nutritional value and is beloved by louts and the mentally feeble. Footballers invariably enjoy it.

Chicken
This common domestic fowl was once very expensive (though it expressed the alleged intention of Marie Antoinette, it was Henri IV of France who was actually the originator of the phrase that 'there should be a chicken in every pot') and was considered in my childhood as a luxury food. The first time I ate it was for a Christmas dinner in the mid-1950s; this was before the widespread development of battery chickens.

At its best, chicken meat is very flavoursome, but owing to the industrial development of what was once a fowl from the farmyards one rarely comes across a chicken that tastes of very much at all. (The same goes for chickens' children, **eggs**.)

No matter, chicken is now probably the most widely eaten meat in the world. A great many Western children have only ever seen it coated in batter or breadcrumbs and consumed with a wallpaper paste-type sauce, a travesty of the famous dish of fried chicken from the southern states of America. There are a myriad of chicken dishes: so many that entire books have been devoted to recipes using chicken. A few must be mentioned here, though: Chicken Kiev is a classic Russian dish which consists of flattened chicken breasts stuffed with garlic butter, which are then coated in breadcrumbs and fried until golden; Chicken Maryland is a version of **Southern fried chicken** but hails from New England and has as accompaniments fried bananas, gravy and corn fritters; Chicken *à la King* is another North American dish and involves diced chicken in a rich white sauce with green peppers and onions, flavoured with sherry and eaten with **wild rice**.

A seemingly odd recipe is for hindle wakes – chicken with prunes and vinegar. It is a speciality from Lancashire and sounds like the title of a gritty northern English play. (There is indeed a classic play with that title, written by Stanley Houghton and set in a Lancashire mill town.) The dish is, in fact, delicious, if a little bracing.

A mention must be made of soups using chicken. No Jewish mother would be without her chicken soup – Arnold Wesker wrote a play called *Chicken Soup with Barley*, which struck me as strange in that Jewish mommas generally employ rice. (Indeed chicken soup is so much a staple of Jewish households that it is known as 'Jewish penicillin'.) His play was not gritty northern sentiment and was set in London's East End, but it was first performed in the Belgrade Theatre in Coventry. The other great chicken soup is the Scottish speciality cock-a-leekie, a soup not unlike a **pot au feu**, and now a fetish in expensive Scottish restaurants.

Chickens' feet

Rarely sold these days in poulterers, they are regarded as essential to genuine Chinese cuisine and are fiddly things which have to be blanched and take bloody ages to descale. Hardly worth the effort really.

Chickpea
This is a legume common to the Mediterranean area and Asia. Usually used as a pulse, it is the main ingredient of such dishes as the Jewish felafel, or the Greek hummus (also well known throughout the Middle East). Itself essentially tasteless, it remains a major bulk pulse, as does the **lentil**.

Chicory
Though this vegetable is used for salads and features as a vegetable accompaniment in many cuisines, it is as an additive to **coffee** that it is mainly employed: indeed the notorious *ersatz* coffee of the German war years was made out of this bitter-tasting veg, (see also **dandelion**) and remains written on the minds of Germans of wartime vintage. Chicory, however, is the national vegetable of Belgium (thus the alternative name 'Belgian endive'), where it is known as *whitloof*. See **Camp coffee**.

Chilli
The smallest of the capsicum family, it has a strong and fiery flavour and can be red, green or yellow. (Though most chilli peppers are small, thin and pointed, there are some variants that are round, rather like cherry tomatoes (see **tomato**). One such grown in the West Indies is known as *bouda a Man Jacques*. In English this means 'Madame Jacques's bum'. (It is a very hot bum at that.)

The inner core of seeds is the hottest part of this pepper and must be used with caution. Two cuisines are dependent on it: South-East Asian and Mexican. In the latter case there is a Tex-Mex dish that has become universal – *chilli con carne*, a minced-meat stew simmered with onions, red kidney beans and refried beans, usually served with **tortillas** and rice. A genuine recipe I received from my friend Marilyn, who was for many years the interpreter for the Mexican ambassadors to various European countries, included a goodly amount of ground cumin and a glass of strong beer. When she cooked this for me on one of her regular visits to Europe, she included a mix of various chillies she had brought from Mexico itself. She admitted that her years in Mexico had made her physically addicted to chilli, the hotter the better.

Chinese restaurants

It would be absurdly presumptuous in a volume of this size to be able to comment on the vast scale of Chinese cuisine, but mention must be made of the ubiquitous Chinese restaurants of the UK.

Chinese restaurant cookery differs from country to country. The four main cuisines in China itself can be said to be that of the south (Canton), north (Peking), east (Shanghai) and west (Szechwan). In America Chinese food on the East Coast is much influenced by Cantonese cuisine, that on the West Coast by Peking cookery. In France many Chinese restaurants are actually Vietnamese, while in Britain the largest influence is from the former British colony Hong Kong. Chinese cookery has been imported throughout the world because of the widespread emigration of mainland Chinese to virtually every part of the globe. And because the Chinese are remarkably adaptable, they often change their cuisine to take local ingredients into account.

On a quirky note: Chinese cuisine easily accommodates Jewish dietary laws, as long as the meat is kosher. Butter is rarely used, and the only milk used in meat and poultry dishes is coconut milk. (Indeed I cherish a splendid book of Chinese cuisine for Jews who eat kosher, written by Ruth and Bob Grossman, published in 1963 and written in New Yorkese *yidishe*. The Grosssmans could not manage to get round the laws concerning such Chinese necessities as, for instance, prawns, nor could the popular pork *char sui* ever be contemplated. For dietary laws see **kosher**.)

There are a few reasonably authentic Chinese restaurants in Britain's major cities, and they can be easily identified: Chinese eat in them. But for most people the Chinese restaurant of the high street take-away variety provides a travesty of Chinese cuisine, albeit tasty and filling dishes.

Chips

Known in the USA as 'french fries' (chips are what Brits call 'crisps' in that subcontinent) and in France as *frites*, chips have become ubiquitous throughout the Western world. The recipe for the perfect chip is as follows: cut the potatoes, which should be of the waxy variety, fairly thickly and immerse in water for half an hour and then drain. (This is to remove some of the starch.) Heat the oil or fat. It will be seen to be the right temperature if, when one chip is put in, the pan starts to sizzle. Lower the temperature and put the chips in. Allow the chips to absorb the oil/fat at this fairly low heat and remove shortly, draining the chips on paper towels. Reheat the chip pan and raise the temperature, then reintroduce the chips. The oil/fat absorbed by the chips will be pushed out of them, and the chips will be ready when they are seen to be golden in colour and rise to the top. This method produces the perfect chip, crisp and golden on the outside and powdery on the inside. They will not be soft or flabby or oily, as one often encounters in fish and chip shops.

Chocolate

Probably originally a drink made from coca beans by the Aztecs, coca butter was well established in Europe by the early eighteenth century but was first used as the basis for a refreshing drink similar to **coffee**. The origins of chocolate tablet are somewhat inchoate but Holland was making this confectionery as early as the mid-1700s. (Bonnie Prince Charlie brought with him several pounds of chocolate solids when he first tried out his coup in the '45 revolution. Not from Holland though: by then Belgium was the main producer of this sweetmeat. See also **carbonnade** re Belgian chocolates.)

Later a firm called Lindt, based in Switzerland, became the first commercial company to produce this. (Suchard disputes this.) Another Swiss firm, Nestlé, not only invaded the market but became the world leader when it set itself up in America. But the largest *per capita* consumer of this product is the United Kingdom, and as a result the major manufacturers are, oddly, British. Even more oddly, the three great chocolate companies are all of Quaker origin: Cadbury's, Rowntree's and Fry's. The other large chocolate company was Terry's, also a Quaker family. (It is said that the Quakers founded chocolate as a drink because of their firm opposition to alcohol. Very large numbers of British industrialists were of the temperance persuasion: it did not stop them from making fortunes out of their workforce and paying them so little that they could afford neither alcohol nor the products they made for their masters either.)

But there is a reservation concerning the benevolence of the chocolate giants. They were indeed paternalists. Cadbury's Bournville village, for instance, refused to have a public house. An employee who was discovered betting or having a drink was instantly sacked. So-called 'model' employers all seem to have this dictatorial trait. Lord Leverhulme's village of Port Sunlight, near Birkenhead, England, made similar provisions for the workers.

But what is it about chocolate makers? For the largest manufacturer in the USA, Hershey's, also operates an employee-friendly organization, with an entire town with free schools and health services, leisure centres and the like, much on the model of Cadbury's Bournville. Indeed, when Hershey's shares were put on the open market the directors refused to sell, thereby losing several million dollars' worth of profit for each individual director. They wanted to keep the vision of Utopia of their founder, Milton Hershey. Why chocolate makers, in a world of global corporatism, should be so enlightened is a mystery. Could it be that the best-known comfort food inclines towards comfort employment? Whatever, chocolate is addictive, so much so that the word 'chocaholic' has been coined to describe the many millions throughout the world who cannot live without this confection.

Cholent

A Jewish dish for the Sabbath, this is a beef casserole made with beans, barley and vegetables. It is cooked very slowly and is put in the oven before *Shabbat* and removed at midday, thereby avoiding strict orthodox laws which forbid work on the holy day.

Cholesterol

This fat is cycled through the liver and is necessary to health. Indeed low cholesterol is nearly as dangerous as high levels of it. High-density lipoproteins (HDL) are found in such oils as olive, rapeseed and fish oils and counteract the effects of low-density lipoproteins (LDL), which derive from animal fats and dairy produce. However, diets that provide very little LDL are injurious to health too. The Chinese diet, which is low in cholesterol, has to be supplemented by the occasional intake of animal fats. While it was once the custom in the West to spoon **cod liver oil** into infants, it is still common for Chinese mums to medicate their offspring with lumps of butter every day.

Chopsticks

Made traditionally from ivory but today more often from plastic, these anachronisms are used by Chinese diners (throughout the Far East too, of course) and, like a lot of Chinese things, such as their ridiculous alphabet let alone their absurd though aesthetically pleasing calligraphy, are too stupid to contemplate. Yet it remains true, for no reason one can rationally discern, that Chinese food still tastes better when you use chopsticks. Also a dexterity in their use suggests that one is a sophisticated fellow and is useful when showing off to girls: girls tell me the same goes for them with chaps.

Chop suey

A Chinese friend of mine tells me that this literally means, in Cantonese, 'rubbish' and claims that apocrypha has it that in the mid-nineteenth century a Chinese ambassador to America described such a recipe to take the piss out of the Yanks. Nevertheless it is a much-loved dish and synonymous with Chinese food, authentic or not. The dish contains a variety of meats, usually chicken or strips of pork, bean sprouts and other lightly cooked vegetables, a marinade of soy sauce and sherry, and prawns. It is one of those oddities which, invented abroad, has come back to its native country, and is much beloved by the Hong Kong Chinese, few of whom know that it is less than authentic. What the hell, it is so good that nobody much cares what its provenance is.

Chow

An Americanism for a meal, also known as 'chuck'. To this day film companies refer to the caravanserai that provides food to the various actors, extras and assorted mountebanks as the 'chow wagon'. The word has its origin in the Chinese word *chow-chow*, meaning, literally, 'a snack'. There is also

the word *chow*, meaning an attack in the game Mah Jong. See
dim sum.

Chowder

A kind of New England soup made from potato, bacon and
fish, often smoked. Rather a variant of the Scottish **cullen
skink**. The writer and intellectual giant Mary McCarthy gives
a fine receipt for it in her book *Birds of America*. McCarthy is
most famous for her seminal novel, today rather overlooked,
The Group (see **recipe**).

McCarthy was in fact a fine food writer and was often
derided for her cookery columns on the basis that intellectu-
als don't enjoy food, and certainly would never know how to
cook if, that is, they had any intelligence. The French knew
better, and McCarthy was awarded the prestigious *Légion
d'Honneur*, probably not least for the fact that she kept a good
table, thought impossible for an American national. (Though
she spent her last twenty years as a French citizen.)

Christmas cake

An interesting point here. Many home bakers bake this in the
autumn and preserve it in a tightly lidded container until
Christmas Day itself. The high alcohol content preserves it
and thus the cake has time to mature, as it were. See also
wedding cake.

Chutney

From the Hindi word *chatni*, meaning a side dish or sambal
of relishes, this is now a positively English product made
often from apples and other fruits liberally doused in vinegar
and spices. Onions, garlic and sugar are also ingredients.
Originating in India, the most famous chutney is probably
that made with mango. (James Allan Sharwood imported
his mango chutney originally from Bombay in 1890, and it

quickly became a luxury item in upper-class English house-holds.) Lime chutneys are favourites in north India and can be gloriously hot.

Also known as pickles, the best-known chutney in Britain is the brand known as Branston Pickle: though inferior to many other brands, it is the leader in the field. Another relish is **piccalilli**, in which florets of cauliflower and cubed marrow are marinated in vinegar, mustard and turmeric. Chutneys and sambals are characteristic of South-East Asian cuisine, especially that of Malaysia and Indonesia. For a reason unknown Britons tend to buy more chutneys, relishes and **ketchup** per head than any other nation on earth. Well, they help to give a taste to perhaps one of the blandest cuisines on this planet.

Cider

An alcoholic beverage made by fermenting apple juice, its pro-duction in the UK is almost entirely in the south of England, especially in the West Country (though in fact the largest cider manufacturer in the world, with over 40% of the market, is Bulmers of Hereford, and Herefordshire provides most of the orchards used in the Bulmer production). The myth that it is drunk copiously by smock-clad yokels is just that: a myth. In fact cider, though it has undergone a slight revival in recent years, has never recovered the prime position that it once had, even in 'zummerzet'. Once every farmer's wife brewed it, but cider is now almost entirely com-mercial. For some years it was poor in quality, and until recently the commercial giants saw no reason to improve their product.

Cider is a different matter in France – actually in Normandy, where cider is still treated with considerable respect and a great many Norman dishes are created using cider. Norman cookery is very distinctive, and as well as using the vast supplies of apples for cider they use the apples too. And cream, and butter. Thus a very rich cuisine indeed.

Cinnamon

Though this product of the bark of an evergreen tree (*cinnamomum zeylanicum*) is widely used throughout the Middle East and the Indian subcontinent, it is rarely seen in Western food save in confectionery, usually in ground form. Northern and central Europe is liberal in employing it for baked foods. And it made its mark on me in childhood as a dusting for the little sweetmeats made by a local baker which he called 'marzipan potatoes'. See **marzipan**.

Clam

A bivalve shellfish best known as the origin of the clambake, a beach party barbecue and a rite apparently necessary for young Californians. It was also the title of an atrocious movie made by Elvis Presley.

Clootie dumpling

As a Scot, I cannot resist including this unique Caledonian dessert. It is a suet pudding, very highly spiced with cinnamon, ginger, cloves, nutmeg and cumin, containing dried fruits and wrapped in a cloth (cloot) and then boiled. The result is that there is a thick gelatinous skin around the dumpling. Just why, in what is largely a simple peasant cuisine, this Scottish pudding should have evolved and remained so popular is inexplicable. It used to be made instead of birthday cakes, which were in my childhood an English sort of thing and not at all anything like a clootie dumpling. But then, there is nothing in the annals of cookery quite like a clootie dumpling.

Cloud ear fungus

A fungus grown on oak trees in China, this is dried and, when soaked, grows to five times its size, ending by looking much as the English translation has it. Very expensive, even in China, it can be replaced, to good effect, by Chinese dried mushrooms.

Cloves

This dried calyx of a fruit tree is – one wonders at this too – the staple crop of Madagascar, from where most of the world's supplies stem. Widely used in Indonesian cookery, and indeed throughout Asia, it has a powerful taste and aroma. It has two splendid uses, however: 1) it is, or should be, an essential for a hot whisky (hot toddy); and 2) chewing and sucking a couple of cloves removes the smell of alcohol from the breath. This is a useful piece of information for all of us who enjoy a snifter and is especially good news for journalists, doctors and other alcoholics looking for a job.

Coca-Cola

A brand of cola known throughout the world and synonymous with the mercantile expansionism of the USA. It possesses a distinctive logo and an equally distinctive shape of bottle. The artist Andy Warhol famously made prints of the bottle and it is said that an early Coca-Cola advert invented the image of Father Christmas, who was in fact originally clad in green and not in the now familiar pillar-box red. It was, like many other drinks, originally invented by a young chemist (allegedly one Hiram Young of Atlanta, Georgia), and later marketed by a group of Atlantan businessmen who bought the recipe for $100.

In the 1980s Coca-Cola decided to relaunch their product with a different recipe. It was a total disaster and just goes to show that 23-year-old accountants are less to be trusted than small-town apothecaries in Atlanta, Georgia, a century ago.

Cola itself is made from African beans and, though now absolutely harmless, once contained a high amount of caffeine. The beans could be fermented into a thick alcoholic liquor and possessed, it was claimed, strong aphrodisiac qualities. Despite being utterly alcohol-free, Coca-Cola can be said to have similar qualities to this day: no teenage American romance can apparently flourish without a Coke being involved, a drugstore, a soda fountain and all the rest of Norman Rockwell's Americana.

Cochineal
This deep red food colouring sounds so unlikely that it has to be true, and it is. It is made from the crushed bodies of beetles that reside in cactus plants in Mexico. Once again one wonders who thought this up. And why.

Cocida a la madrileña
A Spanish stew using meat, chicken, vegetables and chick peas, it is similar to the **cholent** eaten by Spanish Jews. World Jewry has claimed it in the last four centuries, and it is a favourite Sunday repast in Jewish households.

Cocktail
An alcoholic drink using various combinations of ingredients. The cocktail seems to have become popular first in the USA in the late 1890s but spread as a fad throughout the civilized world until by the 1920s the Bright Young Things everywhere were downing gallons of Dry Martinis (gin, vermouth, angostura bitters), Whisky Sours (whisky, sugar, lemon, orange juice) and other concoctions. At the height of the craze for cocktails there was even a cheerful novel by the then Modernistic novelist Eric Linklater predicated on the search for a perfect cocktail, titled *Poet's Pub*. Some years later the same writer was to write a sardonic novel about the course of

the second World War, *Private Angelo*. By then cocktails were deemed a little frivolous.

The cocktail party coursed throughout the 1930s too and will always be associated with Scott Fitzgerald's Jazz Age. It re-emerged in the 1950s and '60s, but by then had become a trifle effete. But the cocktail never entirely goes away. It re-emerged in the early 1990s (there was even a movie, starring Tom Cruise called, succinctly, *Cocktail*).

Today the new Bright Young Things have made cocktails fashionable once again, and TGI Friday, a prominent chain organization with outlets throughout every continent – there are two of them in Bombay alone – have promoted cocktails once again. The image of the cocktail is simple: it means money, and lots of it. And youth as well. An unbeatable combination.

Cocoa

A British bedtime drink made from the coca bean of South America, which is also a source of **chocolate**, this is, like the celebrated malted drink **Ovaltine**, notorious as a bedtime drink for children and the kind of elderly Briton who wishes to die in his bloody bed with his boots on, blameless and blanched in his moribund morality. In France, and especially Belgium, a hot chocolate drink is vigorous rather than enervating and is often infused with rum or other stimulants. Agatha Christie's Hercule Poirot was, in the books at least, keen on chocolate, hot, with *sirop*. It is especially good with a drop of the liqueur wine **marsala**.

Coconut

This is perhaps one of the most useful agricultural products in the world. The leaves are used for thatching and are plaited for mats and baskets. The trunk of the tree provides a valuable timber known as 'porcupine wood'. The thick fibrous outer covering of this nut of the palm tree (called coir) is used for coconut matting and for rope-making. Even the root of the tree is used – chewed, it is a narcotic and has medicinal purposes. The sap in various stages of fermentation makes palm wine and the ardent spirit known as arrack, and can be boiled down into a sugar called jaggery. And the young terminal bud, palm cabbage, is a delicious vegetable.

But to the fruit, the nut itself. The shells can serve as serving bowls and are sometimes carved decoratively. The flesh inside is eaten fresh and can also be dried. The interior milk makes a cooling drink. Coconut oil is also widely used for cooking and is a major ingredient of soaps and cosmetics, also margarines. The dried copra, the meat or kernel of the coconut, yields a great deal of oil and is also used as a plasticizer in the making of nitro-glycerine.

In solid form coconut oil, as coconut cream, is often used in curry, especially in modern Australian versions of it. The British imported coconuts from Malaysia (though the bulk of the nuts' products come from the Philippines and Indonesia), in the form of dried desiccated coconut. They also imported them for use in fairgrounds, in which they had sporting events called coconut shies, thus giving rise to the phrase 'Give yerself a coconut!' And a song as well, during the Second World War: 'Oh, What a Lovely Bunch of Coconuts!' Somehow coconuts, like bananas, have a faint risibility attached to them.

Cod

Britain had a cod war with Iceland. It wouldn't now because British fishermen have damn near fished it out. It is a large fish and generally sold as steaks. Now almost a luxury, it was once much despised and used for fish and chips, as an inferior to haddock or plaice.

For a reason best known to the Portugese it is the staple and national fish of that country, in which, it is said, there are 1,200 recipes. A very famous one, the title of which I have fortunately forgotten, I ate in a restaurant in Lisbon. It involved stewed cabbage, saffron, garlic and, unbelievably, **cocoa** powder.

Cod liver oil
This aperient was in the fairly recent past often administered to children in the mistaken idea that it was 'good for the bowels'. In fact so ingrained was this notion that the British government distributed the oil free to parents during and just after the war. Mistaken? In fact the regular use of such purgatives actually caused bowel irritation to the extent that many elderly Britons of today continue to have intestinal problems and erratic bowel evacuation. Yet another reason advanced for the application of cod liver oil was that it had a repellent aroma and an especially nasty taste. It was indeed sometimes used as a punishment for wayward weans. See **constipation**.

Coffee
A drink made from roasted and ground coffee beans, which, though originating in Libya and the Yemen (though Ethiopia claims to be its original birthplace and the *harrar* coffee bean from that country is to this day highly prized), are now cultivated throughout the world's tropical regions, especially in Brazil, which is the major exporter, followed by Kenya and Jamaica (whose Blue Mountain coffee is also highly prized). The two main types of beans are *arabica*, of which the once famous **Java** was the best known, and *robusta*, the former being thought superior and therefore considerably more expensive. Most instant coffees are produced from the latter bean, and it shows.

Coffee was substituted for alcohol by Muslims, and coffee shops abound in Islamic countries, where they are the social foci in the same way that pubs are in Britain. Some Western countries took to coffee also, and it is the staple drink in France, Italy, Austria and the USA (though British visitors are often surprised that many Americans prefer tea).

Coffee-drinking seems to have started first in Persia some time in the ninth century, though coffee must have been known to Abyssinians before that, for it was their country from which the beans were imported. It was then drunk only by very rich Arab potentates. Introduced to Europe in the fifteenth century, it was still a very expensive product until the middle of the eighteenth.

The Arab nabobs were concerned about the political chat and talk that went on in the coffee houses and took stern measures to close them down. Sultan Amurat III, the ruler of all Islam, celebrated his ascension, after slaughtering his five brothers, by closing all coffee houses and torturing their proprietors. Much the same notion occurred to Louis XIV, who closed the coffee houses in France.

The British had their coffee houses too, and indeed the great days of chaps such as Samuel Johnson and Alexander Pope and the like were spent by the *literati* idling away in coffee houses. A great many of the famous London clubs (White's, Boodles) started as coffee houses. The drink remained a beverage for the aristocracy in the UK until the late nineteenth century, but in France the coffee house replaced the tavern with the **café**, as it did also in Italy and Austria. Alcohol was also served, and later, food.

Coffee rooms, like tea shops, became a major feature of British life from the late Victorian age, partly promoted by the appalling, but powerful, temperance movement. But as late as the 1960s my native Glasgow still had its coffee rooms, where a great deal of business was done. They were not strictly teetotal either, because of the Scottish habit of completing a deal with a handshake and a dram. I worked in the late 1950s, as a boy, in one of the famous 'smoking rooms' as they were called – entirely male environs – George Murray Frame's, and witnessed some considerable captains of industry such as Lord Fraser and Isaac Wolfson rattling out their hip flasks as they passed millions of spondulicks between them.

Sadly the old smoking rooms passed away, just as Fraser and Wolfson did. But the coffee shops have re-emerged in the last decade, and such places as Starbucks are found worldwide. Alas the days of sedition in coffee houses are over. So is business of a straightforward kind.

But a word here about the quality of coffee and coffee houses. The Italian genius in food and drink has produced **espresso**, usually drunk black but in the Milan cafés often with a little cream (*macchiato*). The Turks have a sweet muddy liquid which is surprisingly refreshing. In Vienna the coffee houses, which are a major feature of this most romantic of cities, where East and West and North and South meet, provide a coffee flavoured with figs (see **Viennese coffee**), drunk with a small glass of water and accompanied by the most exquisite sweet cakes.

And then there is Irish coffee. This is hot strong coffee laced liberally with Irish whiskey and topped with cream. It was invented by one Mickey O'Neil back in the 1920s, when he was head barman at the then Dublin Aerodrome (now Dublin Airport), which the Bright Young Things of the age would visit in the early hours of the morning after a night dancing and in need of both a hangover cure and another drink. This may seem a paradox, but so are the Irish.

Cognac

This is a twice-distilled brandy from France and is distinguished from brandy itself, the name protected by law. It is, like brandy, distilled from grapes, and much nonsense revolves around it. For instance, true Napoleon brandy is unlikely to have more than a thimbleful of the spirit from the days of old Boney, and today is an entirely meaningless term. Brandy and cognac are described by the oldest spirit in the cask, thus a twenty-year-old cognac is a blend, the bulk of which may be merely a year or so old. Scotch **whisky**, however, has much more stringent labelling rules and may only cite the youngest whisky in the blend: thus a ten-year-old whisky may well have a thirty-year-old malt in the cask. In short, the French, as they often do, cheat.

Colander

I only mention this bowl-shaped perforated utensil because the nicest and most ingenious colander I ever saw was the tennis racquet that Jack Lemmon utilised for **spaghetti** in the 1969 film *The Apartment*.

Colcannon

Yet another potato dish familiar in Ireland. It is exactly the same as **bubble and squeak**, though is often left to cool and then refried in lard or butter.

Cold collation

Today an old-fashioned term (though still occasionally in use in Scotland and Ireland) for a selection of cold dishes, often as a **buffet**. In the past a cold collation, instead of lunch or dinner, was reserved for fast days, which is rather cheating really.

In the USA selections of cold meats are offered and are known as 'cold cuts'. Then there is what is often called 'the cold table', sometimes known as 'the open table'. This is popular, oddly one would think, in cold climates; thus Sweden has its **smorgasbord**, Denmark its *koldtbord*, Finland its *voleipapoyta*, while Russia delights in its *zakuski*.

Cold food

Though there are many hot dishes that can be eaten cold – **moussaka** and the classic French dish *boeuf à la mode* come instantly to mind – there are cuisines, such as that of Greece, which prefer their hot food to be served when tepid. I do not like food to be excessively hot myself, though many Britons complain horribly when their dinner doesn't appear at the table spluttering and steaming on the plate.

Then too there are certain dishes that I actually prefer cold, even if I like them hot as well. It was many years ago that I discovered that the take-away curry of the night before was delicious cold for breakfast. And I always make too much spaghetti bolognese for the same reason (see **spaghetti, bolognese sauce**). This discovery, made by many others as well, was of course the result of the previous night's heavy course of libations.

Collops

Small pieces of thinly cut meat, usually beef steak, sautéed or sometimes stewed in onion gravy. It was a common dish in the eighteenth century in northern Britain and a famous recipe had added pickled walnuts. You will find frequent references to it in R.L. Stevenson's *Kidnapped*, in which the term is used to describe any cut of beef. More recently it has come to mean stewed minced beef. Some smart Scottish restaurants, anxious to provide traditional fare with a European accent, now have the original collops on the menu and charge accordingly.

Compote

A French term for stewed fruit. Even the French despise it as a dessert.

Condensed milk

Much the same as **evaporated milk** in its manufacture, but thicker and much sweetened. It was a favourite in the UK in the 1950s and was often spread on bread. As a child I loved it: as an adult I feel sick at the memory.

Confectionery

There was a time in the UK when the sign over every baker's shop was 'Baker and Confectioner'. You still find it, even though few bakers are confectioners in the strictest sense of the word: indeed few real bakers outside the chain companies exist any more at all.

Consommé

A clear soup based on meat, fish, poultry or vegetables. It is a tiresome soup and takes a tiresome amount of time to make. Traditionally it is the task given to the most junior apprentice chef and has a cachet that it does not deserve. You can do a simple version with a stock cube with no more effort than boiling a kettle.

Constipation

What, you may think, is this subject doing in a book about food? There is a very good reason indeed for its inclusion (see **diet**). Owing to a ridiculous false modesty many girls and young women in the late Victorian and Edwardian ages actually died of constipation, not helped by the widespread fashion for too tight corsets. Though physicians inveighed against them both for over half a century, it took the liberated bright young things of the post-Great War years greatly to eradicate this largely avoidable medical problem.

Constipation should not occur in a normal healthy child, and diet is the answer to any problems that may arise. The use of preparatory commercial laxatives or such preparations as, for instance, **cod liver oil** should not be necessary in a balanced diet. The daily ingestion of fresh fruit, green vegetables, sufficient fluids (which should be largely sugar-free) and wholemeal bread or such cereals as porridge oats will ensure a healthy child.

Junk food, except as an occasional treat, should be avoided. These injunctions should be especially noted by young women, expectant mothers and young girls during their menstrual periods.

There are so many spin-offs concerning ill-health, including fatal conditions, that constipation is not to be considered lightly. To mention one of them, it should be noted that many heart attacks occur when the subject is straining at stool because their diet is so unhealthy that an easy and not unpleasant evacuation of the bowels is difficult. The widely observed, and rather risible at that, practice of men reading in the lavatory during defecation, a phenomenon rarely noted in the habits of womankind, is not to be discounted. Any process that aids a daily bowel function should indeed be welcomed.

Cookbook
This is, of course, usually a nonsense. A cookbook would be a book about cooks: if it is a volume on cookery it is properly a cookery book. So there.

Cookie
In Scotland this is a bun. A cream cookie, a plain bun filled with, invariably, artificial cream and dusted with caster sugar is not to be sniffed at – it is delicious. But in America a cookie is a biscuit. In America, as I pointed out earlier, a biscuit is a scone.

Cooks
A **chef** is just a cook with a taller hat (Carême invented the tall hat; before him cooks wore a baker's skullcap). But there is an element of both social caste and sexism here. P.G. Wodehouse frequently refers to Bertie Wooster's Aunt Dahlia's French chef

Anatole: in his stories when the purveyor of the baked meats is a woman it is always a cook. And bear in mind that crack of Saki's: 'She was a good cook as good cooks go; and as good cooks go, she went.'

The word 'chef' simply means 'chief' but it has become imbued with a dignity that 'cook' does not possess. Yet some of the best exponents of cuisine, especially women, would not think of themselves as anything but cooks. Delia Smith is a fine example of this, as is the amazing Marguerite Patten, who began her long career in food as an adviser to the Ministry of Food at the start of the Second World War, and the legendary Irish 'Cookin' Woman', Florence Irwin, who likewise had kicked off as a government instructor and adviser on food.

There is, too, the example of the legendary cook and caterer Rosa Lewis, owner of the Cavendish Hotel, who cooked ten-course dinners for hostesses such as Lady Randolph Churchill and Mrs Murray Guthrie. Mrs Lewis presided over society dinners for over a quarter of a century and was considered essential if the Prince of Wales (later King Edward VII) was on the guest list. (Rosa Lewis had been a mistress to the then Prince of Wales and acted as a procurer of young women for him. She was the model for Mrs Lottie Crump in Evelyn Waugh's 1930 novel *Vile Bodies*.)

Besides her extraordinary competence and the vast array of, entirely female, cooks and waitresses Mrs Lewis had two further qualities: 1) she was very discreet (her hotel had four separate exits for those who pursued extra-marital dalliances); and 2) she did not drink, as was common among cooks. When the artist James McNeill Whistler interviewed a prospective cook, he always asked her if she drank. If the answer was 'no', he did not engage her.

And Sir Clement Freud (though he accepted the knighthood he deeply resents being called 'Sir Clement') began as a cook in the Army Catering Corps and recalls the age-old forces sally: 'Did you call the cook a cunt?' The reply was ever: 'Well, who called the cunt a cook?'

Coq au vin

In the late 1950s and early '60s this chicken casserole was present at every Chelsea or Hampstead dinner party, soon to be emulated in every chic middle-class home for special occasions. It is in fact somewhat of a peasant dish and not only easy to make (and hard to ruin), but good fun to cook as well. The chicken is lightly sautéed and then cooked in stock and red wine with lardons of bacon, and small braised onions are added, as are sautéed mushrooms at the end of cooking. Usually the chicken and bacon are flambéed with brandy or whisky at the sauté stage.

Though it fell out of favour among the fashionables for a while (like **baked Alaska** or **Black Forest gateau** it was seen as having descended to the lower orders), it is a staple of Burgundian cooking. Every restaurant in that region of France will have it on its daily menu along with, of course, the ever-present **boeuf bourguignon**.

Cordon bleu

Fancy French term for fancy French food. It means, of course, 'blue ribbon', which was a ribbon bestowed on chefs who had made the register of *haute cuisine* known as the Association de Dégustion, founded after a campaign by a famous French gourmet, the novelist and journalist Edmond About.

Coriander

Used widely in Indian food, it is now common in Western cookery also. The leaves have a parsley-like appearance, and the seeds have an orangey flavour. Greek cookery uses it often, and one of the most magnificent pork dishes of all – afelia – uses both red wine and coriander seeds to great effect.

Coriander is popular in Hungarian cookery and, as one with Hungarian antecedents, I use it myself, both leaves and seeds, as often as I would **thyme**. It is also used in baking and confectionery.

Corn
See **maize**.

Corn on the cob
Perhaps the most irritating dish ever. There is no way of eating this without looking gross.

Corned beef
This is brisket or sometimes silverside of beef which is soaked for a fortnight in salt, bicarbonate of soda, sugar and saltpetre, which renders it a red colour. (The term 'corned' has nothing to do with corn: it refers to 'corns' of salt.) Also known in Britain as 'bully beef', it was, canned, a staple of the soldiers, who naturally came to hate it. My father, who spent nearly twenty years as a member of the brutal and licentious, would not allow it in the house.

Canned corned beef is a major export of Argentina, but the Fray Bentos company, ever associated with the product, hails in fact from Uruguay. It was years before I discovered that Fray Bentos is a place, situated in the middle of that country.

Americans are fond of corned beef, and their corned beef hash is a favourite Monday dish. Made with corned beef, coarsely mashed potatoes and onions, and then fried rather as **bubble and squeak**, it is topped with a fried egg. Accompanied by **chilli** sauce, it is both nutritious and cheap. And very good eating at that. (There is a German version called *Labskaus*, which is probably the origin of this in American cuisine.)

Cornflakes

A breakfast cereal made from maize, which was almost ubiquitous in the days when British parents gave their children a breakfast at all. Kellogg's were the main manufacturers. The founder of this company, an American called J.H. Kellogg, not only became very rich indeed on his product but was also a health freak. He was even loopier than most health faddists. In 1824 he published, at his own expense, a pamphlet titled *The Moloch of the Species*, in which he luridly detailed the dangers of masturbation. He was in little danger himself: he was rumoured to be an avid customer of ladies of the night.

Cornish pasty

There are so many travesties, especially commercially, of this simple meal in itself that it would make you greet. My proud Cornish grandmother made such pasties every Saturday and, as tradition had it, each of us had our pasties personalized with our initials marked on them.

Though there are pasties made from all types of meat and game, fish or even fruit, the Cornish pasty proper is made of a mixture of top-quality rump steak, with no fat or gristle, onions, diced potato and salt and a deal of ground black pepper. At one time barley flour was used for the pastry case as wheat flour was too expensive (this had the added benefit of hardening it, enabling pasties to be dropped down the pit shafts to the miners below), but today a wheat shortcrust pastry is employed. Incidentally most Cornish cooks crimp the pastry at the side, not across the top as one generally sees in shop-bought pasties. Minced meat is not generally used. But the result of this simple recipe is a hearty meal which somehow possesses a sophistication worthy of rich **en croûte** versions in the most expensive restaurants.

This pasty would be a rare treat for Cornish folk of the past. Cornwall has always been a poor part of England (many

Cornish people dispute that they *are* English and claim Celtic descent). The staples of the traditional diet were barley, potatoes and pilchards. Despite these limitations, Cornish cookery has some very distinctive features, and at least one of its dishes has become famous, though rarely seen these days: stargazy pie, in which the heads of pilchards are seen looking skywards through the pastry lid.

Cottage pie

There is a confusion betwixt this and shepherd's pie: the difference is, of course, that the latter is made of minced mutton, while cottage pie contains minced beef. The mince is topped with a layer of mashed and creamed potatoes and is a typically British dish. There are many variants of this – the Balkan **moussaka** comes to mind – but nothing can match the sheer *ennui* of this UK nursery rubbish.

Incidentally, shepherd's pie was served by the mendacious British criminal and former Cabinet minister Lord Jeffrey Archer along with **champagne** for the vulgar lunches he invited fellow idiots to in his country mansion, the former home of the poet Rupert Brooke, in Grantchester. There may well have been honey still for tea there, but Milord Archer, the famous old lag, insisted also on this dish. Shepherd's pie is a fine example of the nadir of British cuisine.

Courgette

This variety of the marrow family is also called **zucchini** in the Italian language. In Rome zucchini are often cut into chips, and like chips, are deep-fried. As Elizabeth David pointed out, marrows are tasteless and worthless, but the baby marrows like courgettes are splendid. Courgettes also work well in stews and estouffades, especially with chicken joints. They are also a necessary ingredient of **ratatouille**.

Couscous

Made from one of the more disgusting cereals, **semolina**, a staple of school dinners, this is a north African dish and is quite awful. A culture that promotes these minuscule semolina dumplings and yet abhors alcohol (despite the fact that the very word stems from the Arabic *alcool* and that the Arab world was probably the first to distil the product), would suggest that modern-day Arabs have somehow got everything wrong.

Crab

I do not like crabs. Frankly I find the look of them rather frightening, and there is doubtless some Freudian explanation for this. They are very expensive and not worth the money, for there is little meat. Crab bisque, a speciality from Louisiana, is much prized. So once was Huey Long.

Cranberry

Sometimes known in America as a 'bounceberry' (because the ripeness is established by how well it bounces off a table surface), this now seems to be used exclusively as a relish provided with roast **turkey**. It is a sharp and tart sauce, and whoever the genius was who discovered the marriage of cranberries and wild turkeys, he or she was, indeed, a genius.

Cream

Fat of the milk combined with water, this is one of the most useful ingredients in the entire world of food. There is no area of cuisine in which this product cannot be used, savoury to sweet, baking to meat and poultry, fish to fruit. Its use varies from Hungarian stews and the Russian **beef Stroganoff** to the famous cream teas of Britain's West Country (tea served with scones, or Cornish splits, and served with jam and clotted cream, a speciality of Cornwall).

Single cream is a pouring cream much used in cookery, double cream more often used as an accompaniment to fruit desserts such as strawberries. (A noted proponent of this lovely combination was Samuel Pepys, who recorded his enjoyment of the dessert twice in 1674.) The Wimbledon tennis tournament would scarcely exist were it not for Strawberries and Cream, itself a euphemism for innocence (Dylan Thomas wrote of 'the wild boys innocent as strawberries'), health and a lovely English girl's complexion.

Clotted cream is, incidentally, complicated to make but my Cornish grandmother, to whom I have referred earlier, always had a couple of pans of milk on the go throughout the day to make it. Her neighbours thought she was a witch but were bewitched all the same by her clotted cream. Cream was, in my childhood, a luxury food and difficult to obtain in urban areas – for most city-dwellers of the 1950s it came in tins.

Cream cakes
The height of sybaritic opulence, cream cakes were the ones to go for when having **high tea** in my Scottish childhood. Truth to tell, real cream was rare in 1950s' Glasgow: almost all cream in such pastries was artificial. No matter: they were delicious.

Crème de menthe
Liqueur made from mint or peppermint. It is disgusting.

Crêpes
French term for pancakes, the most famous of which is the crêpe Suzette. This is a pancake simmered in a buttery orange sauce and flambéed in either brandy or the orange liqueur Cointreau.

Though the French claim crêpes as their own, the most magnificent hail from the cuisine of Austria-Hungary, especially the world-famous Gundel pancakes, created by the Gundel dynasty of Budapest restaurateurs headed by Janos Gundel and then his son Karoly. Hungary has a long tradition of pancakes – *palacsinta* – as savouries, often eaten with sour cream and stuffed peppers, but it delights in pancakes as desserts. The Gundel crêpes are incredibly rich and sweet. They are also unbelievably alcoholic, with enough rum used to run a speakeasy in Prohibition days. I first ate them in a restaurant in Buda run by a chef called Gyula Gullner. The cookery writer Tom Vernon has also discovered Gyula's cookery and, like me, found that this dessert is a main course. Even the fittest gourmand can barely survive a course of *palacsinta Gundel*.

Crisps

I do not like crisps. They always seemed to me a bit like eating toenails. They once came in greaseproof bags with a small sachet of salt, but later commercial concerns developed all sorts of flavours. All of them artificial. Crisps are thinly cut slices of potato, deep-fried. In America they are called chips (they call chips 'French fries' in the States). They appear to be a major part of the modern child's diet and are harmful in the amount of sugar, salt and cholesterol they contain. Add sweet artificial, fizzy drinks and a lack of rigour in the teaching of English grammar and you have the perfect recipe for adolescent idiocy.

Croissants

On my first visit to France as a young fellow celebrating my twenty-first birthday I met a young girl called Miaitie and we spent a hot passionate night in a bedroom of a casino in St Valery en Caux on the Normandy coast. We could not go to sleep because she was also the local baker's daughter and had to be up by five in the morning so that she could assist her papa in his bread-making. She also made the croissants.

The process she displayed was nearly, but not quite, as sexy as her ministrations of the wee small hours earlier. I may well be the only person on Earth who becomes erectile at the sight of a croissant. Few British versions can approach the quality of what a small French boulangerie can manage. But even a British baker's daughter can surely achieve a similar reaction in a young man on the cusp of his twenty-first birthday.

Croquette
See **potato**. Croquettes are made of meat, fish etc. and bound with beaten egg and dredged in breadcrumbs. Potato croquettes are popular throughout Europe but are often rather bland in Britain. Italians add ground nutmeg and thyme, as do Hungarians. This recipe is much superior to the UK version. Another thing: make them yourself and enjoy them.

Crudités
A selection of prepared raw vegetables served with dips of sauces or mayonnaise etc. and of no earthly use at all. Veggies like them. My view is that civilization started the moment we *cooked* our food.

Crumpet
A flat, round cake made from a yeasted batter which has a pitted appearance owing to the yeast. It is part of Oxbridge mythology that crumpets are toasted in undergrads' chambers. When a small boy, I once asked my father why crumpets were different from **pancakes** (in Scotland what are elsewhere known as 'drop scones'). He promptly picked up a pancake, put it through the adjacent washing wringer, and then furiously stabbed the result several times with a fork. 'No difference, Son', he said nonchalantly, 'that's how you make a crumpet'. I believed him.

But the word 'crumpet' has another meaning. To most Britons it also means a fanciable girl or several of them. And sometimes it is a term for the female pudenda, as can be evinced in the rugby-club song: 'And on her crumpet, on her crumpet/ Louis Armstrong played the trumpet . . .'

Cullen skink

A Scottish dish, half soup, half stew; it is made with smoked fish (traditionally smoked haddock), potatoes, milk, butter and sometimes bacon. The North American chowders were imported from Scotland and are similar. The food writer Catherine Brown recently pointed out on *The Food Programme* she does with Derek Cooper who, despite his plummy tones, is also a Scot, that cullen skink is yet another peasant dish that has reached the menus of the most sophisticated restaurant tables of the world. Indeed I was offered this hearty repast under its Scottish name in the famed Le Bernardin restaurant in New York (without the bacon): the waiter described it as 'invented by Rob Roy MacGregor', which is, to say the least, a little over-romantic. Romantic or not, it is a dish to kill for.

Curry

Curry has now become Britain's national dish, though what passes for it in most Indian or Pakistani restaurants possesses but a passing relationship to genuine Indian food. Originally from the Hindi word *turcarri*, though this itself derives from the Tamil *kari*, meaning 'a stew', it was brought to the UK in the early nineteenth century by returning sahibs who had learned to eat native food. When James Allan Sharwood began to import spices and chutneys, it became a staple of middle-class cuisine often, unfortunately, as a mask for left-over roasts on a Monday. Queen Victoria was given a 'gift' of two Indian servants on her accession as Empress of India, and thereafter always included Indian dishes on her luncheon menus. George V, however, was a curry addict and had a phalanx of Indian chefs preparing it for him every night. (He took to curry after his first visit to India as a young prince.)

But it was not until the 1960s that curry became truly popular in the UK. Today there are some 12,000 Indian restaurants in Britain, and 3 million curries are served every week, a third of them at weekends. Few of them are even remotely genuinely Indian, but truly Indian food still exists in some restaurants, and of course in Indian homes.

Curry is common throughout the Far East, beyond the subcontinent, and there are distinctive differences in South-East Asian cookery. Burma is exceptional in the amount of garlic used; Ceylon has pork curries which are very hot; throughout Malaysia coconut flesh and milk are common. But the largely Bhuddist Thais are usually vegetarian and also have fish as a staple. Despite that, Thai cookery has now become a well-known restaurant cuisine in Europe, partly because it has a definitive taste – the fish paste known as **blachan**, coriander and hot chillies impart a unique flavour – and partly because Thais are a remarkably aristocratic people who have evolved a highly decorative style of dining, from their crockery to interior design.

Elsewhere curries evolved according to native custom. Australia has created curries that are part indigenous but influenced by Indonesian cookery and that of Java and Thailand. And in Britain, of course, new-style curries have been developed to suit the British palate – balti curries and the famous chicken tikka masala, which the late Robin Cook MP once said was now the national UK dish (singling it out of all the variety of curries available) are inventions and unfortunately now constitute what the Brits think of as 'real' curries. I once took a young colleague, a restaurant critic, to an authentic north-west Indian place, and she complained that the food was not genuinely Indian: she had been corrupted by the sort of curries that are all cream and **garam masala**.

For some reason the west of Scotland is a haven of Indian cuisine, mainly of Punjabi origin (both Indian and Pakistani Punjabs). In the early 1960s the city of Glasgow alone had over forty Indo-Pak restaurants, while London had a mere handful. Today Glasgow has over two hundred Indian outlets, and the city is renowned in Indian restaurateur circles throughout the UK for the quality of its food. Incidentally, if you want to find authentic (and inexpensive) Indian food in London take yourself down to Brick Lane, where you will find splendid curries in what are simple caffs for Indians. And if you are lucky enough to have Indian friends, you will discover the subtlety of Indian and Pakistani cuisine, a subtlety so often lost throughout its history in Britain.

Curry powder

Few Indians use ready-prepared curry powder, preferring to make their own according to their tastes. Curry powder reached Europe through the importation by the afore mentioned John Sharwood, who, legend has it, discovered its existence when dining with the Maharajah of Madras, who mentioned a spice grocer called Vencatachellum. To this day, Sharwood's most famous curry powder is titled by this long-gone Indian epicier's name. There is a large variety of curry powders on the market in Britain. At the 1889 World Exhibition in Paris, the French Colonial Ministry fixed the legal composition of curry powder sold in France (a mixture of Chittagong **saffron**, **turmeric**, cumin, Kerala **coriander** and a selection of Orissa chillies), and, though this is no longer enforced, the fact is that French curry powder is frequently superior to that sold in Britain. There are also curry pastes which are used in traditional Indian recipes, but sadly a number of them in the UK were often poor versions, though in recent years some more authentic pastes have come on the market.

Custard

An amalgam of milk and eggs, in the UK it is personified by a cornflour-based powder, today utterly dominated by the Bird's company. This was originally created by one Dr Alfred Bird for his invalid wife who liked custard but was allergic to eggs. Other custard powders were developed, notably Cremola and Monk and Glass, but Bird's remained, and does to this day, very much the brand leader.

Until recently it was impossible to encounter any pudding that was not smothered in this muck. Indeed I remember a greasy spoon establishment I patronized as a young advertising chap which refused to serve apple pie without custard. When I asked for the apple pie without the custard, the owner claimed such a request was 'not natural'.

D

Dab

A flatfish popular in Europe but for some reason not in Britain. It is delicate and can be compared to lemon sole in flavour and texture, though it is considerably less expensive.

Dairy

When I was a child in the 1940s and '50s, the dairy was the equivalent of what would now be called a mini-market. The reason for this is simple: because they did indeed sell dairy produce such as milk and butter, these premises were exempt from the laws that forbade openings on Sundays or on whatever early closing day prevailed in the local area. (On such afternoons dairies were not permitted to sell tea or bread as this was considered an infringement on other traders. A lovely example of the idiocy of licensing laws.)

A dairy is any establishment that produces dairy produce. Marie Antoinette insisted on having her own toy dairy, where she played dairymaid for fun. Dairy produce is, of course, milk, cream, butter, cheese etc., and virtually every domestic mammal provides such.

Dandelion

A prolific and hardy flower (the name is an English corruption of the French *dent de lion*, literally 'the lion's tooth') thought by gardeners to be a weed, this is, like the nettle, a useful plant, the root of which when roasted and ground was an ingredient of the German *ersatz* coffee of the Second World War. The leaves can also be used in salads and are the basis of a refreshing soft drink that was once popular, dandelion and burdock; also a country wine. The distinguished graphic designer Canadian-born Leslie Forbes encountered a dandelion soup made by a Montalcino grandmother which she mentions in her exquisitely illustrated cookery book *A Table in Tuscany*. I much recommend this beautiful book, published in 1985, not least for the drawings: the recipes are quite as stunning.

Danish pastry

A puff pastry sweetmeat usually incorporating thick custard and jam, often apricot, and raisins. It was once popular as a mid-morning treat with coffee, the ritual known in Britain as **elevenses**. The snacks are especially popular in New York lunch counters, where they are simply known as 'Danishes'.

Darjeeling

This expensive tea is grown in the snowy foothills of the Himalayas. It is much exported to Russia (see **tea**).

Dates

Grown mainly on the coast of north Africa, though they are now also cultivated in North America, these are rarely encountered fresh elsewhere. The exported and dried dates are to be seen in their characteristic oddly shaped wooden boxes, usually with a luridly coloured illustration of exotic Berber tribesmen and a camel and a palm tree hanging about. Dates and walnuts are often combined as ingredients of specialist breads or cakes.

Daube

Elizabeth David wrote rather beautifully of *les daubes* in *French Provincial Cookery* (1960), and rightly so. But not as elegiac as Pierre Huguenin, from whose book, written in 1936, she quoted. Here is what Huguenin wrote: 'O, scent of the daubes of my childhood! The daube had been murmering gently on the stove since midday, giving out sweet smells which brought tears to your eyes.' He goes on a bit after that, and no wonder. The very aroma of a rich daube, scents of thyme or rosemary, wine and stock, the meat itself, onions and garlic, sometimes the Provençal *pistou* (a Provençal version of the Italian **pesto**), is enough to have you writing verse.

But to be a little more prosaic, a daube is just a casserole, a stew, usually with the meat previously marinated in red (or white) wine, with vegetables. The classic daube is **boeuf bourguignon**, a rich casserole with mushrooms and onions, but there are many variants. Whatever, the daube is a major dish in every French household, and nothing can be more comforting on a cold wet day in northern climes.

Decant

Decanting is sometimes necessary in the case of some wines, especially old **port**, and some very old wines which have too great an amount of sediment. It has to be said, however, that most of us who have decanters use them for spirits such as **brandy** or **whisky**. It does look good, though, and is helpful in disguising the cheap rubbish you have provided for your guests.

Delicatessen

Today this simply means a shop in which exotic, and often expensive, produce is for sale, though the word simply means 'food delicacies'. The delis that you will find throughout Europe and America were a lifeline for immigrants missing their native foods. Thus there were Italian delis, which provided olive oil and pasta etc., Polish and German shops, which allowed those immigrant communities their sausage and pumpernickel, and so on. Today every supermarket has an extensive delicatessen counter, and those under forty take them for granted. Anybody older than that will remember with nostalgia the little delis owned by Jews and Italians and other ethnic groups. My father, who was much travelled as a professional soldier, was an *aficionado* of such shops and was instantly drawn to them. The result was that, while everybody else in my working-class childhood was eating such Scottish fare as mince and tatties or Scotch broth, my family dined on minestrone or cassoulet, green peppers and other rarely seen comestibles. The dear old Dad was probably the only school caretaker in Britain who fed his family on *poloni* and rye bread while listening to Wagner. It was a difficult childhood.

Dessert

At the end, usually, of any meal comes a course designed to lighten the load of the heavier meat or fish courses and so there is a refreshing, though sometimes pretty heavy itself, last course which is more often than not sweet. In European dinners the last course is frequently **cheese**, often in circumstances in which dessert is itself abandoned. I usually adopt this practice myself.

Yet the European tradition is for fruit and puddings to end a feast. As the poet Keats has it:

> Of candied apple, quince, and plum, and gourd;
> With jellies soother than the creamy curd,
> And lucent syrops, tinct with cinnamon;
> Manna and dates, in argosy transferr'd

From Fez; and spiced dainties; every one,
From silken Samarkand to ceder'd Lebanon.

They do go on a bit, these poets. Samarkand, when I visited it, looked a little like an especially dreary British New Town with a certain Soviet element of pomposity, and was a great disappointment. Lebanon is a battlefield without the notion of romance about it. Keats died, aged twenty-six, having never seen either.

Dhansak

Often seen on Indian restaurant menus, this is a Parsee dish from Persia and contains lentils (see **lentil**) and fried onions. Though it is highly spiced, it is not a curry proper and, in the hands of my friend Feroud 'Freddy' Moghbelli, an academic from Persia (he refuses to call his country 'Iran' and oft claims that he has a 'Persianal' interest in this matter), dhansak is a remarkably subtle dish.

Diet

Simply meaning the food we eat, this is now often used as a term for **fasting** or what was once known as 'banting', after William Banting (1797–1878), who recommended such a process. Generally dieting is designed for weight loss, and I know of few women who do not, at some time, decide to slim by abstaining from food. Common sense suggests what and how much we should eat, and it is worth pointing out that French women are among the most elegant females in the world and eat like horses. On the other hand, so do Italian ladies. And a lot of them are fairly large, at least in later life. There is surely something indecent about fasting to fit into a size 8 dress when half the world is starving.

On the other hand we ignore dietetics at our peril (see **medicine**). Despite many nonsenses put forward by some publicity-seeking dieticians in the popular press, the fact is that a healthy and balanced diet is about the best barrier against disease and illness you can find. This means that a normal intake should include a great many foodstuffs (where this is possible), and meat, fish, eggs etc. should be included, despite the beliefs of many vegetarians and vegans. Also that too great an emphasis on flesh, whether it be red meat, fowl or fish, is not recommended. And probably the best injunction of all. Most people in the West over-eat, with too large portions on their plates, and too many meals and snacks in the day.

Digestive biscuit

This magnificent sweetened wholemeal biscuit was once invariably an accompaniment to the mid-morning ritual known in Britain as **elevenses** and will for ever be associated by me with the aroma of coffee, the sound of *Housewives' Choice* on the wireless, and my Mum.

Eaten with a good mature Cheddar cheese, nothing can touch the digestive, which is also used as a base for **cheese-cake**. The brand leader is McVities. Lightly toasted with butter, a digestive biscuit is another taste explosion. There are those who extol it as a biscuit for dunking: we dunking experts go for the **gingernut**, but there is no denying that the digestive biscuit is one of the splendours – one of the few at that – of British food.

Dill

A distinctive herb much used in Scandinavian cookery. When introduced to gherkins and so becoming dill pickles, it becomes a major part of the New Yorkese, and especially Jewish, diet.

Dim sum

These Chinese specialities are delicate dumplings, usually served in little baskets, and can be sweet or savoury. I first encountered them in the late 1960s in an off-beat Chinese after-hours restaurant in Edinburgh which was not really a restaurant: it was a gambling den with food. My Chinese chums saw dim sum rather the way that Europeans saw sandwiches (see **sandwich**) and for much the same reason: it provided something tasty while you lost your shirt at cards or, in the case of Edinburgh's Loon Fung restaurant, Mah Jong. Thank God I abandoned Mah Jong, but I still cannot resist dim sum.

Diner

Though this does indeed mean one who dines, it is also a term for a small, cheap, unpretentious eating place, as against the grander restaurant. It is largely a word used in the USA, as is the term 'lunch counter'. An American friend, the artist Todd Garner, tells me that the latter is frequently used in urban areas while a diner more often describes a rural or small town eatery. He described it thus: 'one is Edward Hopper, the other is Norman Rockwell'.

But all other countries have generic terms for cheap food outlets. In Britain 'snack bar' was until recently in common use, as was 'café' – not as one might think a coffee house but a place usually selling soft drinks, frothy and often very weak *cappuccino* coffee, mugs of over-brewed strong tea, and such dishes as egg and chips. In south-east England the word was usually pronounced *kayf*, as in Wolf Mankowitz's 1950s' play *A Kayf Up West*. France has its *bistros* and *routiers*, Italy its trattorias, India its *dhabbas*.

But a final point about the diner. Some years back in my native Glasgow a former prominent sommelier called Terry Ashe opened a splendid restaurant which concentrated on classic British food, with a European slant. He was a little ahead of his time, especially in his choice of title for his expensive, up-market restaurant. He called it 'Nick's Diner'.

This may have touched a sense of irony in sophisticated circles elsewhere. In the Glasgow of those years people thought it was a transport caff.

Dinner

The title itself divides us all. In the north of the UK it means a mid-morning meal, what the soft southerners call **lunch** (luncheon), and the veteran columnist Godfrey Smith has pointed out that there is a class divide as well. 'Any Englishman who calls lunch dinner indicates at once and for sure to any other Englishman that he hails from somewhere below the middle of the middle class.'

But until recently dinner was in fact a mid-afternoon meal, and the gentry had **supper** in the evening. An especially aristocratic Scottish advocate (the equivalent of a barrister in England) once confided to me that he thought dinner suits were vulgar: 'One sups in tails', he said. I have ever since thought this a splendid title for a novel.

That being said, a formal dinner is a pain in the arse, especially when you are an 'after dinner speaker'. I earn the odd crust out of this tedious activity, though not as much as some distinguished people do. It is said that the so-called comedian the late Bob Monkhouse could demand ten thousand notes for this. Prominent politicians such as Lady Thatcher can command forty grand. Ex-President Bill Clinton goes into the stratosphere of fees. Why this should be so is unclear. The actual grub at most formal dinners is awesomely awful, there are copious numbers of drunks, and people only attend such functions to be seen.

Dinner parties are today much derided and the notion of inviting 'amusing' people to mix and, perhaps, match has long since gone. But all this is straying from the point. Among the working class, lunch is still dinner and there is no dressing up about it.

Dolmades

Stuffed vine leaves of Greek origin, usually filled with rice, fried onions, currants, nuts and parsley. Sometimes also with minced veal. I first met these in a Greek restaurant in Munich. It was a starter but was so good that it became a finisher as well: I over-ate. The Turkish version is *yaprek dolmasi*, though there is a variant called *labani dolmani*, in which cabbage leaves are substituted for those of the vine.

Doner kebab

Of Turkish origin, this meat mixture has become a feature of many a take-away meal. The meat is usually lamb and is finely minced, wrapped round a huge cylinder on an upright and rotating spit, and then roasted. Served with salad and in a split pitta bread, it is filling and savoury. In Britain it helped to make a living for immigrant Cypriots, few of whom would ever dream of eating what they sell to the indigenes.

Doughnuts

There are a goodly number of doughnuts. In Spain there is a variant of the breakfast dish of *churros* called *buñuelos*, which can be found at every fiesta and are essentially doughnuts. In north India and Pakistan there is another version, a dessert known as *gulab jamin*. Austria and Hungary have their versions. (Indeed in Hungary their savoury doughnuts, called *langos*, are the national street food and you will find stalls selling them at every railway station.)

Essentially doughnuts are a yeasted flour mixture made into rings, which are deep-fried and are much beloved by urban Americans. The British have a rich version with an interior of jam. (So do the Germans, and this led to a splendid gaffe by President John F. Kennedy, who in a stirring speech in Berlin at the height of the Cold War stated 'Ich bin ein

Berliner'. The crowd laughed themselves sick. A *Berliner* in German was and is a jam doughnut.) At this point you should note **diet**.

Dressing

The scene is a dining room in a small bungalow in a remote and isolated area of the Federated Malay States, some time in the late 1920s or early '30s. ' "You needn't have bothered to dress on my account, you know," said Cooper. "I didn't. I always dress for dinner," Mr Warburton said. "Even when you're alone?" "Especially when I'm alone," replied Mr Warburton, with a frigid stare.'

This is Somerset Maugham in one of his East Asian short stories. Cooper, in the story, is a man of low birth, an inverted snob with a chip on his shoulder; Mr Warburton, a fairly minor government official, is probably doing as most such gentlemen of his class and age. He dresses for dinner, no matter the climate or the circumstances.

Today surely only a very eccentric person, male or female, would, save on formal occasions, dress themselves up like that to eat. But until the start of the Second World War that was exactly what many people of even moderate middle-class status did.

If you read novels written before that war which depicted characters of this class and above it, you will find that nightly dressing up in the boiled shirt and accoutrements was the norm, even in your own home. Bertie Wooster never fails to hit the dinner table at the country houses he visits in what he always refers to as 'the soup and fish'.

Yet if we do not sport a white tie or even a dinner suit or evening gown outside special occasions, most people do indeed consider what to wear when dining out, either at a small dinner party or visiting a good restaurant. I recant a little here. Most women.

These days a lot of otherwise quite decent fellows don't even bother to shave or wear a tie (though there are yet many establishments in which a jacket and tie are demanded, hence the sometimes ludicrous sight of diners in smart restaurants or clubs being issued with some vile remnant of a jacket and impossible neckwear which the management reserves for such a crisis).

But women continue to dress for the occasion and very pleasant it is too, for both the ladies and the gentlemen, who take in the sometimes rare sight of a well-groomed and smartly dressed woman. As Escoffier pointed out about the Ritz just as public dining in restaurants was coming into vogue: 'It allowed ladies to show off their magnificent dresses.' Women liked to show off their 'magnificent dresses' in public then, and they still do.

Dried fruits

The most common fruits that are dried – i.e. have the moisture taken from them – are apples, apricots, dates, figs and, of course, grapes, which subsequently turn into currants, raisins and sultanas. Plums also turn into **prunes**, thereby making one of the loveliest fruits into one of the most unpleasant desserts the world has ever known: prunes and semolina are a staple of British school dinners. Fat dinner ladies love this dish, aided and abetted by mad school nurses who believe the above has laxative qualities. It is indeed true about the laxative, but prunes in my view can lead to an equal egestion by mouth. The very word 'prune' suggests something nasty. Spinsters and ministers of religion of an especially rigorous morality come to mind.

Dried milk

This has its uses and was much in evidence in the years of the Second World War and the immediate post-war period, when every household had large blue and white tins of what was called 'National Dried Milk' (originally 'Household Milk'). The 1960s saw a return to favour of granules of dried milk. It has to be said that it is not successful when added to, for instance, tea or coffee and should be mixed with water first. Dried milk now has a bad reputation because of its use in Third World countries, where it was distributed widely as aid food. Unfortunately the drying process also processes out a number of the nutrients needed by infants, and dried milk is not suitable for babies.

Dried mushrooms
Chinese dried mushrooms are very powerful, and there is no substitute for them. Nor is there for the Italian dried mushrooms known as *porcini* (though this in fact refers to the cep type of mushroom which is generally used: the correct Italian title is *funghi secchi*). They should be soaked for a few minutes in water and added near the end in cooking. They are, or should be, very expensive, but you can obtain cheap *porcini*, nasty black things which should be avoided. Old dried mushrooms have a strong and unpleasant taste. But good *porcini* have a very long shelf life and are immensely useful for an impromptu quick spaghetti sauce.

Dublin Bay prawn
This is not a prawn at all but a member of the lobster family and is known in France as *langoustine*. It is harvested in both the Mediterranean and the North Sea, and the tail meat provides us all with what we call scampi. The wee lobsters were for many years landed in Dublin, though that is all the connection they have with the Emerald Isle.

Dublin coddle

Despite its title, there is nothing specifically Dublinesque about this: it is a traditional country dish of bacon rashers, pork sausages, potatoes, onions and stock. There is an almost exactly similar recipe in Cornish cookery called 'raw fry', which adds sage and nutmeg. Today Dublin coddle can be seen in some smart Irish restaurants which in recent years have been rediscovering their traditional country cookery.

Duck

There is very little meat on this bird, but what there is is wonderful, rich and gamey, and dark-coloured. There are two famous duck dishes in French *haute cuisine*: pressed duck, (for which the expensive Rouennaise duck is bred) and the orange-flavoured dish known throughout the world by its French name, *caneton à l'orange*. This comes with segments of fresh oranges, but it is the sauce that counts. It is a rich brown gravy with the addition of port or **madeira** and heavily laced with orange liqueur (such as Cointreau). Duck must never be overcooked as it becomes dry very quickly.

There is also the Chinese restaurant speciality of Peking duck. Though I know of one occidental who makes this, the fact is that it requires Herculean efforts and is best left to good-quality Chinese eateries. The duck is served as three separate courses: first as rolls of crispy skin, served with plum sauce and thin Chinese pancakes, then as the meat itself, stir-fried with bamboo shoots, and lastly as soup. This princely dish is naturally very expensive, but in its favour I can tell you that the famous chef of the Dorchester Hotel, Anton Mossiman, once told me that if he could ever invent a dish as wonderful as Peking duck he would die happy.

Duck eggs

The shells are of an almost translucent turquoise blue, and the flavour is rich and creamy: thus they are very much gourmet food. Wild duck lay their eggs in their own ordure (to protect them from attack) and therefore these must be well boiled, as the shells are porous. The advent of extensive duck farms, however, has allowed us to discover soft-boiled duck eggs which, when combined with thin shavings of truffles, make one of the most magnificent dishes ever (see **truffle**).

Dulse

A sea vegetable eaten widely in northern Europe. Oddly, it is chewed raw by the Irish, who regard it as especially healthy. It is similar to another Irish speciality, carrageen.

Dumplings

Dough balls generally with suet and usually simmered in broth of some kind. There are dumplings in every known world cuisine, but they are inescapable in Hungarian cookery, in which they are called *galuskas*. The legendary Hungarian goulash should always contain these little dumplings. But any good stew is immensely enriched by dumplings.

Germanic cookery is also awash with dumplings, especially in the Tirol, where a very famous dumpling is the filling and savoury *speckknödel*, made with cubes of hard bread, flour, onions, chives and bacon. They are usually served in a beef broth. Exactly the same dish exists in the German-speaking region of Italy, the Alto Adige, where they are known as *canaderli tirolesi*.

E

E-numbers
These are the means by which European Union law identifies food additives and colourings. The latter are numbered from E100 to E180, preservatives E200 to E290, anti-oxidants E300 to E321, and emulsifiers, stabilizers and artificial sweeteners from E322 upwards. Most supermarket ready-prepared foods contain a staggering array of all of these. Few shoppers ever notice.

Earl Grey tea
This blend of China and Indian black leaf teas is infused with bergamot oil and is named after the British diplomat Lord Grey, who, it is alleged, created this delicately aromatic speciality tea, much enjoyed by ladies it seems.

Earl Grey was not the effete aristo he is often thought to be. When he was the administrator of the newly founded colony of Rhodesia, he planted a gum tree to celebrate the Golden Jubilee of Queen Victoria. (This was a rather bizarre demand made of 'every stalwart Briton' by the Foreign Office of the day.) Lord Grey planted his tree personally, the noble lord in his shirt-sleeves in front of a bemused collection of African natives. 'I am glad of the opportunity', he later observed, 'of showing by my personal example what bloody nonsense all of this is.' After his hole-digging he went off, presumably, for a cup of his special tea.

Eccles cakes
Originating in the little town of Eccles in Lancashire, these are oval cakes of puff pastry filled with currants, mixed peel, butter and spices. They were once very popular in tearooms and coffee shops. Rarely seen these days.

Education
Though the schools and colleges of cookery and catering are excellent in the Britain of today (though still not a substitute for experience in the kitchen itself), paradoxically in an age when television cookery programmes are in abundance cookery is hardly taught in our secondary schools at all. For generations schoolgirls were taught basic cookery in their Domestic Science classes, later renamed Home Economics (see **Victoria sandwich**).

A number of reasons for the decline in cookery teaching can be advanced. The practice of putting often unwilling boys into Home Economics classes in a mistaken attempt at sex equality did not help to popularize the subject with girls. The cost of ingredients was often a bar to such lessons too. The over-crowding of the school curriculum was also detrimental to what used to be a whole morning or afternoon of instruction in the art of cookery.

But perhaps the greatest blow to what was once an integral part of every girl's education was the influence of modern feminism, which bizarrely saw and still sees girls being taught skills in the kitchen as an attempt to subjugate girls and women and keep them tied to the stove. The same has occurred in the instruction of sewing, needlework, knitting etc., and thus modern women cannot manage such traditional skills. This is a great pity. I recollect as a one-time art teacher being inundated with pleas by small girls to try out their apple pies and such. The Home Economics classes were a haven of peace amidst the madness of most of school life.

Eels

This catadromous fish (that is, a fish that is born at sea but spends its entire life in fresh water before returning to the sea to die) was once highly prized in south-west England, and eel and pie shops were an authentic flavour of East-End life in London.

Jellied eels are still a feature of traditional London pub grub. There are many, however, who refuse this delicacy because eels do indeed look like snakes. (This is one reason, though not the only one, why they are forbidden fish to Jews who are **kosher**.) Myself, I find them over-oily, but I recollect eating some wonderfully grilled eels in a superb little *ristorante* in Cagliari in Sardinia, which was unusual in that, despite inhabiting an island, Sardinians rarely eat fish. See also **gerookte paling**.

Eggs

Eggs are perhaps the most legendary and magical of all foods. Regarded in almost every culture as symbols of fertility and rebirth, they have many magical properties associated with them. Mrs Beaton wrote that 'philosophers saw in them the emblem of the world and the four elements. The shell, they said, represented the earth; the white, water, and the yolk, fire; and air was found under the shell at one end of the egg.' The philosopher she was referring to was Diderot, but then I'm sure you knew that.

There is also considerable magic in an egg to anybody born, like myself, during or just after the war, in that eggs were incredibly scarce, with a ration of one per person per week. (This of course was not observed in rural areas. See **wartime food**.) Those of my generation are thus incensed when we find children and teenagers throwing eggs at each other to 'celebrate' some chum's birthday or, as is increasingly the custom, doing the same as a 'trick or treat' for Hallowe'en.

Eggs can be fried, boiled, poached, scrambled, pickled, made into omelettes (see **omelette**) or used for sauces as diverse as Hollandaise (see **Hollandaise sauce**) or **mayonnaise** and as ingredients for baking. The white is used for meringue mixture and for soufflés (see **soufflé**). The egg-nog is made with rum, and the **prairie oyster**, which lays claim to be an antidote for hangovers, contains a whole egg along with bitters and **Tabasco**.

Virtually every egg-laying creature finds a market for its eggs, from ostrich to alligator. Chickens' eggs are, of course, the common variety, and **breakfast** is hardly complete without the breakfast egg. When the Egg Marketing Board decided to promote their product, they ran an advertisement with the famous slogan, said to have been coined by the novelist Fay Weldon, 'Go to Work on an Egg'. Later a rather silly British politician, Edwina Currie, caused severe reductions in egg consumption when she declared that virtually every egg contains the bacteria **salmonella**. The claim is quite true but only rare salmonella bacteria causes any problem.

To add to the magic there are, of course, Easter eggs, decorated lavishly and hand-painted and lacquered, and though it is no longer common in the UK, this practice still exists in Russia. (The Fabergé eggs are an exquisite and horribly expensive bejewelled development of this old custom.) Today's

Easter eggs are usually made of chocolate and range from small to exorbitantly large.

Though there are some elaborate egg dishes (such as the classic *eggs florentine*, in which poached eggs on a bed of spinach are coated with *béchamel* sauce), to my mind nothing can match a plate of fried fresh eggs and good smoked bacon. And talking of good, the highest praise for a fellow in the words of Bertie Wooster is that he is 'a good egg'. It is even higher praise for a girl.

Elevenses

There was a time when Britain was civilized enough to stop for tea or coffee, sometimes called a coffee break, at around eleven o'clock in the morning. Even housewives, when such things existed, would interrupt their mid-morning and have a coffee and perhaps a **digestive biscuit** or two, even a chocolate one, and perhaps a Danish pastry. This splendid ritual was observed by everybody from working men, with their 'tinnies' of hot sweet **tea**, to office clerks and clerkesses, all the way through to the very captains of industry. As I have written earlier, there were also coffee, or smoking, rooms in which mid-morning coffee was consumed and much business done.

Throughout the continent of Europe there is still an elevenses, but the UK is now one of the most Stahkanovite countries in the world and thus this lovely practice has long since disappeared, as has **lunch**. There has been no consequent increase in productivity, but then the sort of bloody awful nimminy-pimminy accountants who think up notions of sour productivity which ensure misery for us all imagine that productivity equals slavery of some kind.

En croûte
Meaning 'served in its crust, usually pastry'. *Pâté en croûte* is one such dish, but meat and fish are often treated in this way. An especially sumptuous example is beef wellington, in which slightly pre-roasted fillet of beef with a stuffing of **pâté de foie gras** and duxelle of mushrooms (there are those who add shavings of truffles, which I think overdoes it), shallots, sometimes **garlic** and a little **madeira** wine, is wrapped in pastry. I can assure you that no French cook ever refers to *filet de boeuf en croûte* with the name of the Iron Duke. The British may well have won the war against the Little Corporal, but they lost, then as now, the battles of the table.

Endive
A term used in North America for chicory. Another form is *radicchio*, much used in salads and fairly expensive.

English cookery
There are many wonderful dishes in English cookery – the roast beef of England with its horseradish sauce and roast potatoes with accompanying Yorkshire pudding is stunning in any context – but English cookery is a byword for bad food. This is unfair, for there are English regional dishes that excite admiration from the rest of the world. Indeed the same roast beef is extolled throughout France and has become a staple of many French households, being known as *rosbif*. It figures heavily in the very odd but influential novel *A Rebours* (1884), by J.K. Huysmans. He died in 1907, having outlived Oscar Wilde, whose *Dorian Gray* was partly drawn from this strange book. Oscar, however, did not like *le rosbif*: his tastes were towards the French cuisine.

Yet there are many splendours in English cookery. It is good to see that more restaurants are taking on board such items as **jugged hare** and **bubble and squeak**, not to mention one of the greatest breakfast dishes of all: bacon and eggs.

Epicure

One who delights in the sensual pleasure of food and wine. The term refers to the Greek philosopher Epicurus (341–270 BC), who managed to combine a clear rationality in mathematics with an argument for hedonism, especially when it came to the delights of the table. This Greek chap espoused the pleasures of luxury in all its forms – clothes, food and sexual exploits – but it is in food that he is celebrated.

Eroticism

Following on from the above, Epicurus was not unique in his belief that eating was indeed the most sensual of all the arts. There is a powerful scene in the film *Tom Jones* (1963) in which the lusty Tom, played by Albert Finney, dallies over food with Sophie Weston (Susannah York) in a clearly sexual manner. Food as a prelude to love-making is common to all cultures, and the most common approach to a prospective partner is taking her out to dinner. (Until recently men always asked the woman. Even today, in these times of feminine independence, it is extremely rare for a woman to ask a man out for a meal. I suspect this is because even in these times women have no intention of paying for the food.)

There are obvious reasons why food plays such a part in love-making. Physically, of course, the mouth and lips are fundamental to sexual activity, and the idea of oral consumption inextricably links food to sex. There is the phenomenon, seen in all cultures, of licking foodstuffs from the bodies of partners, even intimate parts. And, as Juvenal often notes and Petronius wickedly observes, such astounding perversions as coprophagia (seriously, eating human excrement) were performed by a number of especially depraved Roman emperors in that empire's declining years.

(A wee anecdote here. In the early days of the Second World War there were attacks on Italian shop-owners by some demented native Britons. One such attack was attempted on a fish and chip shop in Glasgow, owned by a widow called Emma Cadona. She quelled the mob by threatening them with a basket of hot oil and yelling in broad Italian Glaswegian: 'Fuck Mussolini! Fuck Hitler! Fuck you. Youse would all eat shite if I fried it!' The mob shamefacedly dispersed. But the Roman emperors might well have taken her up on the offer.)

In many Eastern cultures some foods are considered as aids to sexual potency, as aphrodisiacs. Few of these foods medically bear out their reputation, however. See **aphrodisiac foods**.

Escargots

These are snails and are bloody awful, but there was a time when I would order them in expensive restaurants and even make a pretence of enjoying the things. A speciality of Burgundy, they come with garlic butter, though the taste of *escargots* is earthy and rather like mild mushrooms. The texture is, as you imagine, like something that has come out of your nose. Stick to mushrooms.

Espresso

There used to be some confusion in the British mind about this strong, thick, bitter coffee in that the coffee bars of the 1950s and early '60s had Italian machines called Expresso, pioneered by the Italian firm Gaggia (see **savarin**), which utilized hot milk and made *cappuccino* coffee.

For twenty years I have had two small cups of espresso every morning, and put a little sugar and **evaporated milk** into the coffee. It is worthwhile to pay a little extra for the best *arabica* Italian coffee. There are a great many splendid brands in Italy itself, but in the UK I can recommend the brand Lavazza Rossa.

Estouffade

Some use this term to mean a pot roast, but in France it is most often used to mean a stew heavily cooked with wine and vegetables. It is cooked on the top of the stove for a considerable time, with a strongly sealed lid. Basically a **daube**, it becomes an estouffade when the meat consists of a large joint. The most famous of all is a large sirloin or joint of fillet.

The Greeks have their *stifado* and the Italians their *stufato*, though both these are usually stews with the meat cut into smaller pieces. There is also a Creole dish from Louisiana called *étouffe*, which is similar but always includes **capsicums** (green, yellow and red peppers) and often a marinade of rum.

Evaporated milk

This is an unsweetened condensed milk made by evaporating milk in a vacuum container which reduces the water content by 60–65%. It is canned and may be diluted, in which case it is safe for infant feeding. The prominent brand in the UK is Carnation. I use this evaporated milk in my two little morning cups of **espresso** coffee (*espresso macchiato*, otherwise known as *espresso con latte*) and also in an occasional cup of hot chocolate. It is richer than plain milk but less fatty than cream and does not separate, as cream tends to do.

Extracts

Perhaps the most famous of concentrated flavourings are such beef concentrates as the brand **Bovril** or the malt extract **Marmite**. Much beloved in the United Kingdom, both are now quite popular in northern Europe. Bovril is splendid as a drink but worthless as a spread on hot buttered toast. It is exactly the opposite with Marmite.

F

Fadge

A thin triangular scone made of mashed potato, flour and butter, first baked and later often fried, this Irish speciality is also popular in Scotland, where it is often a feature of a fried breakfast.

Faggot

An English meatball made of minced liver, salt pork, seasonings and spices and traditionally wrapped in pig's caul (the membrane covering the head); it is sometimes described as 'poor man's goose'. Faggots are rarely encountered in these days of cheap hamburgers, but were once a common dish among the poor of London's East End.

Farmers

The English poet and clergyman, and friend of Edmund Burke, George Crabbe (1754–1832) summed up the farmer in an 1805 verse rather succinctly: 'Our farmers round, well pleased with constant gain,/ Like other farmers, flourish, and complain.' Nothing much has changed. There is perhaps no other occupation that moans as much. Nothing is ever right for farmers, and everybody else, especially those who live in towns, is a work-shy ingrate. This would seem to hold true for bucolics throughout the world.

Yet it is true that the origin of human civilization lies in the decision to cultivate crops rather than rely on hunting as a means of providing sustenance. Though farming is the principal occupation in much of the Third World, farmers are in a minority in Europe and North America. Farmers do, however, have an astounding level of political clout in both continents, and the European Community can fairly be said to have evolved as an agricultural cartel (there are those who would maintain that it still acts as such).

In recent years times have been harder for farmers, much of their more painful vicissitudes brought upon them by themselves. The venal rapacity displayed by many farmers has brought about problems with livestock and crops alike owing to the overuse of fertilizers and other artificial elements. The feeding of herbivorous cattle with meat slurry which ultimately led to the so-called 'Mad Cow Disease', is a case in point.

There are sociological reasons for the habits and attitudes of farmers, among which can be included isolation, the preponderance of aristocratic landowners who contrived to hold sway over agricultural communities, and a highly developed subsidy culture. Another feature must surely be the mores of philistinism, if not downright ignorance, among many farmers. I once courted the daughter of an extremely wealthy Perthshire farmer and visited his luxurious mansion of a farmhouse many times. He and his wife were very pleasant people. But there was not a single book in the house.

Fast food
Every culture has fast food and its take-aways. Fish and chips are a British example, but inroads have been made by

American food chains such as McDonald's or Kentucky Fried Chicken outlets. Increasingly, though, fast food is considered to be the ready-made meals one encounters in freezer departments of supermarkets. In the hands of some imaginative cooks some of these ready-to-microwave frozen meals can be rather good (indeed a high-quality **delicatessen** can often provide very well-made frozen dishes), but most fast-food platters are simply awful.

Despite the plethora of TV cookery shows, fewer and fewer people in Europe, even in France and Italy, cook these days, and some dieticians are now voicing their concern that the common diet is now being run by the great food outlets that provide these ready-made meals.

Fasting

Though there are those who at times abstain from food for health reasons and some who are simply over-ascetic in the attitudes to life's pleasures, most of those who fast do so for religious reasons, for all the major world religions either demand such an obligation on the part of their flock or did so in the past.

The Muslim observation of a month's fasting during daylight hours during Ramadan is well known and observed by all Muslims, though a dispensation is made for very young children, the frail and many of the elderly. This fast is indeed seen by most dieticians as injurious, owing to what they see as its unnecessary severity.

The Christian churches too have their tradition of fasting but have got round the injunctions to the extent that in recent years the fast is for most Christians, especially those who practise the Roman Catholic faith, a mere token. Most Catholics, if they observe fasting during Lent at all, translate this as not drinking alcohol during the Lenten month, say, or abstaining from sweets and confectionery. Even then on a holy day, such as the Sabbath, Catholics can enjoy such pleasures. Even the practice of eating fish on a Friday, intended by the Church to be a meatless day – the consumption of fish was rather a cheat – has more or less died out as a principle, though many people, including non-Christians in the West, like to preserve Fridays for eating fish.

It is somewhat of an irony that the custom of fasting helped to develop many splendid dishes as the populace strove to find the most ingenious ways of eating well despite the restrictions forced upon them. See also **xerophagy**.

Feijoada completa

A hearty stew of beans and salt beef with pig meat, including ears and trotters, this is the national dish of Brazil and is derived from Portuguese cuisine. It takes, like **cassoulet**, days to make.

Felafel

An Israeli speciality, these are little balls made of chickpeas (see **chickpea**) and cracked wheat and served with pitta bread and salads, and with tahini (sesame seed paste).

Fennel

Though the fennel bulbs and stalks can be used in salads, it is the seeds that are the more important. They impart a subtle aniseed flavour with a hint of orange and are much used in French Provençal cookery. Also used regularly in north Indian cuisine.

Fenugreek

Used in curries and chutneys, the seeds of this plant have a taste rather like an odd combination of mint and caramel, and almost all curry powders contain them. Fenugreek leaves (*methi* in the Urdu tongue) are used in many Indian dishes, including the celebrated potato dish *methi aloo*.

Feta

The most famous cheese in Greece, it is principally made from ewe's milk and soaked in brine. All it takes to think of Greece is feta and a glass of retsina: you are back in a taverna in instants.

Figs

Anybody who has only ever tasted the dried variety will be unprepared for the taste bomb that is the fresh fig. Sweet and juicy, it is often offered as a dessert in Italy. There is a quite unique dessert of figs marinated in **whisky**: this marriage of Mediterranean sun and Highland mist is said to have been created by the British diplomat Sir William Bonaparte (1826–92), a scion of that famous family, who lived out his days in Avignon and is revered in Provence for his poems in praise of his adopted country.

Another literary reference. In the eighteenth century Lady Suffolk received a gift of figs from Turkey in a willow basket. Her neighbour the poet Alexander Pope planted a wand from the basket in his garden, and from it grew Britain's first weeping willow tree. This anecdote, of course, has got very little to do with figs really.

The Cornish figgy pudding or figgy 'obbin is not made from figs: in Cornwall a fig means a raisin. In the Royal Navy a favourite dessert is figgy duff, which my brother assures me was made using dates. His reminiscence dates from 1958, when he did his basic training in Arbroath in Scotland. He said, with some irony, that the pudding was somewhat heavy.

Fillet

To fillet is to cut flesh, be it fish fowl or any meat, from the bones. Virtually all fish sold commercially is filleted, i.e. disembowelled, but in meats such as pork, lamb, beef or veal the fillet cut is prime and expensive. Fillet steak can be, and often is in France, roasted as a joint, but commonly a fillet steak is cut into thick slices and then grilled or fried.

Fillet steaks come in a number of forms. Chateaubriand is a double fillet steak cut from the head of the fillet. It feeds between two and four persons and can vary in thickness from 2 to 5 inches. Tournedos is 1–2 inches thick. The classic method of cooking both these is by grilling, but many, including myself, prefer to lightly sauté in oil and butter and use the pan juices to make a sauce with red wine and a clove of garlic.

Though it has less flavour than, for instance, rump or sirloin, fillet is more tender, and a rare fillet steak is still the height of luxury. Much beloved by footballers and entrepreneurs of the Del Boy type, fillet steak is seen as bestowing prestige.

Fish

Over twenty years ago I watched in astonishment as groups of young, and rather drunk, men unrolled wads of notes to buy rounds of drinks in a bar in the fishing port of Stonehaven in the Grampian region of Scotland. Each man must have had some £2,000 in his pocket. These were the deckhands of the fishing boats. Later in a local hotel I saw the captains of the trawlers: they had tens of thousands in their jackets. That's how much money was made then by the fishermen. Today it is a different story and, though fishermen are by no means poor, such largesse has gone from the industry. Over-fishing has seen to that. Another odd result is that, paradoxically one would think, fish is now very expensive.

In some countries, or parts of them, fish is the staple of the diet, and even in landlocked countries such as, say, Hungary, freshwater fish is eaten. In Hungary the major fish is carp, taken from Lake Balaton, and if you wish to make a truly Hungarian fish dish there is no substitute for this creamy and moist fish, which is difficult to obtain in Britain.

Fish was once seen by wealthy diners as merely a course to precede the main meat dish. But there have been restaurants specializing in fish and seafood in general since the late nineteenth century, and such restaurants are more popular than ever among the more discerning epicures. Sadly this is not so with the bulk of the population of the UK, where few eat fish at all unless it comes as fish fingers, a horrid travesty of pressed cod or other food fish which are widely marketed by one Captain Clarence Birdseye, and which would now seem to be the only fish dish that children ever encounter. Apart from, of course, **fish and chips**, now often a travesty as well.

Fish is such a source of protein and vitamins that legend had it that the regular consumption of it aided brain power: that was certainly the view of P.G. Wodehouse's splendidly asinine Bertie Wooster, who ascribed the towering intellect of his manservant Jeeves to a massive ingestion of fish. In this he may not have been far off the mark. Research into dietary habits has proved that in cultures in which fish is a principal source of food, mental illness is much reduced, and depression and schizophrenia are very much less common. Which depresses one when considering that so few Brits eat this aquatic creature on a regular basis.

Fish and chips

Fried fish warehouses were first recorded in literature by Charles Dickens, who wrote of one in *Oliver Twist* (1838), but the fried fish was sold by itinerant peddlars along with a baked potato. Christopher Mayhew mentions this early take-away meal in his *London Labour and the London Poor* (1861), in which he describes the common incidence of this cheap food. Gerald Priestland, the religious affairs broadcaster and author, in his splendid *Frying Tonight: The Saga of Fish and Chips* (1973), disputed the claim that the oldest chip shop in Britain was Malin's in London, said to have traded in this now traditional British dish in 1865. Priestland claimed that Lancashire was a more likely home of origin in Britain.

But, whoever first thought of marrying French fries with fried fish, it was a stroke of genius. Many of the first fish and chip shops were started by Italian immigrants, and to this day almost all the chip shops in Scotland are owned by Italian families. The veteran, and now sadly retired, Joe Pieri, restaurateur, chip shop owner and author of several engaging books, once, during the post-war shortage of oil for frying, purchased gallons of the holy oil used for Mass in Catholic churches, which was readily available. He claims that his subsequent fish and chips were not only the best he had ever made, but 'helped the flock quicker to glory'.

Unfortunately many present-day fish and chip shop proprietors buy inferior oils, fish, potatoes and even stint on the necessary batter, and fish and chip *aficionados* such as myself have to travel considerable distances to obtain a really good 'fish supper'. But despite the attractions of other take-away outlets, fish and chips is still a favourite with the British: it was the first thing the troops called for after retaking the Falklands.

Flambé

There are a number of dishes in which this method of cooking is employed (see, for example, **coq au vin**), but the process is most famous in the splendid showmanship of such desserts as crêpes Suzette. A small glass of such spirits as **cognac**, **brandy**, **whisky** or even **rum** (there is a very good dessert of baked bananas flambéed in rum) is poured into the food and ignited. In the case of savoury dishes such as the aforementioned coq au vin or in some recipes for **boeuf bourguignon** the flaming helps to add colour and flavour. Most chefs warm the spirit lightly before pouring into the pan or casserole, as this helps to ignite it. Immediately after adding the spirit, put a match to the liquor: it will light immediately. Roll your pan about until the flames subside.

In the case of such desserts as **crêpes** flambéing is done at the end of cooking, almost always at the table for it makes for a wonderful piece of melodrama. Incidentally there is always a little *frisson* when one flambés, a heart-stopping, for a moment, culinary delight.

Flour
This is meal ground usually from cereals such as wheat, though there are flours made from some vegetables such as potatoes or bananas. Wheat flour comes commercially in many different forms. Plain wheat flour has a gluten content of 7–10% and is used for baking; self-raising flour is plain flour to which baking powder has been added; wholemeal flour is a brown flour that contains the entire wheat grain. But there are a multiplicity of flours – north Indian cookery, for instance, uses gram (**chickpea**) flour, which is more highly flavoured than that used in Europe.

Flowers
There are a number of flowers that are indeed edible and can be used as a decorative element in salads as a garnish. The petals of the flowers of chive and thyme, as well as the wonderfully peppery nasturtium (I've only ever tried the pungent leaves) and such colourful splendours as marigolds, primroses, violets, roses, pansies and pinks, are used in salads and sometimes desserts.

Folic acid
Here are a few of the medical problems that occur when there is insufficient folic acid in the diet: anaemia, diarrhoea, insomnia, weariness and shortness of breath. The acid can be

found in liver, nuts, yeast, soya flour, wheat and bran and green vegetables. A deficiency can occur as a result of excessive alcohol consumption, the use of the contraceptive pill and, most of all, during pregnancy. Many pregnant women seem to know innately that their condition leads to megaloblastic anaemia, and thus the famous sudden demand for strange foods.

Expecting mothers should have a diet that includes vegetables and wheat, though some doctors say that liver should not be eaten during pregnancy: it is said to contain an element that can have effects on the foetus similar to that of an excess of alcohol. As to the latter, many doctors, while by no means recommending a high level of alcohol during pregnancy, used to suggest a bottle of **stout** a day for prospective mums.

Fondue

This was once very fashionable in the 1960s, when fondue parties were popular. The simple cheese fondue is, like most other fondues, of Swiss origin, and consists of such cheeses as Emmental and Gruyère cooked in a large, wide pot called a *caquelon* and melted along with garlic and often kirsch. Other cultures have similar preparations, especially in the Far East, but Switzerland has this as its national dish.

A favourite also from the land of mountains and yodelling is *fondue bourguignonne*, in which cubes of beef are cooked at the table in hot oil by the individual diners. *Fondue chinoise* is rather similar, but the meat is sliced thinly and is cooked by being speared and lightly cooked in hot stock or bouillon. (The similarity to a Chinese fondue called, in English, the Chrysanthemum Pot is so obvious that the Swiss version must have had its origins in the East, though I don't see how. The Swiss are hardly renowned as sailors.) I remember much fun at these fondue parties when I was an art student back in those splendidly hippie days of peace and love. Actually I don't: as the legend has it, if you remember the Sixties you weren't there.

Food
See **nosh**.

Food colourings
There are natural food colouring such as **cochineal**, **paprika**, **saffron** etc., and most of them also impart a flavouring as well. But the vast majority of food colourings are synthetic and include the azo dye group, of which the most commonly used is the yellow dye tartrazine. Such colouring agents are commonly found in most processed foods and can be injurious to children's health. One of the reasons why much baby food looks quite so disgusting is because the manufacturers of such quite rightly refuse to employ synthetic dyes in their products.

Food critics
These are part of a fine tradition among literary people on the Continent. The dazzling array of French novelists of the nineteenth and twentieth centuries who wrote widely and well on food includes Alexandre Dumas, both *père* and *fils*, the Goncourt brothers, Flaubert, Proust of course, André Gide, Camus and Sartre, and Colette, all of them following on from Racine and François-Marie Arouet, better known as Voltaire.

American food critics are in short supply, though the splendid A.J. Leibling, a chap who initially made his reputation, like Ring Lardner and Damon Runyon, as a sportswriter, was such a gourmet that when he was sent to cover the Second World War in Europe he wrote almost entirely about food.

Britain has seen few food and restaurant critics of note, though Oscar Wilde, no mean gastronome himself, was one of the first journalists to write a restaurant report, which he did for the brief years when he was editor of *The Woman's World*, which later became *Woman's Weekly*. (The magazine had started as *The Lady's World*, and it was Wilde who changed the title, stating that, though not all women were ladies, all ladies were women.)

Two British critics who have made their mark on the restaurant scene are the remarkable Raymond Postgate and the equally strange Hungarian *émigré* Egon Ronay. Postgate was a left-wing detective story writer and Classical scholar who produced, in the dark days of post-war austerity, a slim volume called *The Good Food Guide*. The *Guide* has become a veritable bible of restaurant lore. It is often wonderfully literate, even literary. An entry for the Betjeman restaurant in London's Charing Cross Hotel even managed a Betjemanesque touch:

> Vegetables are best forgotten
> Chocolate mousse will not be missed
> Coffee's decent. Cloths are cotton
> Wine's good value. Pianist.

The Egon Ronay guide employs full-time inspectors, some of whom I know are trained chefs.

Both guides do something rare in restaurant criticism: they never reveal who their critics are, never tell an eatery in advance, or indeed in retrospect, and never take a free meal. Because in my native Scotland I can hardly go unrecognized, I have never been a restaurant critic. For some reason this makes me feel as though I possess both integrity and importance.

Food hygiene

The last decade or so has seen a considerable increase in cases of food poisoning, which, at first sight, seems very strange indeed. The most probable reason is thought by the medical profession to be the fact that increased hygiene in the home and in retail outlets has adversely affected consumers' natural immune systems: in short, we are too clean. Yet many other medical experts believe that, though this is a contributory factor, the prevalence of frozen foods, and indeed foods bought in bulk rather than on a daily basis, is a major cause of what seems to be an epidemic of food poisoning.

Myself, I take elementary measures such as washing my hands and utensils and cutlery between the preparation of each ingredient. But I do take risks such as, for instance, preferring to cook both meat and poultry rare. It is indeed a risk with chicken, owing to the high incidence of **salmonella** in this fowl, but I prefer a pinkish flesh in which the juices have just begun to flow: risk is greatly reduced if you buy a fresh, rather than a frozen, chicken.

Food writers

I am making what some readers may think an odd, even pedantic, distinction here between food critics, writers who have touched occasionally on the pleasures of the table, and even cookery writers and food writers. There are a few writers who have written exclusively about food, including giving recipes, but whose prose style lifts them into the small genre of truly inspirational writers on food. Most of them are women, of course, and in recent years it has been a delight to read works by Claudia Roden and Jane Grigson. (Mention must be made of the Irish cookery writer Florence Irwin, who wrote a marvellously amusing book (see **Irish cookin'**) and of Scotland's Catherine Brown, who often works in concert with Derek Cooper, a rare male food writer of distinction.)

Most women food writers are pretty awful, though: gushing, inaccurate, with a style that reminds you of daisy chains, fairies and lovely little bunny rabbits. Invariably they 'divide their time' between their London flat, their Cotswold cottage and their farmhouse in Provence or the Dordogne.

Such vapourings are to be avoided. Yet there is one who rises above all this, one who unfortunately and through no fault of her own gave rise to such farragos perpetrated by others in her wake. Her name is Elizabeth David, and her influence on British food for over fifty years of the last century is incalculable, not simply in cookery – and she did write cookery books – but also in the British attitude to food, to eating out, to how we see world food. Her first book, written at the height of rationing just after the Second World War, was actually rather slight. It was called *Mediterranean Food*. In 1950, the year it was published, British food, never highly regarded, had reached its nadir, with not only a lack of actual foodstuffs but a lack of cooking expertise, the culmination of a process that began after the Great War. Her next book, on French country cooking, which came out a year later, was also fairly slender but just as influential. Then came two blockbusters, a book on Italian food, and then in 1960 her seminal volume on French provincial cookery. In ten years she had changed the face of British food. Every aspect of cookery, from dinner parties in smart London townhouses to chic little restaurants, to even the food outlets, was influenced by her work. Another odd thing too: despite Mrs David's impeccably upper-class origins, in the post-war years, in which domestic servants were no longer feasible, she introduced a new classlessness to the world of eating. Equally strange was that she was diffident of her own writing style and was genuinely astonished at the response by writers and savants to her books. (Evelyn Waugh, no less, pronounced her book on Italian cuisine as his book of the year for 1954.)

I met her just the once, at a Glenfiddich award reception. She had a reputation, in her later years, for a certain irascibility – she disapproved of much of the pretentiousness of food writing in the aftermath of her own work – but I found her graceful and charming. And devastatingly knowledgeable.

Forelle bleu

Despite its French title, this is actually an Austrian dish and consists of an absolutely fresh trout, which still has its slime on its body: it must have been recently caught and killed. When put into boiling water with vinegar and lemon juice it turns a splendid blue colour.

Maxim's of Paris used to serve this on Bastille Day with boiled potatoes, which are of course white, and red tomatoes, thereby denoting the tricolour. It cost a fortune. (Italy has a similar burst of culinary patriotism in its *risotto tricolore*, made with tomatoes, boiled rice and green peas.)

Forfar bridie

This Scottish speciality is a pastry turnover with a beef, suet and onion filling. Made throughout Scotland, and not only in the town of Forfar in Tayside, it can be, like the **Cornish pasty**, disappointing to those who know what a true bridie should be, instead of a piece of flabby puff pastry with a nauseous sausage meat filling. The real Forfar bridie is made with finely chopped or minced prime beef and can be made with both short and puff pastry. The horseshoe-shaped pasty is said to be so-called either because the horseshoe shape was considered lucky (it was consumed at weddings) or because a woman called Bridie (a diminution of Bridget) hawked them around the town of Forfar. No matter, a really good Forfar bridie (and McLaren's of Forfar make just that) is a rare treat.

Fortified wine

The best examples of this are **port** and **sherry**, which can be very, very expensive indeed. Both are wines to which brandy is added, and the vintage can be very old. But what is mostly known as 'fortified wine' has a different provenance. It is much abused by the urban proletariat and is largely both cheap and potent. Once, as an advertising studio artist and also a copywriter, I described a brand of cheap fortified wine with the slogan: 'Very cheap and gets you drunk *quick!*' The former Prime Minister Harold Wilson was said erroneously by the satirical magazine *Private Eye* to have an especial liking for a cheap fortified wine called Wincarnis. There was nothing wrong with this brand, though it was horribly sweet.

Frankfurters
Originally from the area around the German town of Frankfurt, these cold-smoked sausages of finely ground, high-quality pork meat are now made throughout the world and, eaten with finger rolls, **mustard** and tomato ketchup (see **ketchup**). Known as **hot dogs**, are a ubiquitous take-away snack throughout the USA and Europe. A visit to the cinema is incomplete without a hot dog.

French cuisine
The origin of much French cooking as we know it today is said, with some truth, to lie in the circumstance of Catherine de Medici marrying Henri II, then the Dauphin, in 1533, when the young bride brought her Florentine cooks to the French court. (And later Marie de Medici married Henri IV in 1600.)

But the prominence of French cookery, at least in the eyes of the world, stems from the explosion of the French Revolution (see **chef**). For when this astonishing conflagration burst into flames, the cooks who had flourished in the kitchens of the aristocracy were forced to flee or were at least made unemployed. A few of the more politically suspect found themselves in the same tumbrils as their former employers. (Others in the food trade too. It was a grocer, Jean Cortey, who attempted to rescue Louis XVI on the morning of his execution. Despite his failure he also unfortunately tried, along with the Chevalier de Maison Rouge, to save Marie Antoinette and her children. He went to the guillotine in his turn.)

After the Revolution many chefs opened up restaurants in Paris and elsewhere in France and later in other parts of Europe (see **restaurant**). A goodly few went to work for the great households of the British aristocracy. As has been mentioned elsewhere, Beauvilliers, the former steward to the Count (previously Duke) of Provence, escaped the Terror to open what is perhaps the first modern restaurant of Paris at 26 Rue de Richelieu, and Boucher, who had been Talleyrand's chef, was to influence the career of Marie-Antoine (Antonin) Carême, who was twenty at the time. Carême became the most influential French chef of the nineteenth century, writing on every aspect of French cuisine. His influence courses through the cookery of that country to this day.

From Carême, who wrote in French, to the great French chefs who migrated to Britain and America the reputation of French cuisine reigns supreme in the eyes of the Anglo-American world and certainly in the world of **haute cuisine**. But France has also a long tradition of bourgeois and country cookery and an equally imposing tradition of writing about it. And here I have to make an admission. Though I delight in many different national cuisines and generally admire the now polyglot approach to, especially, restaurant cookery, it is to French cuisine that I look for the nonpareil. Some years back I wrote a piece on what I would have as my last meal before I went to the gallows or electric chair, as is common practice among those nations barbaric enough still to maintain a policy of capital punishment. My intention was that celebrities' choices would follow as part of a series. A dashed good idea for my newspaper, I thought, and I still do. But newspaper editors are not as fanciful as myself and, though they printed my piece, they did not follow up my suggestion. I think one of the reasons why my proposal was rejected was that my then editor, the late and lamented Arnold Kemp, was deeply suspicious of anything that he considered high falutin', or in his near obsolete schoolboy contumely, 'swanky'. What he objected to was that my proposed repast was all French, and very, very *haute cuisine* indeed. In short, when I think of the greatest cuisine in the world, I think of France.

Fresh

There are foods that are required to be actually rotted or at least stale. The seasoning known in South-East Asia as **blachan** or *trasi* consists of dried prawns or shrimps, salted and then left to rot, and is absolutely necessary for many of the region's dishes. (The ancient Gauls had their own version of this rotted fish in what they called *garum*, a sauce made with decayed mackerel or anchovies. The Romans had a mania for this. It was one of the most expensive foods the world has ever known and a litre of the sauce would, in today's terms, cost over £1,000.)

In Japan an especial delicacy is made with rotten eggs. (Very smart restaurants refer to this as 'thousand-year-old eggs', which is erroneous as that delicacy is in fact Chinese and consists of eggs buried for some months in a mixture of paddy, tea leaves, lime, clay, saltpetre and spices. The shells turn a marbled black, and the eggs themselves are green-veined. They are perfectly safe to eat and, of course, costly.) Other less than fresh foods: all throughout the Himalayan region rancid yak butter is much preferred and, if you come to think of it, most game is sold when it has become stinking.

But fresh is what we generally ask for in most foods. We like our fish fresh, for instance. Fresh butter is actually unsalted butter; fresh bacon simply means unsmoked. Fresh **pasta** is a revelation to anybody who has never eaten anything other than the dried variety.

But to eggs. Because of the emergence of mass production

and distribution of eggs, in Britain few under the age of fifty have ever encountered a rotten egg. Thus instructions about how to tell when an egg is fresh are virtually redundant in the UK, though this subject frequently crops up in cookery books. But here is the secret. A fresh egg will have a domed yolk, and the white will be viscous and fairly solid with a thin ring of transparent white. And if you put an unbroken egg into a bowl of cold water, a fresh egg will sink to the bottom and lie parallel to the base. If it moves upwards the egg is stale. But then there was the dried egg powder, which was about all city dwellers could get during the Second World War and the subsequent years of austerity. This was a time when eggs, fresh or not, were hard to get. My mother would urge myself and my siblings to eat a cake with the recommendation that 'there's an egg in it'. It remains true that 'fresh' is a recommendation with almost any foodstuff, not least because anything else can be a source of food poisoning.

Fricadelles

Meat patties but, especially when made with minced veal, considered a chic little luncheon dish. It is a very French dish, but for some reason the Danish national dish, which is similar, is called *frikadeller* and is often served at parties along with a great deal of lager beer. A Danish girlfriend of mine (a fellow art student) used to offer this splendid meal, along with the lager, at Sunday lunches she held for fellow students. I later discovered that *frikadeller* was all she could cook. But she *was* a real blonde.

Fries

When they don't mean chips, they mean the testicles of lambs and calves. There is practically no part of an animal that cannot be eaten, but one wonders why anybody would wish to consume wee bulls' bollocks. See **pickles**.

Fritters

Food coated in batter and then fried. There are fruit fritters, popular in Chinese cookery, and meat, poultry and fish fritters. The most famous of fish fritter dishes is the Italian *fritto misto di mare*, in which shellfish and small pieces of fish are cooked in this way. See also **Spam**.

Frogs' legs

The only edible parts of a frog (in French, *grenouille*) are the legs (*cuisses*), considered a great delicacy. They taste rather like chicken and, like **escargots**, are hardly worth the effort. Why the French are pejoratively known by the Brits as 'Frogs', on the basis that they live on a diet of these little amphibians, is a mystery. Very few French diners have ever eaten them. When I asked for them in a restaurant in Lyon, it caused much amusement to my Gallic friends, who pointed out that French ignoramuses believed Scots lived entirely off **haggis**. I was suitably abashed.

Fromage

French for **cheese**.

Frozen food

Though refrigeration of food goes back many centuries – fish from the Rhine, the North Sea and the Baltic was packed with ice and further insulated with furs before being sent to the markets of Ancient Rome – it was the Chinese who probably created the first ice industry when they combined ice and snow with saltpetre and it is said, as it so often erroneously is, that Marco Polo brought the technique back to Italy.

In the mid-nineteenth century several pioneers invented refrigeration machines, though they could not prevent some rotting of meats and vegetables when they were finally defrosted. It was left to an American, Captain Clarence

Birdseye, to solve the problem, which he did by developing what is called 'fast-freezing' in 1929. Though this was an inauspicious time – with the Wall Street Crash and subsequent years of the Great Depression – Birdseye caught the attention of the great beef companies of Argentina, who had already embraced the refrigeration of previous years. By the advent of the Americans into the Second World War Birdseye was, as it remains, the largest frozen food company in the world, and the domestic freezer is no longer the luxury that it was seen to be outside the USA, even as late as the 1970s.

Yet there remains among some a snobbish disdain for frozen foods. It may well be true that absolutely fresh vegetables straight out of your garden are superior in taste to frozen, but they would have to have been picked the same day – frozen vegetables are frozen within hours of picking. Fish is said to be better when not frozen, but people forget that fish is packed with ice on the fishing boats, and indeed Sweden, possibly the greatest fish-eating country in the world, has been fast-freezing fish since the mid-1930s.

Fructe coapte la flama
Fruit fritters flambéed in brandy, and a restaurant speciality in Romania. The late dictator Nicolae Ceausescu, who liked to be called variously 'the Danube of the Thought' or 'The Genius of the Carpathians', was especially fond of this dessert. His subjects didn't even know what it was. During his dreadful regime few urban dwellers ever saw much fruit, flambéed or not.

Fudge
A soft and very sweet confection made from boiled sugar, it seems peculiar to Britain, Commonwealth countries and the USA. Only a child, and one determined on sufficient caries, can possibly enjoy it.

Fufu

A speciality from west Africa in which sweet potatoes, yams or sometimes plantains are boiled and puréed and served with meat. In recent times it has become popular with Afro-Americans as what they call 'soul food'. The latter is hardly new: in my Scottish childhood a very similar dish was made with parsnips (see **parsnip**) and was served with thin slices of beef called frying steak.

G

Gaeng mussamen

This is a famous curry from Thailand. *Gaeng* (or *kaeng*) is Thai for curry, and *mussamen* is from the British word for one of the Muslim faith, *mussulman*. This dish is said to have originated from the appetites of the Indian civil servants whom the British Empire exported to Thailand: a ridiculous notion, for Indians had been emigrating to the rest of South-East Asia for centuries. *Mussamen* curry is a rich beef curry with *blachan* paste, creamed coconut, and peanuts and chillies. It is very hot, unusual for Thailand, but a favourite dish in any Thai menu. (Thais are prodigious eaters and usually have five or more items for a meal, along with rice.)

Galettes

Filled pancakes. As *galettes sablées* they are little sweet biscuits. The famous nineteenth-century Moulin de la Galette, painted by artists including Van Gogh and Toulouse-Lautrec, was a dance hall that doubled as a pancake house.

Gallimaufry

A combination of foods, often a mixture of whatever is available, the word means 'hotch-potch', itself a corruption of *hoche-pot*. (See also **salmagundi**.) I once discovered a restaurant menu in Elgin, Scotland, in which the enthusiastic English couple who owned it had decided to put on the menu a gallimaufry-style dish which they called 'houghmagandy'. They based this title erroneously on the fact that one of the ingredients was potted hough, a jellied delicacy made of shin of beef and once popular in Scotland. So too is houghmagandy in that land of mists and mountains: it is an old Scottish word for fornication.

Game

Roughly speaking, this term refers to birds and animals which are hunted by sportsmen and -women. Thus where turkey was once a game bird, it is now farmed and has lost that status. Britain's own version of turkey, the rare capercaillie, is a game bird. Other game birds include **pheasant**, **grouse**, **partridge**, and pigeons, some of which are protected by game laws forbidding hunting during the breeding and rearing periods. Generally the hunting season for all game, including such mammals as deer, is from August to March.

In Italy sportsmen will kill any bird at all, and very small birds such as thrushes, robins, larks, quails, blackbirds – anything that flies – are killed and eaten. Some of these smaller birds, such as quails and woodcock, are also eaten in Britain. To the astonishment of most of us, the Italians will even shoot and eat such birds as eagles, flamingos and albatrosses. (Clearly Italians are not acquainted with Coleridge's epic poem.) Game also includes deer, rabbits and hares; though hares are protected, rabbits are not.

But if you think Italians are psychopaths, you should note the British royal family's penchant for slaughter: on one day in November 1913 the royal party shot over four thousand pheasants on their Sandringham estate. The British public was not amused.

Game has to be hung, though the absurdity that occurs in smart restaurants in hotels of a competition to see who proffers the first grouse on the Glorious Twelfth means that a flavourless and tough bird is served. Grouse and pheasant should be hung for at least five days.

Game pie

This magnificent raised pie is made with hot water crust pastry and filled with a mixture of sausage meat, raw game such as pheasant, grouse, partridge or pigeon, rump steak, herbs and seasonings, sometimes with chopped nuts; aspic jelly is added at the end through a funnel. It is usually baked in an elaborate mould and looks very splendid indeed. Often served with a creamy potato salad.

A lovely pub, The Dove, in Fulham in London, used to serve this in wedges and a measure of how good it was is that, when I once took the French singer Charles Aznavour (my editor thought it would make a change from the usual gushing female journo) there and introduced him to this traditional British pie, he ordered a whole one the next day to take back to Paris. I found it difficult to understand why the ladies fell for this diminutive little chap. What he looked like to me was, well, a Glaswegian. But he liked game pie.

Gammon

This is the hind leg and thigh of cured bacon and is most often encountered either as gammon steaks (invariably served with pineapple rings) or as cooked thinly sliced cold meats. For some reason I always think of gammon as a genteel working-class item.

Garam masala

The Indian academic and food writer Dharamjit Singh insists that the use of this spice mixture has distorted the subtleties of Indian cuisine, and he may be right for it is today much overused. It is a recipe involving, usually, coriander, cloves, cinnamon, cumin, fenugreek, turmeric, ginger and pepper, and is added at the end of cooking curries, providing a spicy crust. The Indian (and Scottish) restaurateur Navdeep Basi claims that garam masala has aphrodisiac properties: he should know.

Garbure

A French vegetable soup not dissimilar to the hearty broths for which Scotland is famed. Often contains pieces of pre-served goose. The title is said to be derived from the word 'garbage', which in fact originally meant 'left-overs'.

Garibaldi biscuits

Biscuits containing currants and named after the great Italian revolutionary Giuseppe Garibaldi. It is interesting to note that no foods seem to have been named after such revolutionaries as Lenin, Stalin or Hitler, though Napoleon has given his name, or at least his reputation, to countless French recipes.

Garlic

It is no myth that this member of the onion family fairly makes the breath reek. But it is also true that a large quantity of garlic in a dish will somehow cancel out the odour that a lesser amount causes. This bulb was popular in England during the Elizabethan age (though even then olfactory references were made: Shakespeare has Dorcas say of Mopsa in *The Winter's Tale*: 'Garlic to mend her kissing with'), but later became a byword for the French diner, indeed for the

French in general, who are disparaged as a nation of 'garlic-eaters'.

Lovers of garlic, and here I include myself, cannot do without it and there are some magnificent dishes that seem to consist almost entirely of garlic, such as the sauce **aioli** (garlic is *ail* in French) or the Greek version of it, *skordalia*. I have encountered a roast chicken in a Basque restaurant in the Sorbonne student district in Paris in which twenty cloves of garlic were used, according to the chef. And there is a classic Indian dish from Madras in which chicken meat is marinated in a mixture of a whole bulb of garlic and **papain** (papaya): it is heavenly.

Garlic is said to have magical properties and to afford psychic insights. It is also famously said to ward off evil spirits and such phenomena as vampires. Garlic contains sulphur of allyl, said to be a powerful aphrodisiac. But there is one attribute that it actually does possess: garlic is of considerable medical use as it helps to prevent excessive clotting of the blood, and a diet that includes its regular use is a healthy one.

Gastronome
One who is a connoisseur of food and wine. This word is often confusing in that there are also the terms 'epicure', 'gourmet' and 'gourmand'. Do not get too confused, though. A gourmet is an epicure. A gourmand is a greedy bastard.

Gateau
French for cake, now usually meaning an elaborate one. See **Black Forest gateau**.

Gay-Lussac
A French chemist who first developed the system of measuring alcohol by volume. For some reason this seems important

to real ale drinkers. Och, I know the reason. Real ale drinkers are anoraks.

Gazpacho

A cold soup from the Andalucía region of Spain, this is made with tomatoes, garlic, red peppers, vinegar and oil, herbs and breadcrumbs. The French writer, novelist and leading decadent Théophile Gautier described gazpacho as a 'hell-broth'. But then, nobody reads *Clarimonde* any more, and the Andalucians are still supping their hell-broth.

Gefilte fish

No story by Damon Runyon is ever very far away from this appalling dish, a favourite with the Jewish community, which consists of raw fish boiled in water with onions and carrots. Runyon's narrator (always unnamed) was ever consuming gefilte fish in Mindy's restaurant. Actually it was Lindy's restaurant on Broadway, near 50th Street, owned by Leo Lindemann, who opened his first shop in 1921. It closed in 1949, having chronicled the Jazz Age. (An early customer was Scott Fitzgerald.) Lindemann's other restaurant, also on Broadway, shut its doors in 1957, but a chain company opened several eateries bearing the name in the late 1970s.

The original Lindy's was famous for its wisecracking waiters, and when the new Lindy's kicked themselves off, they employed, at vast expense, the comedian Richard Pryor to write gags for their staff. There is no joke that can cheer up this Jewish speciality, though. Despite the astonishing achievements of the Jewish people, it has to be said that cuisine is not a strong point.

Gentleman's Relish

This is an **anchovy** paste marketed under its alternative name *patum peperium*. It is generally eaten spread thinly on hot buttered toast and is thought traditional for Oxbridge under-graduates in their rooms for a midnight beanfeast. Evelyn Waugh had every undergrad endlessly consuming this delicacy, and quite right too. It is a taste explosion.

Gerookte paling

Find yourself in Amsterdam and you cannot be five minutes away from the street vendors of this smoked eel snack. The distressing voyeurism of the many tourists who gawp at the famous prostitutes of the city is to be deplored. So is *gerookte paling*.

Ghiveci Calugaresc

This Romanian speciality, for some reason known as 'monk's hotch-potch' is a vegetarian meal of potatoes, onions and other root vegetables, together with aubergines. The novelist Olivia Manning (whose *Balkan Trilogy* is surely one of the great achievements of twentieth-century English literature) told me she once ate this in a Bucharest restaurant in the company of a young communist activist while he was being searched for by the Iron Guard just before the country decided to join the war. He was Nicolae Ceausescu, later the despotic ruler of that unhappy country. (Incidentally the tyrant's father was the local police informer and not very bright: he named both his sons Nicolae, which must have led to some confusion.) But no matter, this peasant meal is very good.

Gigot

This French term for a leg of lamb is still used in Scotland (that country employs many French words in its cookery owing to its long alliance with France, the best example being their ashet pies, named after the French word *assiette*). To add to the confusion gigot chops is the term used in northern England for lamb chump chops. In Scotland gigot chops are cuts from the leg of lamb, and in my childhood it was my mother's Wednesday dish. It was then cheap; it is not now.

Gin

A colourless and flavourless grain spirit said to have been much favoured by the late Queen Mother. (The flavour derives from the addition of juniper berries, a word deriving from the Celtic *junupus*, meaning 'bitter', and the word 'gin' is derived from the French word for the berry, *jenever*.) The widespread distribution dates from 1575, when the Dutch distillers Bols started its commercial manufacture. Because of a very daft law enacted by William of Orange that proscribed imports of Dutch gin, the British dry gin became a potent and dangerous alcohol often illicitly distilled, and in Hogarthian days was much abused by the proletariat, leading thus to its title of 'Mother's Ruin' and prompting Tobias Smollet's aphorism 'Drunk for a penny; dead drunk for two'.

A transformation somehow occurred with gin: by the 1920s it was a toff's tipple enjoyed especially by the Bright Young Things and the basis for many a **cocktail**. And when the British Navy discovered that angostura bitters, which were used as a preventative medicine, could be added to gin, the fabled pink gin became the classic drink for marble-mouthed naval officers. Similarly in British India quinine tonic water, used to combat malaria, was added. Probably more young British imperialists died of gin rather than malaria at that. Gin is also the base for Pimm's Number One. Pimm's no longer make any of the other five Pimm's, and Number One is the only one to have gin as its alcohol ingredient.

Ginger

A rhizome (underground stem) of a tuber which is washed and dried in the sun. It is used in dried and powdered form, but its use in oriental cookery is mainly in the form of so-called 'fresh' or 'green' ginger. It is absolutely fundamental to any **curry**, in which the base is a *masala* of **garlic** and this strong spice. It is also widely employed in pickles and chutneys and, too, in many confections such as ginger snaps and gingernuts (see **gingernut**), sweet biscuits strongly flavoured with powdered ginger. Gingerbread, a treacly and very sticky cake much admired in Scotland and, indeed, in Grimm's Fairy Tales, also uses it in large quantities.

The appearance of ginger, fresh or powdered, in European cuisine seems to be confined to northern parts of that continent. It is today virtually unknown in France and Italy, and only makes a rare appearance in Iberian cookery, when recipes of Moorish origin are invoked. Some very old Gascon recipes in the Bordelais region of France mention ginger. The writer and gourmet Count Austin de Croze wrote in a collection of regional recipes he published in 1929 that ginger was once commonplace in the cuisine of old Bordelais because of the long occupation of the English Plantagenet family. 'When they left', he wrote, 'they took their cookery with them, and ginger has not reappeared in La Belle France.' Yet ginger was once fashionable in other parts of France. Nostradamus (Michel de Notre Dame) was a fan of the then expensive ginger and publicized a recipe for a cheap ginger substitute. He did not, however, predict that the use of this spice would virtually disappear from his country's cuisine.

The use of ginger extends far elsewhere, though. There is ginger ale, a soft drink occasionally added to **whisky** by such *naïfs* as North Americans. Ginger beer is generally lightly alcoholic, though the restaurateur and publican Gay Graham brews an especially lethal beer using ginger. Some of her customers maintain that her brew is a 'leg-opener' as young women do not realize the alcohol content until it is too late.

Gingernut

Frankly I do not know the difference between a gingernut and a ginger snap and suspect they are one and the same. They are round, sweet biscuits made with syrup and heavily flavoured with ground ginger. As I mentioned in my entry on the **digestive biscuit**, gingernuts make for perfect dunking in tea or coffee. They seem to be exclusive to the Anglo-Saxon world, being popular in both the USA and the UK. Certainly when I introduced French friends of mine to these delectable biscuits, they had never tasted the flavour before in their lives.

Ginseng

In the 1970s this root was thought by those of the Alternative Society to have tonic qualities. The Chinese say it has aphrodisiac qualities too. The Chinese think every food has the same, and they may be right.

Goose

This large bird is of the **duck** family and was once regarded, before the advent of the **turkey**, as the traditional fowl for Christmas dinner. (Thus the famous ditty 'It was Christmas Day in the workhouse/ And the geese were getting fat'. My father was wont to give his family a splendidly ribald version of this poem every Christmas. It ended with 'We don't want your Christmas Pudding/ Stick it up your arse'. This signified the point at which he was led by my mother to his bed to sleep off the alcohol.)

The goose is an extremely fatty bird and today is thus rarely eaten by most Britons. Yet it is this very fat that makes for the splendour of the cuisine of the Béarnais region of France, where the *confit* is the basic cooking fat and is used often as a preservative. And of course the fattened goose is the origin of the magnificent **pâté de foie gras**. The fowl also figures in one of my favourite lines of poetry – apart from the workhouse one – Auden's 'As I Walked Out One Evening'. I cannot resist giving you the entire verse in which the bird figures:

> I'll love you dear, I'll love you
> Till China and Africa meet
> And the river jumps over the mountain
> And the salmon sing in the street
> I'll love you till the ocean
> Is folded and hung up to dry
> And the seven stars go squawking
> Like geese against the sky.

And very oddly there is a fine recipe for roast goose with a purée of – what else? – gooseberries.

Gooseberry

This fruit of a small prickly bush was until recently widely cultivated in private gardens and was so popular in the UK that there were gooseberry clubs dedicated to it. Cooking gooseberries are sharp to the taste and need large amounts of sugar to counteract this, but the result is surely the best fruit pie ever, as well as the splendid gooseberry fool.

Why this marvellous fruit has become rarely used in recent cookery I cannot say, save that fewer people seem to cultivate their own fruit and vegetables than they did during the last world war and its aftermath, when digging for victory was still alive. The gooseberry is long overdue for a comeback. But the origins of the word 'gooseberry', being a third person unwanted when there are two people, usually of opposite genders, is lost in the mists of etymological time. (Since writing this I have discovered that the *Oxford English Dictionary* traced the use of the word to mean a chaperon, hence an unwanted third person, as far back as 1837, the year when Victoria ascended the throne. Seek and ye shall find.)

Goulash
See **Hungarian cookery**.

Grapefruit
This large spherical citrus fruit with its sharp flavour is most often served chilled, in halves, which are then sprinkled with sugar, and is traditionally served at breakfast. It is very refreshing indeed. Grapefruit is also commonly an ingredient of many fruit cocktails and also makes a pleasant juice. The fruit comes in both yellow and red varieties. Though I can discern little difference in taste, I prefer the red variety (which has been cultivated in many countries and developed from a North American variety called Texas Red) because of its dramatic appearance.

Grapes
Why grapes are the fruits that visitors bring to hospital patients and how the practice came about I do not know, but it is a grand idea at that. And who first discovered that grapes and cheeses such as **brie** and **camembert** make a grand combination was a near genius. There are also poultry and fish recipes that use grapes as a garnish known in French cuisine as *véronique*, of which the most famous is *sole véronique*.

These are dessert grapes, of course, but the greatest amount of grapes is cultivated for wine-making. The fruit contains many varieties, though in the trade they are classed as either white (green) or black (from red to black). Some grapes are dried and become raisins, currants or sultanas.

Grappa
An Italian coarse brandy distilled from grape skins; in the Veneto region sometimes plums are the base, and there is even a particularly vicious grappa which utilizes juniper berries. It is very similar to the French **marc**: both, like the

Irish *poteen*, are often illegally home-distilled. Very much an acquired taste, it can be extremely potent. The late Jack House, the Scottish journalist who in the 1950s enlivened many listeners to the popular wireless programme *The Brains Trust*, was wont to have several glasses of this following a meal. He was a noted diner, albeit a refreshingly unpretentious one – his favourite repast was **steak and kidney pie** – and he would imbibe wine, malt whisky, gin and tonic, and anything alcoholic, besides his *grappa*. It was, of course, a more robust age, when journos consumed vast amounts of liquor, but even then Jack House was prodigious in his endeavours. Furthermore his intake never seemed to affect him at all, and he never appeared any the worse the wear for his astounding consumption. He died in his eighties with his boots on, a lasting testament to the powers of grappa.

Gravlax
The Swedes marinate their raw salmon in salt, sugar, peppercorns and saltpetre (sometimes **dill** is added) and then refrigerate it. There are those who, for a reason I cannot fathom, prefer this to Scottish smoked **salmon**.

Greengage
This juicy sweet fruit was introduced to Britain from France by a family of importers called Gage in the eighteenth century. The family remained in the trade for over a hundred years. Greengages are still popular in France, though they are rarely seen in the UK today. So common are greengages in the Champagne district of the Marne that it is common to enjoy an afternoon glass of their famous sparkling wine with plates of the sliced fruit. And it also inspired the writer Rumer Godden to title her evocative and elegiac novel set in that region *The Greengage Summer*.

Grocery

Grocers were originally simple spice merchants – pepperers in England, *épiciers* in France. Both sometimes doubled as apothecaries, as many spices and herbs were used medicinally. To this day there are regulations in France dating from the Revolution that prohibit, albeit in theory, the sale of non-foodstuffs such as soap or candles by grocers (from the old French *grosser*).

The grocer as we know it, a provision merchant, emerged in the mid-eighteenth century and was among the upper classes often a term of abuse, suggesting a greedy and low-class person, a *nouveau riche*. As late as the 1970s the so-called British satirical magazine *Private Eye* was wont to describe the former Prime Minister Edward Heath as 'Grocer Heath'. Later the same magazine was cock-a-hoop when former grocer's daughter Margaret Thatcher became Prime Minister too. This is par for the course for the snobbish Right (and Left) in British politics.

Grouse

A medium-sized game bird native to moors in parts of northern England, Wales and, most famously, Scotland. It has a reddish-brown plumage with a distinctive red comb above the eyes, which is more prominent in the cock. Both sexes have feathered legs and feet, which are often made into kilt pins. Other members of the grouse family are the blackcock, **capercaillie** and ptarmigan. All grouse are wild birds and, unlike the pheasant, cannot be reared by hand.

According to the feeding available in its habitat, grouse differs greatly in flavour from place to place, but it is a strong-tasting fowl and requires hanging, preferably for at least three days. Thus the absurdity of that theatrical nonsense of flying the birds by helicopter straight from the slaughter on the grouse moors to smart London hotels on the same day. And another thing: though the Glorious Twelfth is part of the Society calendar, it is not the best time to buy a brace of grouse, owing to wretchedly ill-shot birds.

Guga

I met this once in Lewis in Scotland's Western Isles and have never entirely managed to get it out of my psychological nostrils. It is gannet, allowed to be rotted underground (see **hakarl**) and then fried in its own rank fat. Nothing can possibly explain the allure of this item for Hebrideans, and no writer can convey the odour and taste of this truly awful atrocity.

Guinea pig

Though this small South American rodent is indeed eaten and regarded as a great delicacy by many inhabitants of the interior, it is to its use in experimental laboratories that it owes its history in food. It was in 1907 that the animals were experimented on by a team of Swedish medical scientists headed by one Gustav Horn who were looking for an antidote to scurvy. Though limes and other citrus fruits had proved efficacious in the prevention of this disease (see **lime**), the fruits had to be very fresh as stale fruits lose their vitamin C content. Dr Horn injected the little creatures with scurvy and subjected some of them to dietary experiments. (Guinea pigs, like humans, cannot produce their own vitamin C.) It was found that green vegetables (see **cabbage**) and fresh milk, as well as citric fruits, were remarkably effective in combating scurvy. This is the first recorded use of guinea pigs in laboratory experiments, and the origin of the use of the word now to describe any animal that is subjected to experiments of which the outcome is at the time unknown.

Gumbo

This soup is a speciality of Louisiana and is made with chicken, prawns, peppers, rice, spices and herbs, thickened with the mucilaginous **okra** (sometimes known as ladies' fingers). Broderick Crawford once said of the late Huey Long, the assassinated Louisiana governer who inspired the film *All the King's Men* (1960), in which Crawford starred, that 'Gumbo explains Huey Long: it is a menacing meal'. The cuisine of New Orleans is a very peculiar amalgam of French and American and deserves to be better-known than it is.

Guvec

A dish known throughout the Balkans but especially popular in Turkey, where it is a staple casserole food in working-class restaurants, though it was once a royal dish. Eric Ambler mentions it in his classic thriller *The Mask of Dimitrios*. This moved me to order it in an Istanbul inn. It was, as my Turkish journalist friend had warned, a great mistake.

Haddock

A soft fish, less oily than its parent family member the cod, this is now a relatively expensive item. Interestingly, the dark brown spots just under its head are said to be the marks of St Peter's thumbs. The same is said of the fish known as John Dory.

Haggis

There are many myths surrounding this Scottish speciality immortalized by the poet Robert Burns in his 'Address to the Haggis'. Scots are fond of asserting to English chaps that it is a bird with three legs that is caught only on mountain tops. Actually the so-called 'chieftain of the pudding race' is a mixture of offal such as the chopped heart, liver and lungs, usually of sheep, and including oatmeal, suet and spices, which is then stuffed into a bag made from a sheep's stomach. Though it does indeed look horrid, it is a Scottish institution eaten not only at Burns suppers – the commemoration of perhaps one of the greatest of European poets – but is widely consumed in the country of this national bard. This peasant delicacy is most often accompanied by heavily creamed mashed potatoes and highly peppered neeps – also known as swedes or turnips (see **turnip**): root vegetables, mostly used elsewhere as cattle food. At Burns suppers, held on the poet's birthday on 25 January throughout the civilized world, or anywhere Scots have ever assembled, the haggis is celebrated along with the tatties and neeps and considerable amounts of good malt whiskies too (see **whisky**). This rather absurd Caledonian ritual usually involves a piper, and elderly drunk bourgeois men who would never dream of speaking in the Scottish demotic will then intone such verses as:

> Ye Pow'rs wha mak mankind your care,
> And dish them out their bill o' fare,
> Auld Scotland wants nae stinking ware,
> That jaups in luggies,
> But if ye wish her gratefu' prayer,
> Gie her a Haggis!.

Basically Burns was extolling the virtues of honest toil in the form of the simple fare of the working man, as against the French fancies of the Scottish aristocracy. Thus is Rabbie beloved by socialists the world over. There are, of course, the usual paradoxes here. Burns himself, though indeed a rustic, was highly educated for his time, and by no means averse to the company of the great and the good and the food they provided. And despite his tilts at the fashion of his day for French cuisine, the fact is that the word haggis is derived from the word *hachis* or *hacher*, meaning to chop up or mince meat. It is, of course, a French word.

Hakarl

This very odd speciality from Iceland is shark meat ripened by being buried underground for several weeks and then allowed to rot for some weeks. It smells dreadfully (see also **guga**).

Icelanders accompany this appalling delicacy with their own version of schnapps called *brennivin*, which is known as 'Black Death'.

Halal

To halal is to slaughter an animal according to Muslim law, similar indeed to **kosher** slaughtering, in that the animal is prayed over before slaughter and all the blood drained. There are those who deplore this method of slaughtering animals and claim that it is cruel. There is, however, little evidence that it is any more distressing than other methods, and it is said that a skilled halal butcher can dispatch a sheep, cow or chicken as quickly and efficiently as a Western slaughterman.

But in the West a new dispute has appeared, in that in the production of most so-called halal meat the animal is stunned by electric current before slaughter. In Britain the Halal Food Authority finds this acceptable because the Koran could hardly have foreseen such technologies and thus there can be no injunction against this process. Furthermore it is considerably more cost-effective.

Fundamentalist Muslims have discovered that over 80% of their lamb and chicken meat is stunned before slaughter and are appalled. One Muslim told me that she felt sick when she found out this fact and that no amount of common sense could persuade her that the Halal Food Authority was acting within the dietary laws. Similar nonsense often comes from members of the Hasidic Jewish community.

Some, myself included, claim that meat slaughtered in this way, stunned or not, is more tender. Certainly if you want good-quality lamb or mutton, go to an Asian butcher.

Halibut

The largest flatfish and regarded as a luxury item, as is a close relation, the **turbot**. It is usually sold in the form of steaks and is difficult to come by these days. The late Bernard Corrigan, a fish merchant of considerable repute throughout the restaurant trade in the UK, was wont to have a whole halibut at one sitting: he was a prodigious eater.

Halva

Made from sesame seeds, this is a sweetmeat popular in the Middle East. It is sold in the bazaars and is as common as chocolate is in the West.

Ham

As mentioned previously (see **bacon**), not all bacon is ham but ham is always bacon. Ham is the hind leg or thigh of bacon, though, and can be served cold. There is a paucity of dishes involving ham in most cookery books, which rather surprises: it can make a quite marvellous cold buffet. A really good ham can be served as a treat along with potato salad and other cold offerings.

Some hams are regarded as delicacies, and such world-famous hams as the Bradenham ham (which figured as an element in the solution of a murder in a Dorothy L. Sayers murder mystery) can be very expensive indeed. The German Westphalian ham is similarly expensive and highly regarded. The reason why ham is so rarely mentioned in cookery literature is probably that a good boiled ham needs no tarting up of any kind. And no sandwich can beat a ham one.

Hamburgers

These round patties of minced beef are said to have originated in Hamburg, in Germany, but in truth hamburgers in essence can be found throughout the world. In Italy, where they are known as *polpette*, they are regarded as a chic little luncheon dish. Indian cuisine sees them as *shami* kebabs and as a staple of street food. So too in the Balkans and in the Middle East.

But it is to the USA that we look for the explanation of the hamburger. Only **Coca-Cola** is more American than this homely, simple fare. Today it is known throughout the world as a 'burger', or sometimes 'beefburger', and the world chain McDonald's is synonymous with the hamburger, which is a great pity in that, while the corporate organization provides a reasonably nutritious rissole, a real hamburger is a very fine specimen of a cheap and easily made meal.

For once I give a recipe: finely mince a half-pound of good quality beef, with very little fat and no gristle; then add a chopped onion, coarsely ground black pepper, a good pinch of thyme (or parsley), a crushed clove of garlic and a slice of bread first soaked in a little milk, and bind with a beaten egg. Put the lot together and allow to rest. Make into small patties, and then lightly flour. Fry in good oil. Serve with salad and sauté potatoes (see **potato**). Why am I telling you this? Simple. When my nieces and nephews were very young, they all wanted to go to McDonald's and, though happy enough to take them skating or to bowling alleys or whatever burst of false consciousness they required, I balked at this hamburger chain and instead took them back to my house, where I made the genuine articles and served them with buns and tomato ketchup. To this day the younger generation of McLeans make their own hamburgers and haven't been inside a burger joint in years. There.

Hare

Often thought of as a big rabbit really, this animal has flesh that is gamey and comes up as an especially rich stew in **jugged hare**, in which pieces of the rodent are simmered with stock, onions, root vegetables, peppercorns, port and redcurrant jelly. The hare cannot be hunted out of season, unlike rabbits.

Hash browns

This North American speciality is made with raw grated pota-toes and resembles the Swiss **rosti**. I once had this essential ingredient of an American breakfast served up to me in a USAF base in Erlangen in Germany, along with a huge steak, gravy, two eggs sunny side up, green beans and a dollop of maple syrup. As I looked around me, I realized that everybody was about eight feet tall. The Yanks can eat a bit.

Haute cuisine

This has had a bad press for over half a century, even in the land of its birth, France. There were, of course, a great many excesses, and the snobbery of *La Belle Epoque* in food matters was bound to lead to a rejection of the high traditions of elab-orate cookery. In the UK the work of Elizabeth David meant that many domestic cooks embraced the new philosophy of bourgeois and country cooking. So too, of course, did a great many restaurant chefs, especially those who lacked the proper culinary expertise. Mrs David, who had great respect for the *haute* tradition, did not mean to do this, but there came about a ludicrous inversion whereby expensive restaurants offered fried bollocks instead of an exquisite pressed duck *au truffe* or a *lièvre à la royale*. Yet all the great chefs of the high period of cookery – Boulestin, Escoffier, Carême et al. – stressed sim-plicity in even the most complicated of dishes on their menus. Later French cooks created the *nouvelle cuisine*. Though the original practitioners of this so-called *cuisine minceur* were all traditionally trained chefs, their followers enjoyed enor-mous reputations on the basis of their amateurish ignorance. My guess is that *haute cuisine* will be back with a (costly) vengeance.

Hazelnuts

An important ingredient in many cakes and confections in northern and central Europe, they are also popular as a dessert nut. The term for them in the USA is 'filbert': thus the music hall comic character Gilbert the Filbert. Just why the word 'nut' should be a euphemism for an eccentric or even a lunatic is not clear, though it may have its origins in the use of the word 'nut' for 'head: thus 'off his head' is 'off his nut'. There is a famous quote from the Mafia mobster Lucky Luciano, when he was asked if Al Capone would be a threat after he was released from Alcatraz in 1939, a hopeless paretic owing to advanced syphilis. Luciano cheerfully replied: 'Al', he said, 'is as nutty as a fruit cake'.

Health food shops

These establishments are often seen as faddy sort of places for weird vegetarians such as George Bernard Shaw and the like. But for many years they were virtually the only venues in the UK where you could obtain fresh herbs and other oddities such as garlic, unpolished rice, real pasta and wholemeal flour. They are still little oases in the midst of the supermarket culture of today.

Hedgehog

I have never encountered this: apparently it is a greasy and dreadful animal when cooked. It is said that Romanies regard it as a delicacy, and certainly George Borrow records it in his novel *Lavengro*, a bestseller in the late nineteenth century. Gypsies were once thought to be horribly romantic, and artists such as Dame Laura Knight and Augustus John often depicted them as such, as did the late poet laureate Walter de la Mare. It is worth pointing out, however, that a genuine gypsy, the guitarist Django Reinhardt, was a noted gourmet and would not have thought of eating a hedgehog.

Herbs

Herbs are almost fundamental to European cookery. Italians could not imagine a life without **basil** or the French one without **thyme**, and Greeks missing out oregano or marjoram would not be Greeks at all.

But in my childhood virtually the only herb in common use in Britain was **parsley**, though there was the exotic sage and **onion** stuffing with the Christmas **turkey**. The astounding food writer and all-round expert Marguerite Patten once told me in an interview I did with her in the 1980s that when she tried to promote the use of herbs during the second World War (she was with the then Ministry of Food), housewives reported that their menfolk did not approve: they said the food tasted 'funny'.

Herring

Anyone who has had the good fortune to have encountered the Para Handy stories by Neil Munro will know that once the herring was the staple food fish of Scotland. 'The herrin' iss an aufy saagacious fush', opines Captain Para Handy, 'it steys awa' maist o' the year and cams up at the wrang time.' Today it is always the wrong time for the herring, for it is almost fished out.

Herring is – or was – popular in northern Europe: it appears as pickled herring in Scandinavia and also as rollmops, which are rolled herrings marinated in brine. Both techniques are used in the marinated herrings dear to Jewish cuisine.

Northern Britain likes herring rolled in oatmeal and fried. But it is as kippers – smoked herring – that the herring comes into its own. Today most kippers are not actually smoked but painted with a strong dye made out of coal tar and tasting of it too. Americans will not accept dyeing, nor will Scots. Surveys show that England prefers it, as does France and Ireland. This dyeing process started in the Second World War and deserves to, well, die with it.

High tea

A meal once popular in north England and Scotland, served in the early evening. Supper would be eaten late. Traditionally high tea would consist of a soup course, a cooked meal such as a mixed grill or perhaps **fish and chips**, bread and butter, and fancy cakes, washed down with tea. It was largely a middle-class repast, much beloved by ladies who had been to elocution classes. Think of cake stands, paper doilies, extended pinkie fingers and the 1950s, and you have high tea. Would that all of it would return.

Himmel und Erde

Yet another potato dish, a speciality of Alsace, formerly in Germany, and means – what else? – 'heaven and earth'. It is made with potato and apple purée and fried onions. It is often served with liver or ham. A supper dish, it is generally combined with a good dry white wine.

Hollandaise sauce

This classic French sauce is an amalgam of egg yolks, butter and lemon juice and is employed most often for fish dishes, occasionally for chicken and sometimes for some vegetables, especially asparagus. ('Plum' Wodehouse's splendid creation Bertie Wooster swears by Hollandaise for this delectable vegetable: I myself believe that melted butter is all that is required.)

Though some purists would argue the point, I agree with the gourmet and cook Prosper Montagne that wine or wine vinegar should be added to the basic sauce to sharpen it a little. (The sauce *mousseline* is Hollandaise with cream whipped into it.) To be honest, I find both a touch too bland and find most of the fish dishes for which the sauce is designed much improved by either simple *maître d'hotel* butter or occasionally by a robust **tartare sauce**. Hollandaise is also fiddly and a source of much frustration for many amateur cooks.

Homard

French for lobster. Thus you have the following fancy titles for lobster dishes: *homard à l'armoricaine* (a classic French dish of diced lobster meat and a mirepoix, flamed in brandy, simmered in white wine and stock, with the lobster coral, that is the roe, added, and finished with thickened butter) and *homard thermidor* (another classic French *haute cuisine* item, which has diced lobster meat in a **béchamel sauce** and French mustard). I once witnessed an exasperated restaurateur who, finally pissed off by the demands of an American customer that the lobster should be absolutely fresh, took the wretched crustacean out of the tank in which he kept his, still very much alive, lobsters and put it in front of the said Yank. The screams of the demented American woman as the *homard* crawled towards her were very satisfying indeed.

Hominy grits

This cereal, made from the husks of maize, has achieved legendary status as the classic breakfast dish for the good ol' boys of the Deep South. Elvis Presley was, of course, addicted to them. They have no nutritional value at all, but to poor Southerners – the poor white trash, that is – they provided a filling dish. It is a paradox that blacks of the same area have a much more exotic and nutritional cuisine than the whites who so despise them.

Honey

> I always eat peas with honey,
> I've done it all my life.
> They do taste kinda funny,
> But it keeps them on the knife.

So wrote the American versifier and staple of the *New Yorker* magazine Ogden Nash. But then, honey is a favourite food-stuff for poets, from Virgil to Shakespeare and for all recorded time. And Mr Nash was not the only humourist to invoke honey. The late comic artiste Chic Murray, confronted with one of those small individual pots of the stuff that one is invariably offered at hotel breakfasts, was once heard to remark to the waitress, 'I see you keep a bee'.

More in line with real poetry, the greatest of the gods, Zeus, was said to have been reared on honey as his sole diet. (Zeus seems to have been surrounded by foodstuffs: in Greek mythology he was said to have always slept on a bed of **saffron**.)

Honey is the sweet substance made naturally by bees and was for many centuries the major source of sweetening in European cookery. Sugar was extremely expensive until the expansion of sugar cane plantations in the Americas, especially the Caribbean, in the seventeenth century. (It is not true that sugar cane came from the Americas: it was imported to that continent by one intrepid fellow, Pedro d'Arranca, one of Christopher Columbus' voyagers. Cane sugar in fact originated in the Indus valley. See **sugar**.)

Honey varies in its consistency, being clear and runny in some cases, thick and viscous in others, and its taste varies also, according to the flowers and herbs from which the bees feed. It has considerable medicinal properties. But it is in poetry that honey most glistens. After all, was it not Rupert Brooke who asked if the church clock still stood at ten to three; and was there honey still for tea?

Hors d'œuvres

How this has become simply the first course of a meal I do not know, because it used to mean – and still does to me – a selection of savouries eaten at any point in the meal and, in northern France, the meal itself. Spain yet continues the prac-tice with its snacks in **tapas** bars.

Horsemeat

Why Anglo-Saxons will not eat this delectable meat is inex-plicable. Perhaps not. While oxen were commonly used as dray animals on the continent of Europe, it was the horse that pulled the ploughs of the Americas and the British Isles. The flesh of an old horse, after years of toil, would be almost inedible. It is true also that, while a cow is a rather soft, stupid creature, the horse, while just as brainless a ruminant as a cow, does look horribly noble. Be that as it may, horse-meat is not eaten in Britain. Yet in France, Spain, Belgium and Italy shops selling this meat abound (Verona has a spe-ciality horsemeat stew deriving from a siege when the inhab-itants of this once garrison town ate their horses). The shops usually have a gilded horse's head above them. A touch of *The Godfather*.

Horseradish

This root (*Armoracia rusticana*) has a hot and pungent flavour and is widely used in Scandinavian and Russian cookery. It is the basis for the British horseradish sauce, which is served, by discriminating people at least, with roast beef. It was once thought to have properties that could be useful as an aid for abortions. (Gin was equally erroneously said to have similar properties.)

Hot dogs

The American writer James Thurber has a fine story concern-ing his search for a really good hot dog sandwich; so too does his compatriot John O'Hara. See **frankfurters**.

Huckleberry

This is the fruit of a small bush and is rather similar to the blueberry or blaeberry. It is very sweet and juicy and is native to the New England region of the USA. Two American literary references here: Mark Twain's magnificent hero Huck Finn is named after this berry (Ernest Hemingway claimed that all modern American literature comes from this astounding novel, and one cannot help but agree), and a line from a song that featured in the film *Breakfast at Tiffany's*, a cleaned-up version of a deftly written novella of the same title by Truman Capote. The song, which won an Academy Award, was 'Moon River' and was written by Henry Mancini, but the lyrics were by the industrious Johnny Mercer. His line was: 'my huckleberry friend'. Later he explained that he didn't know what he meant by the phrase, but it sounded good.

Humbles

The internal organs of deer (originally called 'numbles', later shortened to 'umbles' and then made into a pun as 'humble') were often left for the servants of huntsmen and made into a pie; thus 'eating humble pie' (see **venison**). The Gaelic word for humbles is *gralloch* (it is also a verb, meaning 'to eviscerate'), which is a very nice word indeed.

Humbug

This conical peppermint boiled sweet bears no relationship to the word 'humbug' meaning a shallow or misleading statement or policy. But it was indeed a favoured sweet for especially severe Calvinist churchgoers.

Hummus

Spelt in many different ways (*houmous, houmus, humus*), this chickpea purée combined with the sesame seed paste known as tahini, is of Middle Eastern origin but is now much seen in

Greek and Turkish cookery and throughout the Balkans. It is eaten as a snack with pitta bread. With black olives and a glass of **retsina** it conjures up Greece in seconds, even on the rainiest and most dismal day that Britain can conjure up.

Hungarian cookery

It is very strange indeed that the cuisine of this country has attracted so little attention, apart from its famous goulash (spelled *gulyas* and pronounced *goolyash*). *Gulyas* is more a soup in fact, like a **pot au feu**, but there are a great many stews in Hungarian food and I suspect that what most people imagine as the famous dish of this country has been confused with the large variety of porkolts (see **porkolt**) and *tokanys*, rich stews and braised meats, using sour cream, **paprika** (Hungarian paprika is not to be confused with the Spanish variety, which is essentially a colouring agent – Hungarian or *hot* paprika can be very hot and may be compared to cayenne pepper) and a bewildering number of spices. Hungary is where oriental cuisine – Hungary has been part of the Ottoman Empire in its history – meets the traditions of French and Italian cooking.

Laced with German and Austrian *haute cuisine* and the peasant food of the *gulyas* (cowboys) of the Great Plains, the Hungarians' food is as strange as their language. (Magyar has no relationship with any other language except, oddly, Finnish. Both languages have their origins, though, in the Arabic tongues of north Africa.)

Hungarian cakes and desserts are as elaborate as Viennese patisseries. I have dwelt a little on this cuisine because I was brought up with it, as the grandson of a Hungarian. For a reason I cannot fathom, considering that a large number of refugees from the Hungarian Revolution of 1956 came to the UK as well as other parts of Europe, there are few Hungarian restaurants and the cuisine is largely unnoticed.

Hunger

Cervantes claimed that hunger was the best sauce, but of course it is not. When it merely means being rather peckish, it makes one eat that which one would never think of consuming at all: when it means starving, as so many peoples of the Third World are, it is a very sick aphorism indeed. That's enough morality for now.

Hush puppies

A dish from the southern states of the USA, these are onion and cornmeal dumplings often eaten as an accompaniment to fish. They are said to have originally been scraps of food thrown to puppy dogs to keep them quiet – hence the name. Today also the name of a dreadful type of suede shoe.

I

Ice cream

Ices are said to have originated in China but were known in Arab countries and in Persia and north India (the ice itself came from the snows of the Himalayas) long before their emergence in Italy, which country is likely to have exported the sweet to the rest of Europe. Originally simple fruit sorbets (from the Arab **sherbet**), ice cream was first imported to France probably in the wake of the marriage of the Italian Marie de Medici to the French King Henri IV in 1600. It was later that ice cream parlours came about, when in the 1670s a Francisco Procopio opened the first one in Paris. (Procope's, reputed to be the first actual **restaurant** in the country, is still a famous institution in the French capital.)

The large-scale introduction of ice cream to the UK took place even later and originated for some inexplicable reason in the west coast of Scotland when Luigi Crolla brought his *gelati*, his Italian ice cream, to that part of the world in the late 1880s.

When Elizabeth David launched an attack on British and American commercial ice creams, she was undeniably correct save that in Scotland, particularly in the west, genuine Italian ice cream was still being produced. The extent of the importance of ice cream in that region's diet can be seen in the police statistics. In 1903 there were 89 Italian cafés selling ice cream in the city of Glasgow. A year later there were 184 such outlets. By 1905 there were 336 in that most industrial of British cities. In my childhood of the late 1940s and '50s every area of the city had a large number of ornate ice cream parlours, each vying with the other.

Though such cafés are much reduced in number today, every Glaswegian of whatever age is well used to real ice cream, often topped with what they call 'red stuff' – in reality a sugary raspberry sauce which slightly ferments. There are no additives or artificial flavourings in either the ice cream or the raspberry sauce, which is, though few Scots realize it, the famous *sauce Melba* first created for the opera singer Dame Nellie Melba (who seems to have inspired so many dishes, such as Melba toast and *pêche Melba*).

The secret of Scottish real ice cream, as in the original Italian version brought to Scotland by the large number of immigrants from northern Italy – and indeed mostly from one small town, Barga, in Tuscany – lies in the fact that full cream milk is used – not cream – and vanilla pods and sugar. There are no palm oils, butters, eggs or any preservatives, and only about 30% of air is used to beat it, unlike the industrial disasters.

Ice cream soda

Though this is referred to in the USA simply as a **soda**, and is a necessity for American teenage innocents, it was surprisingly popular in my youth in Scotland. It comprises a soft aerated drink to which scoops of ice cream are added. It is surprisingly popular with myself as well. In recent years I have become somewhat childishly addicted to this simple and effective concoction, to the extent that I often consume this along with, and at the same time as, my morning *espresso* **coffee**. The result is both refreshing and exhilarating. Try the combination for yourself and you will see what I mean.

Ice cubes
The first ice cube-making machine on the commercial market was demonstrated at the Great Exhibition in London in 1851 by its inventor, Frenchman Ferdinand Carré (1824–1900), who went on to become a pioneer of refrigeration. The other pioneer was fellow French engineer Charles Tellier (1828–1913). Note **frozen food**. See also **whisky**.

Imam bayeldi
A Turkish version of **ratatouille**, but which also includes spices and raisins (though there are many variations throughout Turkey and the Balkans – an Anatolian version contains many fresh and dried fruits and is very highly spiced). It is widely eaten, spread on bread, as a snack in the coffee parlours of Istanbul.

Irish cookin'
Ireland contains a most peculiar cookery because it is perhaps the last country in Europe to have a sizeable and influential peasantry. Thus Irish cooking is both rich and poor, and this small country has produced the paradox of one of the most literate nations on earth along with traditionally one of the economically poorest. (This has changed much in the last twenty years, which have seen Ireland become a very rich country indeed.)

It is, then, not surprising that it has also produced one of the most entertaining cookery books ever, *The Cookin' Woman*, by Florence Irwin, first published in 1949 and still in print, though hard to come by. Miss Irwin started as an instructress in Domestic Science in Northern Ireland in 1905 and when she died in 1965 was as famous as Delia Smith is today. Her book is invaluable, not only for its recipes but also for her many anecdotes of Irish rural life between the wars.

Irish cookery is, rather like Cornish cuisine, a peasant cookery often dependent on pigmeat, fish and especially the **potato**. The Irish Famine occurred when the potato crop failed in 1845, and the next year entirely, and then again in 1848, and was the result of the potato blight which had been exported from America. The disease caused famine throughout Europe, but nowhere were its effects seen more than in Ireland because the Irish diet was utterly dependent on this tuber.

Within five years over a million Irish people had died of starvation, out of a population of a mere 5 million, and the world-famous chef of London's Reform Club, Alexis Soyer, was invited to this small country at the very edge of western Europe to create nourishing soups which could be given to the starving of Dublin. By 1849 M. Soyer was feeding nine thousand a day with his soups, the first of the soup kitchens. It was too late. But Irish cookery has revived itself in the last twenty years, and with the coming of a considerable economic miracle has emerged a splendid Irish cuisine beyond the dreams of Miss Irwin.

Italian food

The Italians claim, with some justification, that French cookery derives from the cuisine of Italy and has since been perverted by their Gallic neighbours. It is not as simple as that, however, and, just as the German-speaking Italians of the Alto Adige region have German dumplings and heavy meat recipes, so too the region around Piedmont has much in common with French cookery. Italy was, of course, united by the Garibaldi-led *Risorgimento*, but it is still in reality several countries and the cookery of the different regions are, well, different. Yet Italian food has travelled the world, and two dishes in particular have straddled it: **pizza** and **pasta**.

Italian restaurants outside Italy are often unpleasantly showy and rarely authentic. But there are splendid exceptions, and this I discovered in a good many countries as a young student. I also discovered that some of the best and most genuine Italian *ristoranti* were the least expensive. But one of the few countries that seems unable to manage Italian food is France.

J

Jam

A fruit preserve usually made by boiling the fruits in water, and with a high sugar content. The best-known fruits for jam-making are soft ones such as strawberries (see **strawberry**) and raspberries (see **raspberry**). After the Second World War there was a scarcity of these, and **rhubarb** and **pineapple** jams became common, though not much loved. There has been a decline in jam manufacture in the last half century, not least in domestic jam-making. There was a time when every European household made its own jams, and much pride was taken by housewives in their jams and preserves. Hardly a single Women's Institute was complete without jars of jam in receptacles covered with paper jampot covers. Once thought of as the height of luxury, jam has given rise to one famous aphorism: 'Jam yesterday and jam tomorrow, never jam today'. Why a lucky person is called a 'jammy bastard' is lost in the mists of vernacular time.

Jambalaya

This Creole dish from Louisiana is strikingly similar to the Spanish **paella** and consists of prawns or chicken, or often both, in a mixture of fried onions, capsicums, tomatoes, garlic and long-grain rice. It is sharpened by copious amounts of **Tabasco** sauce. Celebrated in a song by the country singer and yodeller Hank Williams, jambalaya is to be found at every Country and Western festival, as my friend the implausible C&W singer and musician Kinky Friedman (he and his band The Texas Jewboys have had hits including 'There's Been No Good Jews Since Jesus' and 'Get Your Biscuits in the Oven and Your Buns in Bed') found when at a concert in Nashville. A fortnight later it was served at a weekend gig he was doing with my Glasgow-based band at the Munich Bierfest.

Jansson's temptation
A nineteenth-century religious fanatic called Erik Jansson, a Swede who had forsworn meat and other earthly pleasures, is said to have been so taken by this Scandinavian dish of onions, grated potatoes, anchovies, butter and cream that he fell from grace and gorged upon this casserole. The title seems fanciful, and so I thought until I encountered it at a dinner held by the Institute of Scandinavian Studies at London University. Some years later I discovered that it is a popular midweek luncheon dish throughout Scandinavia and is known by this very name.

Java
This coffee, from the *arabica* bean, was once a generic name for coffee in the USA. Both Raymond Chandler's protagonists and those of his hard-boiled writer colleague Dashiel Hammett were forever ordering cups of Java.

Jelly
The basis of this fruit-based pudding, much loved by children and often used for desserts such as **trifle**, is gelatine. Jelly cubes make a refreshing dessert and, though much used in

British cookery, it is in the USA that jelly has taken on mythic status. It was a piece of a Jello packet (a brand name) that ensured the conviction and subsequent execution of the Rosenberg husband-and-wife spy team, who had revealed the secrets of the atomic bomb to the Soviet Union in the aftermath of the Second World War. Jelly is also what the Americans call **jam**. And a jelly roll is what is elsewhere known as a Swiss Roll. The famous jazz pioneer and piano-player (who claimed to be the inventor of the genre) Jelly Roll Morton was said to be named after his fondness for the sweet. (This is untrue: 'Jelly roll' was an African-American euphemism for the penis.) And talking of sweets, two perennial favourites are jelly beans, shaped like kidney beans, and jelly babies, shaped as infants. All children devour these latter and always start by biting off the head.

Jerky
Strips of dried beef once popular in the wilds of the USA and derived from the native American *pemmican*. It became a staple of American troops in the field. Also known as 'jerked beef'.

Jujube
The fruit of evergreen and deciduous trees originally from China and the Middle East and used for the production of fruit pastilles and for throat pastilles and medicines. It was once widely used as a term for soft sweets, but later became prison slang for a slow-witted chap (derived from prison argot for an effeminate homosexual inmate).

Jugged hare
This traditional, though now rarely seen, British speciality consists of a rich stew of hare sections cooked with herbs, onions, peppercorns and **port**, red wine and redcurrant or

cranberry jelly. Last but not least, the blood of the hare is added towards the end of cooking.

Originally the dish was cooked in a large earthenware jug, though today an ordinary casserole is employed. I used to have this regularly in the magnificent Glasgow Art Club, but it is rarely found on the club's menu these days as younger members find it too heavy for them, poor souls.

Hare is quite popular in France, where a similar dish to jugged hare can be found in the famous *civet de lièvre de Diane de Chateaumorand*, named after the rich and beautiful Diane, Marquise de Valromey, a keen hunter. The dish was served to Britain's own Diane, the late Diana, Princess of Wales, at a dinner in her honour given by President Giscard d'Estaing.

Juice

A term for the natural liquids found in meat, game, poultry and fish, this also refers to those found in fruit and vegetables, and it is in the latter context that it is more often used. The most common forms are tomato juice and that of oranges and grapefruit. Oddly in recent years it has come to mean fizzy drinks, given unwisely, except as an occasional treat, to children. Another odd use of the term: my nephews and nieces were told that what I drank was 'Uncle Jack's Juice'. It was whisky.

Junk food

Not always the same as **fast food**, this refers to food and drinks heavily laden with calories and containing a great deal of fat, sugar and salt. Children and stupid people become addicted if permitted to do so.

Junket

A speciality dessert of the West Country of England, and also popular in the New England region of the USA, this is a milk pudding thickened with rennet. My Cornish grandmother made this soothing pudding for her grandchildren, flavoured wickedly with brandy, coloured a delicate pink with black-currant juice and sprinkled with grated **nutmeg**. See **beestings**.

Jus

Though sometimes used as a term for fruit or tomato juice, this usually refers to the pan juices left after roasting meat. Now used by idiot celebrity chefs to refer to any sauce.

K

K rations

Emergency pre-packaged foods, first created for the US troops in the Second World War. Much of it was dried and could be reconstituted by the addition of water. It gave rise to considerable technological advances in preserving foods – and a serious decline in the amount of fresh foods consumed these days. But K rations were emergency foods and included toilet paper and fags. The more complete 'C rations' were more common. The British had their Compo rations, which were also issued to civilians and lasted well into the 1950s. Don't let anybody fill you up with balderdash about how we fed ourselves well in the Austerity years. Anybody who can remember Compo rations will tell a different story.

Kaeng mussamen
See **gaeng mussamen**.

Kail
See **Kale**.

Kalakukko

An extraordinary dish from the Karelia region of Finland, this is made from a hollowed-out loaf of bread which is filled with **whitebait** and pork sausagemeat and then baked in an oven. The composer Sibelius, who hailed from this region and who wrote the famous Karelia Suite, introduced this speciality to many of the world's grand hotels as he insisted on it on every first night of his works.

Kale

A member of the cabbage family and strongly flavoured, this is more often used as cattle fodder, though it has found itself on menus in the more radical restaurants in recent years. An especially fashionable variety is known as *cavolo nero*, an Italian cabbage so dark green in colour that it is almost black. Kale was once so commonly grown in Scotland that it became attached to an especially sentimental literary genre set in rurality in Scottish literature, and there grew up a school known as 'the kaleyard novel'.

Kangaroo

The indigenous Australian peoples rarely ate meat and were largely vegetarian, though they did eat insects and grubs, which provided high levels of protein. However, the tails of kangaroos were considered a delicacy and you will find kangaroo tail soup on some Australian menus – it is similar to oxtail. It is said that the word 'kangaroo' came into being when a white settler saw this odd beast and asked an aborigine what it was called. The native replied 'kangaroo' and thus the animal was named. Apparently the word itself meant, rather succinctly, 'fucked if I know'.

Kartoffelpuffer

Potato pancakes, popular in Germany (*kartoffel* is the German word for 'potato'). They are often eaten with apple sauce. German cuisine is often very odd and has never been exported widely, though you can find influences in French cuisine, in the Alsace-Lorraine region, and in Italy, in that strange area shadowed by the mountains of the Dolomites called Alto Adige, where the Italian people are German-speaking. Incidentally, Austrian cuisine is hardly affected by German cooking because of Austria's affinity for many years with the Austro-Hungarian Empire. It is somewhat bizarre therefore that the most pro-Germanic xenophobe of all time, Adolf Hitler, was in fact an Austrian. Hitler is said to have actually disliked food (he was a vegetarian). And here is a very bizarre notion indeed: throughout the whole of the Second World War, his half-sister Elisabeth Schickelgruber is said to have lived in Liverpool in England, where she had been a refugee for many years.

Kedgeree

Though few Britons have ever eaten this, it remains in legend as an archetypal part of the traditional English breakfast and P.G. Wodehouse almost always includes it on the breakfast tables of his country house characters. Originally an invention of the Brits during the two centuries of the Raj in India, kedgeree consists of flaked smoked haddock, hard boiled eggs, rice, bacon and cream. Often spices, especially **curry** spices, are added.

Something else adds to the spice of this dish. Despite being an entirely British invention, it is now a feature of every *de luxe* hotel breakfast menu in India. Indeed the famed Bhukhara Mausry Sheraton in New Delhi proudly boasts that its kedgeree is made with Finnan Haddie which, apart from the fact that India has its own splendid smoked fishes, would be very unlikely: a Finnan haddie, or haddock, is a Scottish speciality originally hailing from a small fishing village on the Kincardineshire coast. But then India has absorbed so many cuisines over the centuries that it is hardly surprising that the British Raj made its contribution too.

Keftedes

Greek **meatballs**. Who knows by what linguistic process the same are known in North Africa as *kefteji*.

Ketchup

Though this now almost universally refers specifically to tomato ketchup, the word itself is clearly derived from the Indonesian *ketjap*, meaning a *sambal* or dip-in sauce using soy, and is taken to refer to any commercially bottled sauce – usually strongly flavoured such as the British brown sauces, the most famous of which is HP sauce. Actually in Victorian times ketchup was made from oysters, eels, anchovies and mushrooms and was used as an essence in stews and ragouts. It was much prized and had a shelf life of over twenty years.

But to the modern brown sauces, and HP in particular. The name was an acronym for 'Houses of Parliament' and since it was first marketed in 1896 by a grocer called John Garton, it has always displayed a picture of the mother of parliaments on its label. The only relationship with the Palace of Westminster is that when he was Prime Minister, the wife of Harold Wilson revealed that this most intellectual of politicians smothered every dish in it.

Until fairly recently one of the side labels was in French, and it is probably the only *français* that British people know. Certainly it is a party trick of mine when I soujourn in France to recite the old lines starting with 'Cette sauce de haute qualité est un mélange . . .' in an impenetrable Glaswegian accent. It gets a smile from even the most phlegmatic of

Gauls, especially when I go on to the bit about it being free from 'aucun préservatif' – *préservatif* meaning not, as the HP people thought, 'preservative' but in fact a condom. The sauce is made from **dates**, **tamarind**, **vinegar**, **garlic** and **onion**, **spices**, **sugar** and cornflour.

For some reason best known to themselves, the good folk of Edinburgh in Scotland anoint their fish suppers with brown sauce rather than the vinegar preferred by almost everybody else in the world.

But what about tomato ketchup? One thing is certain: no **hamburgers** or **hot dogs** are complete without its application.

Kid

Throughout Greece, Turkey, the Balkans and much of the Arab world kid is a very prominent meat indeed. It is the national meat of Corsica, and the Corsican dish of kid cooked in a **pebronata** sauce is known as *à la Buonaparte*.

Just why western Europe largely eschews kid meat is difficult to fathom, for goats require little herding and can sustain themselves in the most barren of terrains. A German agriculturalist once told me that he could not understand why the Scottish Highlanders didn't populate the sparse heather and bracken tundra with goats: kid meat, he explained, is highly prized throughout Europe.

I once experienced a splendid dinner of whole roast kid (*capretto*) in the expensive and renowned Roman restaurant of the Hotel Lord Byron, the Relais le Jardin, and it was magnificent, served with artichoke hearts and roast potatoes. I had almost the same dish in a taverna in Athens at a tenth of the price.

Kidneys

Kidneys are a rich source of iron and riboflavin, and regular consumption aids health. The vitamin Bs that kidneys, and

liver especially, possess are useful in counteracting the effects of heavy smoking and alcohol abuse. Now there's a nice thing to know. See also **offal** and **steak and kidney pie**.

Kitchen

This is, of course, a place for the cooking and preparation of food, but it is also a metonym for food (though by now surely horribly dated) as in 'the family kept a good kitchen', much as a similar metonym has it 'he kept a good table' or 'he had one of the best cellars in England'. And before you go looking up the *Oxford English* I can tell you that a metonym is a figure of speech, a trope that describes one thing for another, such as 'he took to the bottle' for the hapless fellow drinking himself to an early death. Not for the first time have I strayed into the world of grammatical arcana. The American writer James Thurber has a very good piece about this figure of speech in his 'Here Lies Miss Groby'. There is something about short-piece writers that attracts them to grammar and syntax, the more obscure the better.

Kit-kat

Though this is a brand name for a popular chocolate biscuit, the name has its origin in the title of a Whig literary club in London that existed from 1688 to 1820. It was named after its host, pie shop owner Christopher (Kit) Catling (Cat). Small portraits are sometimes described as 'Kit-cats' after the 36 by 28 inch paintings by Sir Godfrey Kneller made to fit into the low ceilings of the club. One can only express admiration for the advertising chap who came up with this splendidly recondite name for a chocky biscuit.

Knaildlich

These dumplings made from **matzo** meal are part of a traditional Jewish Passover soup. They are dreadful.

Knickerbocker Glory

In Scottish Italian cafés this is an elaborate ice cream sundae packed with fruit and jelly, whipped cream and a glacé cherry. As a child I lusted after this but could never afford the then considerable price. By the time I could, I had sadly lost my desire for it.

Kosher

Food prepared according to the dietary laws of Judaism. Foods that are permissible according to such laws are said to be *kashruth*. Probably fewer Jews today, in the West at any rate, totally observe the very strict rules, which require separate kitchens, freezers, knives, crockery etc. for meat and dairy produce. (In Yiddish non-kosher food is called *traif*. I recently discovered that this is a common word today for any shady dealing among young people, even goys, who will surely not know of the etymological history.)

Most non-Jews see kosher laws as bewildering, but they can find some insight into their origins in the Old Testament, in Leviticus 11:1–47, and reaffirmed in Deuteronomy 14:3–21. There they will find that such animals as rats, rabbits, hares, pigs and camels are unclean and cannot be eaten. (I should have thought the prohibition of camels causes little angst among Western Jews. Yet there is now a considerable trade in camel meat in Australia, especially among aboriginal small farmers. The fat of the humps is considered a special delicacy.) But there is an extensive list of animals that are unclean, some of which nobody in his right mind would think of eating anyway.

There is, however, some method in this. By and large animals that are carnivorous are denied for human consumption, a taboo seen in almost every culture. Carrion-eating creatures also are prohibited, which makes hygienic sense. Very scary sea creatures such as squids and eels are also not permitted. The basic rule is that amphibious creatures that have fins and scales may be eaten but that those without either shall be an abomination, which means that such delights as prawns, for instance, are forbidden. There are other prohibitions that, in the context of a very hot and arid climate, are perfectly rational.

Many of these dietary laws have become merely part of ritual, as, for instance, the necessity of a rabbi being present at the slaughtering of animals. (At one time butchers were also rabbis. They were called *cohens*. Now you know that Jewish people called Cohen are the descendants of these religious artisans of the meat trade. One such was William Turner Palgrave of the poetry anthology *The Golden Treasury*, whose name originally was Cohen. His father was a prosperous meat trader.)

The truth, however, is that in the absence of a religious conviction most of the Jewish dietary laws are a complete nonsense, but these laws have created much grief and heartache among Jews all the same. It is possible that they have prevented Jews from having anything other than a truly awful cookery: on the other hand, the international historian Professor Norman Stone, who claims that the two greatest peoples on earth are the Jews and the Scots, maintains that an excessive love of food is a major source of decline. Says Professor Stone: 'That is why Scots and Jews are so successful in what they attempt.' This may be true, but don't let Jews, or Scots either, try cookery.

Kreplach

A kind of Jewish **ravioli**, usually cooked in a consommé. Back in the early 1960s I used to order this in a Jewish restaurant in Belsize Park in London, where I played in a wee R&B band whose lead singer was a chap called Paul Jones. He introduced me to a South African fellow called Manfred Mann – you have to know the 1960s to know who he was. Nearly forty years later I was taken to the famous kosher restaurant Bloom's in the Old Kent Road, where I met Paul Jones again. He was eating *kreplach*.

Florence Greenberg in her *Jewish Cookery*, a seminal book, claimed the Jews invented pasta – a very unlikely claim at that, but it is true that Jewish cookery has a large number of recipes in which food in parcels figures. But I have encountered something very similar to *kreplach* in Turkey, where it is called *manti*.

Krumpli

A famous Hungarian potato dish, often served as a filler, especially for children, on a Monday; there are variations throughout Europe, and indeed the Scottish **stovies** is a very close cousin. It is made with hot Hungarian **paprika** and onions and garlic, cooked in bacon fat. Egon Ronay, a dapper little Hungarian fellow who came to Britain as a refugee in 1946 and who subsequently produced his splendid food guides (see **food critics**), often ordered this simple peasant dish in restaurants (where he usually had to explain how it was made), and said that it didn't remind him of his native Hungary: it reminded him, he said, of childhood.

Kulfi

Indian ice cream, often flavoured with rose water. Indians, like most Asians, do not include desserts in their courses and usually end a meal with fruit. The exception is ice cream.

L

Ladle

This long-handled spoon has been depicted in cave paintings and has been known to be in use since 1200 BC: you may note that it seems to have been the same shape over all these centuries. The most famous ladle in literature has got to be that wielded by the workhouse cook in *Oliver Twist*, when that somewhat irritating urchin asked for more (see **afters**).

Actually the widespread use of cutlery, apart from the ubiquitous knife and the later spoon, is of fairly recent date – forks were introduced to the rest of Europe by Catherine de Medici and even in the early nineteenth century were rarely used by the British peasantry, who saw them as being horribly effete.

Lamb

There was a time when the meat of sheep was invariably mutton, simply because sheep were principally kept for their wool and slaughtered after a long life. In those early days it must have been unbelievably tough, and there are still recipes throughout the world for long marinades to render old sheep edible.

But lamb, a sheep usually less than a year old, is the preferred meat, being less tough, less strong in flavour and less fatty. In some parts of the world, such as Hungary, it is not as well regarded as **beef** (like the most commonly used meat in that country, **pork**), though Hungary does possess some splendid lamb dishes. It is probable that the Austro-Hungarian aristocracy despised so well-used a meat throughout Transylvania and that the slur remains.

Here the delectable Italian version of suckling pig must be mentioned. *Abbacchio al forno* is a whole baby lamb or its equivalent, *capretto* (baby kid), roasted on a spit. I shared this infant lamb with my companion the late Cardinal Winning, then a mere bishop, in a famous Roman restaurant, Serafino's in the Via Veneto, and not for the first time was taken aback by the sophisticated worldliness of humble priests. (Tom Winning was indeed a man of great Christian kindness, but you could never have called him humble.) The baby lamb was so good that one wonders why it is seen so rarely, if at all, in Italian restaurants in Britain.

But while the Magyars may despise the flesh of sheep, with meat-eaters throughout the Indian subcontinent it is the favoured animal as it upsets neither Muslims, who cannot eat pig meat, nor Hindus, who are not permitted the flesh of cattle.

Lampreys

These exceedingly odd little eel-looking fish, like fellow members of the cyclostome family, have an open mouth with which they fix themselves on to rocks under water, thereby making them easy to gather. The name derives from the Latin *lambere*, 'to lick', and *petra*, 'rock'. The river variety is called a lamproon.

Lampreys were once popular among Plantagenet royalty and were consumed in large quantities – so much so that Henry I allegedly died of 'a surfeit of lampreys'. In turn this phrase became the title of a best-selling detective novel by one of the three celebrated 'Queens of Crime', Dame Ngaio Marsh. Agatha Christie also received her 'damehood'. For some reason the other member of the triumvirate, Marjorie Allingham, did not. (The reason may well be that she was married to Philip Youngman Carter, who was, like many employees of Lord Beaverbrook, left-wing in his politics, despite being for many years the Features Editor of the *Daily Express*.)

Lancashire hotpot

This casserole from the north of England was once more popular than it is now, probably because it got a bad name during and immediately after the Second World War, when inferior meat was used, and sparingly at that. Made with layers of sliced potatoes, rather as in an Irish stew, interspersed with layers of sliced potatoes and lambs' kidneys, a more expensive variation also includes oysters. It is sometimes on the menus of fashionable restaurants today and would astonish those who first encountered it in the school canteens of the 1950s.

There are regional variations in the UK, of which the best known is the Welsh hotpot which, not surprisingly, contains leeks (see **leek**). But this combination of potatoes, and other vegetables, with lamb occurs throughout the world.

Lasagne

These wide strips of **pasta** come of course in many versions, as all Italian pastas do, though the *lasagne verdi* from the Emilia-Romagna region of Italy – flavoured and coloured with **spinach** – are especially popular (though they are also common in the French Alps, where they are regarded as the dish for the harvest celebration).

The dish *lasagne al forno* consists of layers of this pasta with thin layers of **bolognese sauce** followed by a sheet of the pasta and then a layer of *besciamella* – **béchamel sauce** (in Italy always flavoured with grated nutmeg) – and so on until the cake tin in which it is baked is filled. It is topped with the creamy *besciamella* and grated parmesan. It is a rich and filling dish, to which I was introduced by my late sister-in-law Lin McLean, who had herself been taught how to make this deceptively simple meal by an Italian fellow student at St Andrews University in Scotland. Many years later it was the first repast that Prince William ate at his induction to the same ancient Scottish institution. By then, of course, it had become a commonplace and has turned into a gross sort of savoury pudding. My own and authentic version of this excites great admiration from all but Italians, who take it for granted and quite rightly so.

Lassi

This is a drink, common throughout Asia from India to Russia, made from thinned **yoghurt**, iced and flavoured. It can also be made with soured cream, which to my mind is an improvement, or even soured milk. (In **Hungarian cookery** the latter, which is called *aludt tef*, quite literally 'slept milk', is often taken as a reviver on hot days.) Lassi (pronounced *lussee*) can be either sugared or salted. It is very refreshing and is often an accompaniment to food. (Tea is never an *accompaniment* to food, save in Britain.)

Laver

The claim to fame of this sea vegetable, a type of seaweed, is that it has given its name to the home of The Beatles, the British sea port of Liverpool, named after the famous liver birds which once fed off this in the coastal waters of the area. Dried and riced, it becomes laver bread, a traditional Welsh delicacy. It is yet another member of the red algae family, like **dulse** and carrageen.

Lecso

This condiment, if it can be so described, is common in **Hungarian cookery**, in which it is often eaten as a dip, rather like the Italian **bagna cauda**. It is made with sweet peppers, onions, hot paprika and tomatoes, and is turned into a preserve during the summer, to be used in the long, cold winter months. There is also a dish by the same name that consists of the above but which includes rice and smoked sausages. Try it with **hot dogs**, instead of the usual **ketchup**.

Leek

Talking of Wales, we come to one of the few vegetables that has become a national symbol (like the shamrock in Ireland, the rose in Ireland and the thistle in Scotland.) Yet, just as the original emblem of Scotland was the little flower the bluebell, more properly the Scottish harebell, the Flower of the Forest, banned by the English after Culloden, the original emblem of Wales was the lovely daffodil, David's daughter, after the patron saint of Wales.

Enough of this. The leek is a pungent, though subtle, member of the onion family and when cooked has a slightly sweet flavour. It makes wonderful soups, such as the famous potato one known as *potage bonne femme*, the basis of the restaurant soup vichyssoise. And also the Scottish speciality cock-a-leekie, a chicken broth that, like hindle wakes (see **chicken**), is unique in combining this fowl with **prunes**. Considering that this vegetable is easily grown in mild climates such as that of the UK, this is a much underused vegetable. But the French like it: there is a splendid dish made with leeks cooked in red wine. It is called *poireaux au vin rouge*. (Though the French writer, Nobel prizewinner for literature and noted gourmet Anatole France once averred that 'the leek is the asparagus of the poor'.)

Years back, when faced with the demands of nieces and godchildren who were going through the then fashionable fad of **vegetarianism**, I used to make this dish. I called it 'Hercule Poireaux casserole', a harmless, if feeble, pun on Agatha Christie's character Hercule Poirot. When the children got older, they exercised the little grey cells so celebrated by Ms Christie's little Belgian detective and abandoned vegetarianism, thank God.

Leftovers

Some 30% of food in Britain is thrown away, much by farmers for sensible commercial reasons and a lot by households with no sense at all. A great many people throw uneaten food away simply because they can afford to do so, and anyway can't cook and do not know how to make use of what they could not consume from the previous meal. This was not always the case. In fact in the last war virtually every scrap of leftover food made up a subsequent meal. Monday meals were often made with leftovers from the Sunday beanfeast.

Two favourites of mine are the Scottish **stovies**, a **potato** dish involving meat gravy and leftover meat, and a quite wonderful rice ball made from leftover **risotto**, called *supplì al telefono*, which has balls of cooked rice with a centre of cheese and ham; these are then coated in breadcrumbs and deep-fried. If you are making a risotto, prepare more than you need and enjoy this lovely item for a smart luncheon the following day.

Legume

Generally taken to mean vegetables from pods, or even the pod itself, this term also includes climbing plants, one of which, the laburnum, is horribly poisonous.

Lemon

This remarkable fruit of the *Citrus limon* tree is perhaps the most widely used, and certainly the most versatile, fruit in cookery. It is a necessary addition to many savoury dishes, can be used as a marinade and a garnish, and is a necessary ingredient of soups such as the Greek **avgolemono**. It enhances many famous Provençal dishes, especially their daubes (see **daube**), shellfish cannot do without it, and countless desserts command its presence. No kitchen can be called one without lemon juice and the various sweet preserves, such as lemon curd, and the lovely lemon-based *confiture* produced by Robertson's – of **marmalade** fame – known as Silver Shred makes one of the most refreshing spreads on toast of a breakfast morning.

There is almost nothing that this fruit cannot accomplish in cookery. It is even an ingredient of perfumes and toiletries. The Romans called it a queen and used it in their bathwater. The scent itself is so pervasive that the name has been given to herbs such as lemongrass, used widely in South-East Asian cuisine as well as in the Indian subcontinent. Then there is lemon sole, a fish so called because when fresh it gives off a scent of the fruit. Drinks include lemon barley water and lemon squash and, of course, **lemonade**.

Lemonade

There was a time when this was the generic term for any fizzy drink. In England this is generally called 'pop', and in the west of Scotland it is known as 'ginger' (after 'ginger pop'), while in the east of Scotland it is known by the unlovely name of 'skoosh'. Most commercial lemonades are horribly sweet, but a good commercial lemonade is very refreshing indeed and French commercial lemonade is a revelation, being tart and using less sugar. (The lemonades provided for the UK licensed trade also contain less sugar and, though very much cheaper than what you will find in shops and supermarkets, are much superior.)

Lentil

There was a time, back in the days of hippiedom, when lentils made up the diet of, well, hippies. Thus the fleshy and lusty John Lennon changed into a thin and cadaverous freak. Lentils also featured as part of the then stylish macrobiotic diet. Such dietary fads are hardly new and were a feature of many of the intelligentsia of the late 1890s, yielding a crop of raving idjits who took their psychological dyspepsia to public life.

But in my childhood lentils were a staple of many of the nourishing soups of Scotland, and indeed a very good **ham** soup was made using the red lentils that were then found in every Scottish household.

The lentil is usually thought to be a pulse, though it is in fact a **legume** and is very high in protein. It is used in many Mediterranean dishes and also in Asia. The Parsee speciality **dhansak** is based on lentils.

Lettuce

A thoroughly tiresome vegetable which looks like a washed-out cabbage, this figures mostly in **salads** and is often used as a sort of garnish on side plates. Yet few know that when cooked, puréed and made into a soup, it becomes a very dark green and has a very strong taste indeed. Oddly it possesses a more robust flavour when cooked thus than **cabbage**.

Lime

Another citrus fruit, less well known, or at least used, than the **lemon**, this can be made into a juice (Rose's Lime Juice is world-famous) turned into a preserve (Rose's also manufacture a fine lime **marmalade**) and used in many fish recipes.

When the British Royal Navy introduced limes to their ships' galleys to counter scurvy – and the introduction was very effective – the result was that Americans and Australians came up with what they thought, and still think, is a pejorative term for Britons: 'limeys'. Be that as it may, within a few years every national fleet in the world had a large consignment of limes on board (see **guinea pig**).

Limeade, a fizzy drink, is superb when teamed with ice cream, as in an **ice cream soda**. It also makes the Indian lime pickle, which can be mild to wonderfully hot. The last seems to daunt a great many people for it is a little idiosyncratic in its flavour, but once you have acquired a relish for this relish you will never do without it as an accompaniment to **curry**.

Liqueurs

Fruity or aromatic spirits which are usually sweet and can be used in cookery but are generally partaken as an after-dinner *digestif*. Popular liqueurs are anisettes such as Pernod, or the Italian **amaretto** and **strega**. The French are fond of a vermouth-based brand called Dubonnet. Yet none is as popular as a very recent liqueur, dating back perhaps sixteen years or so, which is now the world leader – Baileys Irish Cream, a whiskey-based cream liqueur.

Liquorice

This plant of the pea family is indigenous to Europe, and its name is said to have derived from the Greek *glukus*, meaning 'sweet', and *rizha*, 'root'. It is used mainly in confectionery, the famous Liquorice Allsorts being an example. Another well-known sweetmeat made with this ingredient is the Pontefract cake, a small round and flat comestible from the small town of that name which is now part of the larger Yorkshire town of Wakefield.

Many English people erroneously refer to liquorice as 'lick-erish'. Erroneously because among some other identifications the word means 'lecherous', which hardly pertains to this piece of childhood innocence. Richmal Crompton's school-boy hero William Brown was a devotee of this sweetmeat, especially when made up into a disgusting concoction called 'lickrish water'. Come to think of it, I was once a devotee too.

Literature

Though a great many writers were and are enthusiastic and often very knowledgeable gourmets (as are often many others in the world of the arts, much in contrast to those in the sciences), few writers have included food in their work, save for those who have actually written on food itself. The latter include Norman Douglas, Arnold Bennett and a great many French novelists, such as Dumas *père* and *fils*.

But when it comes to descriptions of food in novels, drama etc., there is little on the subject, which does seem rather surprising, though there is a little more in poetry. (It should be noted, however, that there are a very great many popular songs written about food – where would the great rock'n'rollers be without their endless refrains on sodas and hotdogs?) O. Henry wrote several short stories in which his descriptions have you salivating. Indeed his story *Hostages to Momus* is predicated on the basis of feasting in a community deprived of interesting pabulum. Washington Irving waxes well on grub in his *A Christmas Day in New England*, which, even if read on a blistering hot summer's day, makes you desperate for turkey and clam chowder, roasts and sweetcorn fritters, jellies and trifle.

Virginia Woolf, perhaps surprisingly, writes well about eating in *Mrs Dalloway*. (Just as surprisingly it was she who persuaded Marcel Boulestin to open his famous eponymously titled restaurant in London. Woolf was shy and nervous in restaurants and had managed to persuade Boulestin, an *émigré* from France who had arrived in Britain in 1910, to cook a luncheon in his own flat. The luncheon party was such a success that the notion of a restaurant run by him, manager Robin Adair and the chef Félice Bigorre, took root and, when relocated to Covent Garden, became the most famous French restaurant in London.)

Perhaps the reason, though, why food is rarely written about successfully in novels and stories is that it takes great skill in its depiction. Not so in the case of painters, for whom food is so often a subject for still life.

Liver

Liver is astoundingly rich in vitamins, particularly in the B categories, and medical authorities recommend that at least 8 grams (¼oz) should be consumed per week. It is especially healthy for young people, expectant mothers (though see **folic acid**), the elderly and anyone suffering from anaemia, which is why adolescent girls in the early days of menstruation should be provided with this nourishing **offal**.

There is no reason why this cannot be promoted for the above, as liver is both relatively inexpensive and fashionable in smart restaurants today. Liver is also, of course, the source of interminable pâtés, including the superb **pâté de foie gras**, and gives rise to the stupendous German liver sausage known as *leberwurst*.

Lollipop

When a diminutive young West Indian girl called Millie took a song titled 'My Boy Lollipop' to number 1 in the American charts, the Yanks were bemused because the North American term for this hard-boiled sweet on a stick is a 'popsicle' and usually refers to an ice lolly (see **sorbet**).

Lucullan

A lucullan meal is one profusely lavish and luxurious, elegant enough for any epicure. The adjective derives from Lucius Licinius Lucullus (110–57 BC), a Roman general famed for his banquets but also noted for his fastidious tastes. In this he was a *gourmet* rather than a *gourmand*. See **aristology** and **waiters**.

Lunch

This should always be called 'luncheon' and was originally a middle of the day snack (see **dinner**). I belong to the era of journalism, or indeed any business, that once had lunch: the concept, let alone the reality, is no more. Young journos and young business people have a sandwich at their desks and indigestion in the evening. Here is a prediction. Young journalists will not get old: they will croak it of pressure, idiocy and a lack of the long, liquid lunches of my generation. A phrase had it that only wimps did lunch and the phrase is imbecilic. Lunch is for those of us who can do our jobs in time. Dinner is for those who need to impress.

Luncheon meat

This loaf-shaped cooked meat, usually of **pork**, has a fair amount of cereals as an ingredient and was common during the war and its aftermath owing to the paucity of actual meat. The most famous example, at least in the UK was **Spam**. It was and is pink-coloured, like the more vulgar of ladies drawers, and tastes somewhat similar. Yet there are those who love Spam, especially fried in batter. A variant is **Ulster fry**, made from minced bacon.

Lychee

Though originating in China, this fruit of an evergreen tree is now cultivated in many other parts of South-East Asia. The outer husk has to be removed, revealing a delicate and very sweet fruit. It is often canned in syrup and retains its flavour and lovely aroma. Though once on the menu of every Chinese restaurant in the UK, because they are rather expensive only the better establishments seem to serve lychees these days.

M

Macaroni

Thick tubes of **pasta** (though in Italy it is a generic term for any form of dried pasta), which for some reason best known to the English became popular as a dish mixed with a creamy cheese sauce. This is a simple and somewhat bland nursery/invalid-style repast and featured in many a Lyons Corner House menu.

Earlier, in the eighteenth century, especially effete dandies were known in England as 'macaronis', thereby giving rise to the famous line of the abusive American doggerel about Englishmen dressed as such and riding on a pony.

Macaroons

The same as **amaretti**. There was also a once-popular sweetmeat known as a 'macaroon bar', which bore no relationship to macaroons at all. It was an impossibly sweet icing sugar fondant covered in toasted coconut. The firm of Lees made it and advertised their product on television with a jingle that could hardly be broadcast today. It went: 'Lees, Lees, more if you please . . .' and went on, to the accompaniment of images of happy and caricatured Caribbeans, 'For piccaninnies and grandpapas, it has to be Lees Macaroon Bars'. It was a jolly jingle. That did not excuse the sickly sweetness of it, though.

Madeira

This liqueur, or **fortified wine**, is a touch unusual in that its origin is said to be wine with spirits such as brandy but which in its long voyage to India during the reign of the British Raj, when it was especially popular, tended, in the extraordinary heat, to mature quickly. Actually this is nonsense: the maturation occurs naturally – in Madeira, where it is given extra heat. There is, too, the madeira cake, made from a creamed cake mixture with shredded lemon peel added. It was often presented as an accompaniment to the taking of a glass of the wine.

Madeleines

Perhaps the most famous little cakes in world literature. Just why the remembrance of things past such as these cakes should have sprung to the very odd French writer Marcel Proust in *A la Recherche de Temps Perdu*, one cannot tell. It has to be said that few have ever read, or at least finished, this farrago of *dandyiste* vapourings. I read the first volume in an English translation titled *Swann's Way*.

The English singer and pop star Sting lived for some time in Proust's house in Cabourg, Normandy, with no ill effects. Until his death in 1922, however, the aesthete Proust rarely left his apartment in the Boulevard Haussmann in Paris. Proust was hardly an original: the novel *A Rebours* ('Against Nature'), by Joris-Karl Husymans, a novel that may well have summed up *La Belle Epoque*, published in 1884, is very much a precursor to Proust's work, which most *littérateurs* claim they wish to have read but have never got round to.

To put you out your misery, though, but not much, madeleines are little sponge cakes, in Britain shaped rather like chimney pots and covered in jam and desiccated **coconut**, usually called 'Eiffel Towers'. In some parts of France they are similar. In Normandy they are spicy and fruity little tartlets, not unlike **eccles cakes**.

Maize

Grown worldwide, this cereal is yet another product of the New World and was introduced to Europe as a crop that could reproduce itself every three months. When idiots tell you that space exploration has been able to develop new technologies and the rest, think upon this: about the only useful result of it has been Velcro. But the voyage of Columbus changed the world and one of the changes was the distribution of the cereal that had fuelled the civilizations of the Americas, especially that of the Incas and Aztecs.

For a clear picture of the importance of maize – known in the northern states of the USA and in Canada as 'Indian corn' – you need look no further than Maguelonne Toussaint-Samat's *History of Food* (1987), in which you will find a comprehensive analysis of this staple and its unique story. (Madame Toussaint-Samat's epic book is awesome in its scholarship, though it has to be said that she at times surpasses even Nicolas Chauvin in her portrayal of the importance of France in the history of grub.) One part of this story is that it was much cultivated by the peasantry of central Europe because, being new, it was exempt from taxes and did not make up the dues to feudal landlords.

But it is in Africa that maize has become a major staple, for there it can often be about the only food available to the very poor. It is made into cakes called *mealies*, a corruption of the word 'millet', which cereal preceded maize.

Maize is used for human and animal consumption – the famous Bresse chickens are fed on it, tinging the flesh a characteristic golden yellow – and the stems can be used for animal fodder. The plant also provides manufacture with material for plastics and gramophone records. Bourbon whiskey uses maize and, on a bizarre note, the stems are used to make the corn-cob pipes that General MacArthur was foolishly wont to flourish to give him the look of a famous frontiersman, the oaf.

Malnutrition
Literally 'bad feeding', this condition now generally means a lack of nutrition. It is an absurdity of modern life that a condition known as *anorexia nervosa* exists, mainly among young girls, whereby the fad for slimness can lead to a level of malnutrition that can prove fatal. The pop singers Karen Carpenter and Lena Zavaroni both died of malnutrition. The fad of **vegetarianism** when applied especially rigidly can lead to this, in the West, avoidable condition. But malnutrition is equally avoidable in those areas of the world, especially Africa, where it is rife. All it takes is the rich West feeding these peoples instead of worrying about their own figures, physical or economic.

Malt
The enzymes in barley produce this starch, from which a variety of foodstuffs, and certainly drinks, are made. Beer and whisky result from this fermented barley, and it is a boon, a blessing, and a curse as well, to us all.

Mangetout
In the 1980s you could not avoid a helping of this bland member of the pea family, and very dreary it was too. It means in the French, literally, 'eat it all'. Well, you can if you wish.

Maple syrup

This light sweet syrup derives from the sap of Canadian maple trees and is widely used in North American cookery. My father, who was attached to the Americans in the Second World War, first encountered it at breakfast, where he witnessed the Yankee soldiers pouring what he took to be gravy over their eggs and bacon. My father discovered the 'gravy' to be this syrup and was suitably outraged. However, he took to it eventually and enjoyed it, especially with the waffles that he likewise discovered.

Marc

A spirit, a French version of **grappa**, distilled from grape skins. Simenon invariably had his Maigret quaffing this in the little zincs he seems to have so often frequented (see **zinc**). It is often made illegally and can be very powerful indeed.

Margarine

A combination of animal and vegetable fats, this rather awful butter substitute was once thought to be healthier than what it was intended to replace. It was certainly cheaper. Invented by a chemist who named it after his daughter Marjory, it became a byword for the ersatz foods of the immediate post-war years in Britain. (This may be apocryphal in that the Greek word *margarites*, meaning 'little pearls', could be the original provenance.) Actually margarine is a reasonably adequate substitute for butter in frying. But not for butter on bread.

Marinade

There is a real reason why French cookery often suggests a marinade for meat: much French meat, especially **beef**, is said to be of poor quality and there is a reason for that nonsense too; the marinade is said to be a means of hiding this. The truth is that the French slaughter their animals, especially beef cattle, at a later age than the British do and therefore hang the carcasses longer. And to ensure tenderness they, as a nation that sees wine as a staple, often marinate their meats in it. In the Balkans and the Indian subcontinent meats are often marinated in a mixture of oils and **yoghurt**.

There are some meat dishes that do indeed benefit from marinading: but remember that such vegetables as are employed in a marinade should normally be thrown away. It is the actual marinade liquor that should be used.

Marmalade

The preserve made from bitter Seville oranges is widely recognized throughout Europe, but it is as a British breakfast conserve that it is famous. Popular fiction has it that the name derives from a circumstance in which the tragic Mary, Queen of Scots, was unwell and her maid gave her a compote of these oranges from which the title derives ('Marie est malade'). This is manifestly untrue as the name was well known long before Mary ever sailed to Scotland and her destiny.

Some of the legend is valid. When Mary made her trip across to Scotland in 1561, she was indeed served *marmelada*, a name from the Portuguese, meaning a jam made from quinces. And later, much later, a Dundee housewife called Janet Keillor made a preserve out of increasingly decaying quinces which had been left on a Spanish ship long harboured in the River Tay, and called it marmalade. The firm Keillor's is still a major purveyor of this preserve, as is also Robertson's, who make the delicate Golden and Silver Shred marmalade jellies. Another Scottish company, Baxter's, is famous for its whisky-flavoured marmalade.

But perhaps the most legendary marmalade manufacturer of all is Frank Cooper's of Oxford. Its marmalade (first made by Sarah Jane Cooper, the wife of Frank, a chandler) was taken up Everest by Sir Edmund Hillary in 1953, and a jar of it was found, perfectly preserved, in the provisions discovered in 1980 at Captain Scott's last camp at the South Pole.

Europeans are mystified by marmalade as a breakfast relish but invariably insist upon it when in England. I once interviewed the singer Charles Aznavour (see **game pie**) and discovered that he much enjoyed buttered toast and marmalade for **breakfast**. The other well-known marmalade addict is Paddington Bear.

Marmite
The brand name of a commercial product made of yeast extract, the residue of the manufacture of beer. It is highly flavoured and salted. The little jars instruct you to spread it thinly on toast, which is a little surprising: one would have thought the manufacturers would wish you to use more of it. But in this the makers are right. Thinly spread, it is delicious. It is also highly nutritious and thus very suitable for those daft enough to be vegetarians.

The name itself is taken from the name of a French earthenware pot with small handles. The pot is flameproof and can sometimes come in individual sizes. See also **Bovril**.

Marrowbones
There was a very wee, but enormously effective, television jingle back in, I think, the 1960s for a dog food that went as follows: 'Made with nourishing marrowbone jelly'. To gourmets and butchers alike this sounded very strange in that marrowbone jelly was enormously expensive and rarely discovered in the shops. There was a time when this delicacy was spooned out (with special little silver spoons) on to thin slivers of toast, and it is a major ingredient of the splendid *risotto milanese*.

Marsala

This sweet and fortified wine is the basis for the dessert **zabaglione**, but it is a lot more than that. It is used throughout Italian food: in meat (famously in *piccate* or *scaloppine al marsala* – floured veal escalopes, over which a marsala and butter sauce is poured) and poultry, and in soups and sauces. I met it first in a restaurant in Kilburn High Road in London, where Tony, the Sicilian waiter, chef, owner and friend, provided myself and my brothers with dishes that always seemed to include this Sicilian speciality.

But oddly this most famous of the wine products of Sicily is barely two hundred years old and was the brainchild of an English merchant, John Woodhouse, who had discovered that the wines from the small port of Marsala withstood the trip to British shores better when fortified with alcohol spirit. (A similar conclusion had occurred to British importers in Portugal, which led to **port**. Like port, marsala was imported by British, indeed Scottish, companies – in the case of Sicily, by Inghams, and the firm of Whitakers.)

Though marsala wine is usually very sweet, there are drier products, among which the most famous are Pelligrino, Rallo and the *Superiore Riserva* of Marco de Bartolli. What I can tell you is that sometimes the more expensive the marsala the less useful it is for cooking. Try the very cheap marsala incorporating eggs, *marsala alla uovo*, and you will know what I mean.

Marshmallow

Though this is indeed a plant, which possesses a gum-like root used in confectionery and which has medical properties, the gelatinous sweetmeat of today is generally made with gelatine, sugar and egg white. It is often coloured pink, dusted with caster sugar and sometimes desiccated coconut. In parts of the USA it is then toasted and is a favourite party sweet beloved of college students. Well, supposed to be: most US college students of today are more likely to toast lumps of marijuana. I am reliably informed that Girl Guides once obtained a badge in the toasting of these sweetmeats. Doubtless the Girl Guides of the modern age have a similar badge for joint-rolling and Janis Joplin is an honorary Brown Owl.

Marzipan

As a very small boy I used to watch Willie Tocher, the local baker in our small idyllic village of Cathcart in Glasgow (that sounds a contradiction but it's true and the village still exists, though the bakers doesn't), making what he called 'marzipan potatoes'. They consisted of a small piece of sponge cake brushed with apricot jam, wrapped up in marzipan and then dusted with cinnamon.

What Willie probably didn't know was that this was a traditional item originally from Arab countries and especially popular in Sicily, where marzipan sweetmeats abound, often made into exquisite shapes such as fruits and coloured delicately. Sicilian marzipan cakes and sweetmeats are stupendously elaborate and can be said to be works of art to the eyes as well as the palate. Indeed I once had an array of such wonders put before me which had been made by nuns in a small town in Sicily and which, literally, were almost too good to eat. It took courage actually to consume such visual glories.

Marzipan is made of ground almonds, sugar and egg whites and is very malleable: thus the sculptural shapes. In the UK it is almost exclusively used to top Christmas and wedding cakes and then covered in icing.

Mastic

This gum-like resin from the lentisk tree is sometimes used in North African and Arab cookery and imparts a peculiar smoky flavour. The resin is also used in the manufacture of varnish, cement and spirituous liquor.

Matzo

Passover unleavened bread used in orthodox Jewish cookery, but more than that. Matzo meal can be and is often used to make matzo balls, and this is where we encounter a legendary story. It is said that when Marilyn Monroe started going out with her later husband, the Jewish playwright Arthur Miller, he took the most famous blonde in the world to his mum and dad's home, where she was given a good orthodox kosher meal, including matzo balls. The next week she had a similar meal, also with matzo balls. On the third week she was proffered another genuine kosher repast – with matzo balls. It is said that after the third dinner Monroe turned to her husband-to-be and asked, ingenuously: 'What other part of the matzo can you eat?' If it's apocryphal, it shouldn't be.

Mayonnaise

It is today distressing to discover that the menus of bistros run by horribly jejune young women possess a substance titled 'Mayo', when what is meant by that is the two-century-old egg sauce called mayonnaise. Oddly, because the writer rarely became over-historical, Elizabeth David wrote something of the origins of this liaison of egg yolks and oil in 1956, when French cooks celebrated its so-called 200th anniversary. Legend has it that it was invented by the cook of the Duc de Richelieu in 1756, when the English were being besieged at Port Mahon in Minorca. This is, as the redoubtable Mrs David herself pointed out, absolute drivel and mayonnaise had been known to the Spanish a century before.

There are a number of commercially available versions of this delectable creamy sauce, and none of them is entirely successful, though there is a variant called, in the UK, salad cream: a thinner and more vinegary substitute which snobbish people deplore, though there is nothing wrong with salad cream at all. But back to mayonnaise: it is essential with chips in Belgium.

Meat

The flesh of animals (see **beef**, **lamb**, **pork** and **veal**). It also sometimes refers to the flesh of fish and poultry. Humans are omnivorous and thus also carnivores. There are humans, though, who eschew the eating of meat and even some who will not contemplate the consumption of any animal products at all – vegans they are called. There was a fashion in the late twentieth century for **vegetarianism**, although most dieticians saw it as dangerous to many of its adherents, especially the many young people (particularly girls) who practised this fad. A diet that requires vitamin supplements might be said to have something not sensible about it. Richmal Crompton, whose hero William courses throughout this tome, was splendidly sarcastic about the loony nut-cutleters – mainly of a bourgeois-lefty persuasion – who practised this creed. She once said that 'if God had made people vegetarians, he wouldn't have had animals made of meat'. There is not much of an answer to this.

Meatballs

There would appear to be no cuisine in the world that does not have meatballs. Even **hamburgers** are, after all, nothing but a flattened meatball, as are the Italian *polpette*. The Greeks have their **keftedes**, the Germans their meatballs in a rich sour-cream sauce, *königsberger klopse*, the Turks *kofte*, and the south Indians their similarly titled *kofta*. Now see below.

Meatloaf

Made of minced **beef**, **onion**, breadcrumbs and seasoning bound with egg and baked in a loaf tin, this is a cheap and popular dish especially in the USA. Practically no New York diner is without meatloaf on its menu. It famously figured in the Billy Wilder film *The Odd Couple*, in which Felix made it for his pal Oscar and two delectable but rather blowzy girls. Like the film, meatloaf is very New York.

The dish is less popular in the UK, where it is associated with the rubbish served up in works canteens during and after the Second World War.

Medicine

Like many others in this tome, this heading merits an entire book: indeed there are many on the subject already in existence. Underlying the philosophy of much of the approach to Chinese cookery is a knowledge of the medicinal properties of the ingredients; so too much of the cookery of the Indian subcontinent. The use of herbs and spices is probably due in part to medical purposes.

Undoubtedly tea, coffee and chocolate originated as pharmaceutical compounds. There is, too, the old adage that you should 'feed a cold and starve a fever'. This is true in the first part but not in the second. During fevers an increased, but careful, nourishment is desirable.

Despite the obvious fact that the food we eat is perhaps the most important element in our health, there is an appalling lack of concern in the subject in our medical care services, especially in the UK and North America. Dieticians and food experts are rarely seen in hospitals (a mere four thousand medical dieticians work in Britain's hospitals and outside in the health service: they are grossly over-stretched) and are often marginalized as unimportant. And what used to be termed 'invalid cookery' tended to be bland and unattractive.

There is no need for this ignorance, though, for physicians throughout the ages have written widely on the medical properties of what we eat, and old wives' tales are often a source of much valuable knowledge.

And the benefit of good and healthy food is incalculable when we come to consider mental health. A last thought: what seems strangely characteristic of all the great dictators throughout history is a disregard for, or even dislike of, food.

Melon

A fruit of the cucumber and gourd family, this varies considerably in size, and its flesh, which varies according to its type from green or yellow to red, is slightly sweet. It is very refreshing. The word itself, however, is Ancient Greek for 'fruit'. Though often a starter course in Britain and America, in Greece it is served iced, at the end of a meal. The lovely watermelon slices called *pasteque* are universal in Greek tavernas.

Melton Mowbray pie

The difference between this traditional pork pie from Leicester and the usual British pork pie is that the former is made with minced pork and is highly spiced, while the latter is made of cubed pigmeat and today tends to be bland. Both are made with hot water crust pastry. Melton Mowbray pies are expensive but a revelation to most Brits, who have only ever encountered that soggy crust encasing pigs' gristle and industrial gelatine offered in cheap pubs these days.

Menu

The list of dishes offered in restaurants, cafés, eating houses and the like. In France it is known in the cheaper eateries as *le tarif* because the price is included. But originally the menu was simply what was served at a dinner. Today, when three, or at most four, courses are served at an informal, or formal, dinner it is hard to think of the gargantuan menus that were once prevalent in **haute cuisine**. Queen Victoria, for example – who was considered a diner of plain tastes – indulged her guests with repasts of twelve courses every night. Her gourmet, and gourmand, son Edward VII was wont to provide more. Here is a typical menu for the roistering royal:

Tortue liée
Consommé de boeuf froid
Whitebait à la daube et au naturel
Pain de saumon à la Riche
Sauces Genevoise et Hollandaise
Cailles braisées printanières demi-glacées
Cotelettes d'agneau Rachel
Canetons à la Voisin au coulis d'ananas
Salade de Gobelins
Hanche de venaison à l'Anglaise
Sauce Porto et Cumberland
Granites au champagne
Poulardes roties flanquées d'ortolans
Asperges d'Argenteuil, sauce mousseline
Oeufs de faisan parmentier
Croûte d'ananas
Coupes Petit-Duc
Petites friandises
Fondants au Chester
Petites glaces au café et pain bis vanillées
Petites gaufrettes

Actually this menu, for a dinner given for the King in 1904, was not typical at all: there are only eight real courses in it. Dear God.

Myself, I regard giving the names of dishes in French, unless they are very well known, as a pretentious pain in the arse. Unless, of course, I am in France.

Methi

Another name for **fenugreek**. There is a wonderful Indian dish called *methi aloo*, yet another **potato** recipe, which uses the leaves grown from this seed. See also **bubble and squeak**.

Meze

Greek **hors d'œuvres**, often eaten with dips such as the chickpea-based hummus or cod's roe, known as **taramasalata**. Stuffed vine leaves and such small items as little meatballs, prawns, fried fish etc. are usually included. The Turks have their *mezeter*, which is much grander and constitutes an entire meal in itself.

Milk

Regarded as an essential source of vitamins and proteins (see **dairy**), milk was issued by the British government during and immediately after the Second World War to every nursing or expectant mother and to schoolchildren under the age of fourteen. Later a certain Mrs Thatcher, as Education Secretary in a British Conservative government, withdrew school milk, thereby earning the sobriquet of 'Milk Snatcher'. As a child myself I was made to drink this appalling liquid by overbearing primary school mistresses so that I should 'grow up big and strong'. It didn't work.

Mince

In 1954 Elizabeth David, in her *Italian Food*, told her readers to buy beef in the piece and have the butcher mince it in front of their very eyes on the basis that, and I quote: 'butchers' minced meat is seldom good'. She amended this in a later edition in 1963 with the following: 'Better nowadays, if from a conscientious butcher'. This was probably true, but to this day I follow her former ruling and insist on overseeing my butcher on the matter of mince.

In the USA mince – for Britons this usually means minced **beef** – is called hamburger steak and is often used in such homely dishes as **meatloaf**.

But to Elizabeth David's notion that butchers' mince is seldom good: tell me about it. In my native Scotland it was and remains a staple of the weekly diet. Indeed there are many Scots who assert their Scottish identity, especially their Scottish working-class identity, through this dish of finely chopped beef, always combined with 'tatties' (boiled or mashed potatoes).

The minced beef of my post-war childhood was so awful that for some years I was nearly a vegetarian. I have never eaten this 'tatties and mince'. Never. As a child I vomited on its appearance and thankfully 'now I have become a man I have put away childish things'. One of them is mince.

I am not alone in this prejudice against stewed minced beef. Florence Irwin, in her wonderful book *The Cookin' Woman*, recalls the story of the Derry woman who was entertaining a Donegal man from one of the far-off islands of that Irish county who was about to embark on his first visit to Scotland to seek work, and had set before him a plate of minced beef. He had never seen mince before and just sat looking at it. The lady told him to eat it up. 'Naw, naw,' he replied, 'whoever chawed that can swally it.' As a small boy I knew what he meant.

Mincemeat

Originally this was made, of course, of meat with suet and a combination of spices and fruits along with liquors such as brandy. The meat has disappeared, though I do make this for

Christmas; my friends and family regard this eccentricity as rather similar to the sort of musician who insists on playing medieval instruments.

The modern mincemeat omits meat, though it does include beef **suet**. It is still very good, though, and why one mainly finds such festive mincemeat pies at Christmas is as inex-plicable as why we only get hot cross buns at Easter.

Minestrone
A good test of the authenticity of an Italian restaurant, any-where in the world, is this soup. Most so-called Italian *ris-toranti* serve up a thin liquor with bits of broken pasta and a few kidney beans swirling forlornly about. This is a travesty of what is in fact a main dish, like Scotch broth or Hungarian goulash; more of a stew really. There are so many variants of it that recipe books often get the very idea of it wrong. My view is that a good minestrone should include bacon, tomatoes (or purée anyway), root vegetables including diced potatoes, chopped cabbage, onions, garlic, haricot beans, herbs such as oregano and parsley, pasta such as the large, shell-shaped *conchiglio* and, last but not least, a good glass or two of robust red wine. Olive oil is necessary, and a decent stock cube as well. You can see then that this is a main course and not that silly consommé with bits of macaroni which non-authentic Italian snackeries serve up to you.

Mint
This herb is used throughout the world, though it is usually only grown in the more temperate parts. The British mint sauce, made with vinegar and sugar, is a traditional accompa-niment to roast lamb, a taste now shared by the French, albeit somewhat grudgingly.

Miso

This is bean curd (the famed tofu), which is impregnated with yeast mould and combined with grains such as barley or rice. It is a staple in Japan and is eaten for breakfast as well as at other meals. Miso soup (*miso-shiru*) is based on it.

Mixed grill

There was a time when this was standard fare in UK restaurants. The repast consisted of a bit of frying steak, a grilled sausage, a tomato and a rasher or two of bacon. Sometimes a slice of liver was included. All of it was grilled. Chips were included. Whole generations of Brits grew up thinking this was all you could order on a night out.

Mocha

Though this originally was a type of coffee bean named after the Yemeni port from which the beans were shipped, the name more often than not denotes a mixture of coffee and cocoa powder used both as a drink and as a cake flavouring.

Mock turtle soup

I have never seen, let alone consumed, this favourite of the Victorians. It was made with the broth of a sheep's head. Its inclusion here is due to my fondness for anything written by Charles Dodgson (Lewis Carroll) and the fact that I once dined with Michael Hordern, who played the Mock Turtle in the TV film *The Adventures of Alice in Wonderland*. Afterwards I met the late Sir John Gielgud, who asked Hordern to introduce him to 'your *soigné* friend'. I asked Michael later what had made the famous actor knight (who in fact looked like a very old turtle himself) compliment me in such a manner. 'My dear boy,' said Hordern, 'he probably wanted to get up your *soigné* river.' The lovely man then told me he had been waiting for years to get to make this pun. I forbore to tell him that P.G. Wodehouse had made the same paronomasia many years before.

Monosodium glutamate

As a widely available product this flavour-enhancer is derived from Japanese seaweed, sugar beet and gluten from wheat. It is widely used in the cookery of South-East Asia and is included in many Chinese restaurant meals. It is occasionally seen in Western cookery and is known variously as *vetsin*, *aji-nomoto* or by a French brand name, L'Accent. It does indeed enhance flavour in certain dishes, though its overuse in many European so-called oriental restaurants has resulted in what has become known as 'Chinese Restaurant Syndrome': heart palpitations, dizziness, nausea and other unpleasant reactions are signs of this. As I have myself encountered much the same sensations with the cheaper Chinese outlets, I am inclined to suggest that this addition should be used very sparingly.

Mortadella

This Bologna sausage, which was once made with donkey meat, is common throughout Italy and often used today in pizzas (see **pizza**). A good many supermarkets sell it as salami. Some of their customers pay more for mortadella than they would for salami in the mistaken belief that it is a superior sausage, not realizing that salami is a generic title.

Moussaka

A dish common throughout the Balkans, this is made with layers of sliced aubergines and a mixture of heavily seasoned minced lamb, onions and tomatoes, topped with a crust of an egg custard with cheese. There are a great number of slight variations as the recipe is used throughout such a large area, the Turkish version being richer than the Greek.

However, the one known to Greek-Americans is, to my mind, the most satisfying. In that community's version sliced potatoes are also included and the topping is of what is essentially a **béchamel sauce** which omits the cheese. It is a hearty and filling dish, almost a pudding, and can be eaten cold as a buffet meal. It is surprising that it is not seen on menus in the UK more often, being no more fiddly to produce than the by now ubiquitous Italian **lasagne**.

Mousse

I first encountered this name in one of the William Brown stories, in which William is confused and earnestly believes it is a dish made with a small rodent. For myself I too was no wiser than young Mr Brown, as I had never heard of the word for this dessert made with eggs and fruit, or sometimes a frothy savoury pudding. It didn't help that when I first read of this it was the days of rationing. I wasn't sure what an egg was either.

Mozzarella

Though this mild but distinctive centuries-old Italian cheese is today often made with cow's milk, by tradition it is made with the milk of buffaloes (see **buffalo**). It is widely used for pizzas (see **pizza**), and also in a large range of meat dishes. One of the most famous dishes in Italy is *mozzarella in carrozza* (literally 'mozzarella in a carriage'), which is bread saturated in beaten egg, rather like French toast, with a filling of this cheese. It is a widely made breakfast dish. To be honest I find it impossibly bland. The truth is that continentals don't know how to do breakfast: the British Isles, including Ireland, may not manage much else, but they are ace at brekkers.

Muesli

Though originally a breakfast food made of oats, fruits and nuts soaked in condensed milk and promoted by a Swiss health clinic for patients suffering from consumption, this appalling concoction became hugely fashionable in the 1970s and was often, despite warnings by dieticians, the sole diet of young women who believed it to be slimming. It was indeed, and the result was that thousands of young girls were horribly slim and suffering from malnutrition as, though there are a number of vitamins in the food, it also lacks a number of them. Also lacking, of course, were the **proteins** necessary for healthy living.

Muffins

These traditional English yeasted buns elicited, I recollect as a child, a poem about a muffin man, but the only other reference in literature I can find is to The United Metropolitan Improved Hot Muffin and Crumpet Baking and Punctual Delivery Company, which Charles Dickens's febrile imagination conjured up in his novel *Nicholas Nickleby* (1837).

It is rare to discover a hot toasted muffin these days, though the word is also used to describe an American tragedy of a soft sort of cupcake, often shot through with blueberries. They are bloody awful.

Mulled wine or ale

Wine or beer heated up, usually with sugar and spices. It is traditional at festive occasions and is thoroughly unpleasant.

Mulligatawny soup

Said to derive from a Tamil word meaning 'peppery water', this is a substantial soup from Ceylon, very much like a **pot au feu** and involving beef, onions, curry spices and frequently fruit. Brought back to Britain by retired old India hands, it became eventually a pale imitation of the Sri Lankan original.

Mushroom

Though there are said to be 120,000 species of mushroom and related fungi, only 1,841 of these are edible. This figure is, of course, ridiculous but it has been recorded in the national medical and food hygiene surveys in France. Essentially mushrooms grow in damp soil and the rotting vegetation found there. As a result many mushrooms are poisonous: these poisons can also be used for medicinal purposes.

As to mushrooms as a food, the edible varieties have a considerable nutritional content, being high in proteins and vitamins while low in calories. It is not too fanciful to describe mushrooms as a vegetable meat. (Indeed there are meat substitutes – to be avoided, if you ask me – made from processed mushrooms in a similar process to that which can be manufactured from soya. See **soya bean**.)

Mushrooms are cultivated as well as being harvested in the wild. The USA is the largest grower of the cultivated varieties, most of which are bland and hardly worthwhile, though they are commonly found on supermarket shelves. In recent years such varieties as the Japanese *shitake* have found much favour in the West, especially as they can be bought fresh instead of dried. (Dried mushrooms such as the Chinese *mu* and the Italian *funghi secchi* made from porcini are very strong-tasting and extremely useful in many sauces.)

But varieties of mushrooms such as the meaty and delicate chanterelles and morels are very good eating. Only the very experienced can be trusted with the identification of wild mushrooms, however. Though most poisonous varieties can usually be identified by the presence of scales under the cap and a ring and a small sac on the stem, the absence of such does not ensure edibility. Don't let the above put you off mushrooms, however: because mushrooms possess, as well as their splendid taste, a natural monosodium glutamate, *haute cuisine* would be much the poorer without them.

Music

'If music be the food of love, play on,/Give me excess of it that, surfeiting,/The appetite may sicken and so die', says Orsino in *Twelfth Night*, and too many restaurants in recent years have taken this literally. Not so recently either: Saki wrote a splendid story, *The Chaplet*, in which he satirized the Edwardian craze for orchestras in the exclusive restaurants of the day. His near-contemporary G.K. Chesterton agreed: 'Music with dinner is an insult both to the cook and the violinist', he averred. This much-loved critic, poet and novelist, and early broadcaster, was a noted gourmet, and both he and Saki wrote often and lovingly about food. There is, quite simply, little excuse for music to eat by. And none at all in pubs.

Mussels

My first meal on my first visit to France was in a tiny *estimanet* in St Valery en Caux in Normandy, where we, being Scots youngsters, were royally received by the locals and treated to bowls of *moules marinière*. We were rather dubious about this dish, never having seen mussels other than as discarded shells on seaside beaches. But we ate them with fresh French bread and lots of *vin ordinaire*, and it is still the first thing I order on a trip to France.

Mustard

Most of us know this as the thick and creamy, though hot, condiment we use for ham, beef and chicken sandwiches (see **sandwich**) without realizing that it is in fact made from a member of the **cabbage** family. English mustard is considerably hotter than French mustard, the best known purveyor of the former being Colman's.

A literary reference here: the husband of the detective novelist Dorothy L. Sayers, Oswald Fleming, the author of *The Gourmet's Book of Food and Drink* (1933), wrote a series of recipes for Colman's mustard in a booklet for that company. He was asked to do this because his wife, a former advertising copywriter, had produced the famous slogan for that company, a phrase now in common usage: 'As keen as mustard'. She also coined famous slogans for Guinness **stout**. In this she joins the novelist Fay Weldon as an originator of renowned advertising headlines. See **eggs**.

The French type of mustard sometimes turns up as a brown sludgy travesty, but the splendid wine-flavoured Dijon *moutardes* such as the famous Grey Poupon brand are a revelation.

Mustard seeds are much used in pickles such as **piccalilli**, and in **sauerkraut**. And they are widely used in Indian cooking, as is the oil extracted from the seeds, which is used for frying and also pickling. My father, in his droll military way, had a rhyme about this which delighted his children but scandalized my mother. 'The three turds', he would announce when spooning some Colman's on to his cold ham, 'mustard, custard, and you, you basturd'. Anyway, he thought it was droll.

N

Nam prik

A hot sauce from Thailand using chillies, garlic and the ubiquitous fish paste of South-East Asia, **blachan**, also known as *trasi* (see **fresh**). One of the most common dishes in Thai cookery is vegetables or fish in this delicious sauce.

Nasi goreng

This dish originated in Indonesia and is a made of rice (*nasi*) with a combination of thin strips of meat or poultry and shellfish. Indeed it is similar to the famous Creole **jambalaya** and the Spanish **paella**, though it uses the fish paste **blachan**. It is now a weekly dish in every Dutch household owing to its exportation from Indonesia, for so long ruled by the Dutch East India corporations. The Van Der Valk stories, set in Holland and written by British thriller writer Nicholas Freeling, invariably have their characters consuming this splendid rice dish. (Incidentally Freeling was an internationally known chef, not unlike Len Deighton of the Harry Palmer spy thrillers, who also served his time in the hotel industry.)

Nectarine

This variant of the **peach** falls, like its cousin, into two categories: those which remain free from its central stone and those which cling to it. Thus 'cling peaches'. Nectarines were once more common in Europe than peaches. This was evinced in the line from Marvell in which he writes of 'the nectarine, and curious peach'. In the same poem he is 'ensnared by flowers' and 'falls upon grass'. The reason I recollect these verses is that they were used in a famous poster seen during the great days of 1960s' 'flower power'. The grown-ups didn't quite grasp what the hippies were getting at.

Nettles

The stinging nettle has been used as both a herb and a vegetable from the beginning of cooking itself. It is similar in taste to **spinach**. (Cooking takes the sting out of the nettle.) I have encountered nettle soups in Ireland, Cornwall and Brittany. But use gloves when gathering.

Nightcap

This varies from hot milky drinks such as **cocoa** and malted preparations such as Ovaltine to alcoholic beverages, usually spirits: all are designed to act as soporifics. A favourite, and effective, nightcap which induces sleep is the hot toddy – whisky in which sugar or honey is dissolved, a clove added and mixed with hot water.

Noodles

A type of **pasta**. In recent years a fast-food development has been the appalling pot noodle, literally a pot containing a type of Chinese-style vermicelli, called in China *bee-hoon*, containing artificial flavouring and preservatives. It is very quick to make into a meal and derived from Japanese K rations before and during the Second World War. In terms of the actual value of the original product pot noodles retail with a massive mark-up.

Nosh

From the German *naschen*, meaning 'to nibble', this Yiddish word means snack food, often from street vendors. Some time in the 1950s it first became common usage for a snack in the then burgeoning coffee bars and was then taken up by the Bright Young Things of the day, known as the 'Chelsea set', and it stuck. Today it is applied to any meal from a hamburger to a formal dinner. In short, nosh has simply come to mean food.

Nougat

A sweetmeat made with nuts, honey, egg whites and often containing glacé fruits, especially cherries. Though nougat is of Moorish origin, the French town of Montelimar is its most famous source. A M. de Nougarede, of a noble Provençal family, spent fifty-five years writing a book 8,721 pages long, entirely on nougat, inspired, it is said, by the propinquity of his surname to this confection. Though it should be pronounced 'noogah', the lower orders invariably call it 'nugget'.

Nutmeg

The inner seeds of a fruit that itself is inedible, nutmegs are surrounded by a lacy covering which is mace. In the days when the Dutch had the world stranglehold on such spices as cloves, they were wont to dip nutmegs in lime in order to prevent the seeds from germinating. To this day there is a lime drink flavoured with nutmeg which can be found in bars in the working-class areas of Amsterdam. It washes down the infamous smoked eel dish **gerookte paling**.

Nutmeg is a preserving spice and was used in mummification in Ancient Egypt. But as to its culinary use, Italian cuisine demands it, especially in sauces such as their *besci-amella* or indeed meat *sugos* such as the famous bolognese (see **bolognese sauce**). Nutmegs are in fact slightly poisonous in that a whole nut, if grated and eaten at a sitting, could increase the heart rate inducing a possibly fatal attack. Be that as it may, there is a rather nice verse in folklore that goes:

> Nose, nose, jolly red nose
> Who gave thee this jolly red nose?
> Nutmegs and ginger, cinnamon and cloves
> And they gave me this jolly red nose.

There you have the origin of the British charity-raising drivel of Red Nose Day.

Nuts

Nuts contain high proteins and fats (the exception is **chestnuts**, which are floury) and are widely used in cookery. In recent years there have been scares concerning the increasing numbers of young people who experience severe and sometimes fatal allergic reactions to nuts, especially peanuts. This raises a serious problem in that a great many ready-prepared meals contain nuts or their oils. Many fast-food restaurants, particularly Chinese, use such oils, and affected customers should always check such places. Even slight contact with nuts through cutlery or tableware can induce such reactions.

That being said, the nuts most widely grown for consumption are almonds, pecans, hazelnuts and, of course, coconuts. The days, however, when chestnuts were a common staple in France have long since gone. And so too, regrettably, have the roast chestnuts I remember vendors selling in the streets when I was a child. Some of our most pervasive memories of childhood concern smells. Roast chestnuts was one of them.

O

Oats

One of the earliest grass cereals known to man, they became a staple of the poorer classes throughout the Roman Empire and remain a cereal for the poor. Thus oats and oatmeal were the basic foods in what was traditionally the poorest country in Europe – Scotland: that land, according to the Revd Sydney Smith, of 'Calvin, oatcakes, and sulphur'. And Dr Johnson loftily claimed that oats, while in Scotland being generally given to horses, 'in Scotland support a people'.

The Scots made a virtue out of this necessity – and still do – and their oatcakes and porridge remain popular in that country. The rest of the world regards oats as animal fodder. The origins of the phrases 'sowing your wild oats' and 'feeling your oats' would appear to be from Matthew 13:14. Trollope uses both metaphors in *Doctor Thorne*. I'm babbling now.

Offal

Liver, kidneys, brains, tongue and sweetbreads are all offal. Pigs' and sheep's heads are offal. Calves' feet and pigs' trotters, oxtail and tripe are offal. And some of them are, in truth, absolutely bloody awful at that. Traditionally the bits left over for the poor (see **humbles**), in recent years some of the above have become popular in fashionable restaurants.

Oil
Though animal fats in liquid state are oils, in food oil is generally taken to mean vegetable oil such as that procured from corn, nuts or sunflowers, but the most famous, of course, is that of the olive (see **olive oil**). Oil is not only one of the trinity of the basic foods that make up what we know as civilization; it is also part of the trinity of the sacraments in the Christian faith. Bread signifies the bread broken at the Last Supper, and wine the blood of Christ.

But oil has its part to play. Priests and kings are anointed with oil upon taking up their offices. The very word 'christ' is Greek for 'messiah'. And 'messiah' literally means 'one who has been anointed with oil'. The only time that non-kings, non-priests and non-messiahs are anointed with oil is at baptism and death. Cheery.

Okra
Also known as 'ladies fingers', this mucilaginous vegetable is widely used in Indian cooking (in which it is also called *bhindi*) and is used in the Louisiana dish **gumbo**.

Olive
As a small boy I was intrigued by the jars of stuffed green olives with little red spots at the top in Mr Santonini's delicatessen, and he gave me one to try, explaining that I would not like it. Much to Mr Santonini's surprise, I loved its salty, sweet and sour flavour immediately and I still do.

Green olives are the unripe ones, usually steeped in a solution of potash. Black olives are the mature ones, preserved in brine. In Britain and the USA most consumers see olives as a cocktail snack, but in Mediterranean countries, and especially in southern Italy, Greece and southern France, olives are basic to many dishes, including the marvellous daubes of Provence (see **daube**). A **pizza** without olives and anchovies is a poor thing indeed. Incidentally, the olive branch is known as the symbol of peace because the olive tree takes so long to bear fruit that those who planted them had to look forward to years of peace.

Olive oil

Two-thirds of olives produced go to the making of this wonderful oil. Every country surrounding the Mediterranean Sea has it olive oils. In Spain it tends to be heavy and greenish in colour; Greek varieties tend towards the robust too. In Italy olive oil is ubiquitous, though butter is a common cooking agent in the north (and surprisingly lard or pork fat is mainly used in the Roman cookery of the Lazio region).

Despite the preference for oil in the south of Italy, the most fêted olive oil comes from the north, from Lucca in Tuscany. Most highly prized of all is the expensive Extra Virgin first cold pressing oil, because the first pressing of the olives yields a rich and fruity product. It is by no means cheap. There is also little point in wasting it in deep frying, where a later pressing is in fact preferable, or in salads, in which the lovely subtlety of Extra Virgin goes unnoticed. (Many chefs dispute this. I dispute them.)

One use I learned in Italy, however, over twenty years ago. A small liqueur glass of good olive oil taken first thing in the morning aids digestion and is good for the bowels. Northern Italians claim it makes the hair glossy and the skin clear. It has been part of my morning ablutions these last two decades: without effect, it has to be said, on my hair at least.

Omelette

This has achieved almost mythic status in France, but it is essentially a simple dish made with beaten eggs – but not too well beaten: in fact, as Elizabeth David points out in her *Mediterranean Cookery* (1951) the eggs should be stirred rather than beaten. I part company with Mrs David, however, in that I like an omelette with a hefty filling. One I make with diced potato and bacon; another, perhaps my own invention, with spring onions, oyster mushrooms and Chinese bean sprouts. But no matter the filling, this first-course dish should be light and soft and not like the bits of burnt leather one usually finds in homes and restaurants alike.

Onion

This is probably the only vegetable that is absolutely indispensable in cookery throughout the world. About the only savoury dishes in which the ubiquitous onion does not make an appearance are those made with fish, though even then there are many recipes that blend fish with onions.

There is a great number of types of onions (including leeks, shallots and garlic, which belong to the same genus), and they range from the small so-called spring onions to the mild, sweet Spanish onions and on to the pungent onions of the Middle East. There are dishes that are fundamentally of onions, such as the splendid onion tarts of Germany and France, especially from the Alsace-Lorraine area (see **quiche**).

There is also an astonishing onion starter which the head waiter of the gorgeously decorated Del Cambio restaurant in Turin recommended – it was an onion stuffed with macaroons, raisins, cheese, nutmeg and cinnamon, and egg. The result was indeed discordant but magnificent. But it is not a starter, as the same head waiter told me. He suggested only an **espresso** and a small glass of amaretto after my stuffed onion, and he was right.

ONION JOHNNIES

Onion johnnies

This term properly belongs to the world of sociology, but is worth a mention if only because it is occasionally used by young people who do not recognize its derivation. The first recorded onion johnnie was a M. Henri Olivier, from Brittany, who started up business in Britain in 1828. By 1860 there were two hundred of these traders, and by 1951 over one and a half thousand. The boom in their numbers was because just after the Second World War a lot of poor French people from Brittany came across to Britain and peddled onions, then in short supply in Austerity Britain. They lived exceptionally frugally, and travelled throughout the ravaged UK on big black pre-war bicycles with their strings of onions cascading from the handlebars. Almost a caricature, they always sported little black Breton berets, and often apache-style striped jerseys.

I remember them well as they came to the back door of my home to sell their wares. They were often quite elderly and possessed an air of a sort of jaunty pathos: few could speak much English, and they were clearly even poorer than the Britons of the time. My mother, who spoke reasonable French, would invite the poor wee men in for a cup of tea and was always sorry for them: the result was an onion-rich diet in my childhood.

Orange

Originally from South-East Asia, the orange is now grown in any hot climate (north Africa, Spain, California) and is synonymous with healthy living. But its name derives from Sanskrit. An Indian fable that an elephant died from eating too many of these fruits produced the name *Naga ranga*, meaning 'indigestion of an elephant', later turned into 'orange'. However absurd this sounds, it is also true and is reflected in the word for orange in Spanish (*naranja*), and for

242

some reason in Hungarian (*narancs*) too. It is also, in some cultures, the orange, not the **apple**, that was responsible for original sin. And an Irish tradition had it that oranges were not eaten because of King William of Orange, as his anti-Catholic policies were anathema.

Today the variety of oranges ranges far. The Jaffa derives from the port in Israel from where it is exported. Similarly the Seville orange which turns into **marmalade**. Outspan is a brand name for a fruit sold by a South African company, and Sunkist the same for a Californian firm. Orange juice is undoubtedly the favourite fruit juice of all, and in the Republic of China orange juice is distributed free to all children under five. This was also done in the UK shortly after the Second World War. A strong argument could be made for the reintroduction of this practice as many modern children in the West suffer, despite the availability of food, from a significant lack of the vitamin C found richly in oranges.

Highly sweetened orangeades are popular in the UK, especially as an inducement by silly parents to quieten their children and ruin their teeth. As with **lemonade**, the continentals prefer their orange fizzy drinks with much less sugar. A chilled glass of orange juice and soda water, known as *spremuta* (though this is usually a carbonated **lemon** squash), can be found in every little Italian café and is very refreshing indeed.

Osso bucco
A speciality of Milanese cookery, this dish utilizes stewed shin of veal on the bone, and is served with the famous *risotto milanese* (see **risotto**).

Ostrich
Why the meat of this large and flightless bird is almost unknown outside Australia, the leading producer of the meat

of this African bird, is indeed surprising (though there is some increase in smart UK restaurants in the use of ostrich steaks, and there are ostrich farms throughout Europe). The meat is very similar to **beef** and is very tender. Australian aborigines especially prize the meat of the bird's gizzards.

Ovaltine

The reason I include this malted drink (called Ovalmaltine on the Continent) is that it has a long resonance with the British public as signifying health and childhood innocence. The drink was marketed around 1910 by a Swiss doctor, George Wander, and was an immediate success. Much of this was due to the splendid advertising ruses, and the rosy-cheeked (and splendidly bosomed) Ovaltine dairymaid with her basket of fresh eggs and sheaves of barley can still be found in its advertising and packaging, virtually unchanged since its foundation. Then there was the Ovaltiney Club, with its children's song 'We are the Ovaltineys/Happy girls and boys', which everybody of my generation can, and does, sing at parties and with a wee drink in us.

The other reason for its success was that mothers and nannies discovered that it was a genuine soporific: taken by small children just before bedtime, it induced sleep in the little ones, much to the gratification of tired-out mums. It is an official drink for the Olympics and such intrepid explorers as Wilfrid Thesiger and Sir Edmund Hillary included it in their supplies. It was even issued to the troops in the Second World War, and the brutal and licentious could be found singing the then most famous jingle in the world as they went about their business of defeating the Nazi hordes, and making the world safe for little children and other Ovaltineys.

Oven

There was a time – even as late as the late nineteenth century – when many Western households did not possess ovens and meat was taken to the local bakery for roasting and stewing. As late as the 1950s many households of my childhood possessed old-fashioned kitchen ranges in which the small box of an oven was never used save for reheating food. Older people still sent their roasts off to the baker's.

Today's ovens are of a standard that is near-professional with extremely useful timing mechanisms, and the convection fans with which many modern ovens are equipped can determine more regular results than was the case in the past. Despite this, surveys show that fewer people are using their ovens at all and that microwaves are more often utilized. There are, however, certain types and brands of ovens that are of good quality. I am thinking here particularly of the high-status Aga oven range and hobs, although they too have their limitations.

Ox

Though the ox is still seen in Europe as a beast of burden, it is today largely unknown in Britain. Oxtail soup is, however, a British favourite.

Oysters

Today oysters are regarded as a luxury food, but it was not always so. Indeed this bivalve mollusc was once regarded as for the dispossessed. As Sam Weller says in *Pickwick Papers*: 'Poverty and oysters always seem to go together'. This is a reference to the fact that London's poor gathered oysters from the Thames as a free meal. Oysters were often used as a cheap filler along with meat, and thus we had steak and oyster pudding – the steak and kidney was more expensive. Steak and oysters remains as a dish, known as 'carpetbag steak', an

Australian speciality. Though oysters can be baked or even fried, they are probably best consumed raw, with **Tabasco** sauce. They are widely thought to possess aphrodisiac qualities. It doesn't need Freud (Sigmund, not Clement) to explain this notion.

P

Paan

The English detective story writer H.R.F. Keating has his Indian hero Inspector Ghote consuming this breath-freshener after every meal. It is made from leaves filled with a variety of stuffings, including hemp, **cannabis** and **tobacco**.

Paella

Perhaps the most famous Spanish food of all, this is a rice dish surprisingly common throughout many parts of the world, often known by a similar name: *pilaf* in Russia, *pilafi* in Greece, *pilav* in Turkey and *pilau* throughout India. The truly legendary paella hails from Valencia – the rice-growing area of Spain – and is a massive affair containing lobsters and mussels, steak, pork, ham and chicken, garlic, sweet peppers, beans, peas, saffron and, of course, **rice**.

When working-class British tourists first ventured to Spain for cheap holidays, they were appalled to discover this incredibly rich collation being offered, especially as the Spanish like their food in heavy olive oil. The result has been that most Brits eat steak and chips in Spain, and most Spanish restaurants in Britain put forward a pale imitation of paella.

Pain perdu

This was once a popular super snack of slices of bread dipped in milk and beaten egg, and then fried in butter. Though in France it is often a sweet, served with caster sugar or syrup, in Britain and the USA it is regarded as a savoury and is known as 'French toast'.

Pakoras

Spicy deep-fried vegetable fritters made from gram (besan or chickpea) flour. They are street food in India, usually accompanied by an aromatic dip. Other examples of this deep-fried savoury are filled pasties such as samosas; similar to French *boulettes* or the popular Russian snacks or starters called **piroshki**.

Pancakes

Every culture has some variety of a thin, flour-based version of these batter cakes, often baked upon a griddle (see **crêpes**). In parts of the Western world pancakes are rather more like scones. The Scottish pancake is what is elsewhere known as a 'drop scone' and in the USA is called a 'biscuit'. Traditionally in Britain pancakes are made on Shrove Tuesday.

Papain

The flesh of the pawpaw fruit, also known as papaya, contains an enzyme that tenderizes meat much in the same way as pepsin does in the human stomach. Thus a marinade using this can ensure that meat takes a surprisingly short time to cook.

Paprika

A great deal of nonsense is written about this spice, made from the sweet red pepper, by food writers who often think of it as simply a colouring agent. This is true of some paprikas, but there are a great many different types, especially of the famous Hungarian paprikas which are so essential to that country's cuisine (see **Hungarian cookery**).

Spanish paprika is brightly red and almost tasteless. But Hungarian paprikas go from the mild *kulonleges* variety to the incredibly strong *eros paprika*, which should be used sparingly until you have got a taste for it. The cherry paprikas known as *cerasiforme*, which are essentially chillies, are very hot indeed. I once introduced an Indian friend of mine, used to pungent spices, to the cherry paprika and he subsequently doused himself with pints of cold water for five minutes.

Two famous Hungarian dishes that indulge in this product and are named after them are the potato-based *paprikas krumpli* and the rich chicken stew known as *paprikas csirke*, in which sweet peppers, paprika, wild mushrooms and soured cream combine to make up one of the most satisfying meals you could ever encounter.

Parma ham

A very expensive cured raw ham (*prosciutto crudo*), which hails from the same rich pastures of the Emilia-Romagna region as the famous **parmesan** cheese. Few Italian restaurants in the UK regularly serve this today because of its astonishing price, yet there is still nothing to beat the old cliché of thin slices of real parma ham with a portion of melon and a glass of that odd Italian wine Lambrusco, an oddity because it is a sparkling dry red wine. (A similar ham and melon hors d'œuvre is seen in Germany, using Westphalian ham and German cheeses, accompanied by chilled white German wine.)

In Parma itself the inhabitants often make a meal from the ham, a glass of Lambrusco, bread, local unsalted butter and a peeled pear. I know this because I encountered it in the famous Aurora restaurant there. I was taken there by the artist Rosann Cherubini, who told me that eating is love-making and that Parma ham is the most delicious foreplay (see **eroticism**). D'you know, I could see what she meant.

Parmesan

This world-renowned hard cheese is also known as *grana* (from the grainy appearance of good Parmesan). In Italy it is a controlled product and very expensive. It is not cheap in the UK either, and good-quality parmesan is, after all the years of import to this country, sometimes difficult to obtain. For a reason best known to retailers, ready-grated parmesan is sold in small tubs. This is not only far more expensive than that sold in the piece; it is nothing like as good. Parmesan as an addition to pasta sauces may well be a cliché but, like most clichés, there is a dashed good reason for it.

Parsley

As mentioned in the item on **herbs**, this was about the only one anybody knew in the Britain of my childhood. It is often used as a garnish, and at one time was used in this way especially in New York restaurants. According to Jimmy Breslin, a columnist for the *New York Daily News*, virtually every Manhattan eatery was serving 'meals that were growing lawns'. This was due to a Mafia shakedown in which the Mob insisted that every restaurateur bought tons of the green herb, which had gone from 5 cents to 40 cents a bunch. The Gambino Mafia family owned vast acreages in Ventura County, California. Unbelievably, the innocuous herb was more lucrative, dollar for dollar, for organized crime, than cocaine.

Yet another strange thing about parsley. I have never understood why a washing powder should call itself after this herb: in French it is called *persil*.

Parsnip

This is rather an oddity in that it is a root vegetable that was introduced to America, rather than the other way round, as is usually the case. The more mature the parsnip, the sweeter the taste (rather similar to the **yam** in fact, though it is of the carrot family): if too elderly, it becomes woody. This vegetable is somewhat uncommon in British cookery today, which is a great pity. Though it can be boiled, fried or baked, it is in my view best roasted along with potatoes and should always be included in the Christmas dinner. It also makes a lovely and subtle soup.

Partan bree

The Scots word *partan* means 'a crab', and the bree is a broth using this crustacean with rice and onions and other vegetables. Cream is added to make this rich Scottish soup which, once eaten by poor families in the Scottish islands, is now considered a great delicacy and is accordingly very expensive in smart restaurants.

Partridge

A game bird available during the shooting season. Not as fashionable as the better-known **grouse** or **pheasant**, it is a better buy as the taste is gamier and richer. It is found throughout Europe. Why a partridge should want to nest in a pear tree as the Christmas rhyme has it is beyond me: the partridge nests on the ground.

Pashka

Made from curd cheese, soured cream, eggs, almonds and glacé fruits, this is the traditional cake baked for Easter in the Russian Orthodox Church. Russian woman queue in their hundreds to have their pashka blessed by their priest. This was once common elsewhere in Europe. In Britain it has been superseded by hot cross buns.

Pasta

Myth has it that this was introduced to Italy, where pasta is now a staple, by Marco Polo, who brought it from China. This is not only myth, it is mince (see **mince**). Not only was pasta known to the Ancient Greeks and the Etruscans, but Apicius, the Roman gourmet, included pasta in his *De Re Coquinaria* ('On Cookery').

Pasta is, of course, known worldwide and one of the staples in China and Japan. The Mongols careering across Asia brought it as far as Siberia. It spread all over Europe, especially the Balkans and the Ottoman Empire, where it often emerged as little parcels like **ravioli**. (The Turks have their rich savoury version called *manti*.)

Yet it cannot be denied that pasta is synonymous with Italian cuisine, especially that of the south, where it is ubiquitous. There are literally over a thousand shapes of pasta in all sorts of sizes. Shells and stars, strips and ribbons, long and short, tubes and parcels stuffed with meats or vegetables, cheese, and even fruits.

Italian pasta is made with flour, usually wheat; most industrially produced pasta is made with the fine wheat flour milled from the cleaned endosperm, or heart, of the durum wheat grains. Water or eggs are the binding agents. Fewer Italians make their own pasta (*pasta fatta in casa* – 'made at home') these days, and as manufactured varieties are of high quality this is a perfect convenience food.

For many years it was thought that pasta was fattening. Many pointed to the legendary girth of Italian mamas as proof of this. In fact, peasant women in whatever country, regardless of the produce in the diet, are often thicker bodily in middle age. The truth is that pasta is not fattening at all and the Mediterranean diet is among the healthiest in the world. Athletes, especially professional soccer players, are urged to eat pasta as a staple as it is not only highly nutritious, but the calories also burn off more easily than many other staples. And as final proof that pasta is actually good for the figure I quote the film actress Sophia Loren (real name Sofia Scicolone), who when asked the secret of her beauty replied: 'Everything you see I owe to pasta'. Pasta can have no better recommendation than that.

Pastilles
These little jelly sweets take their name from a Giovanni Pastilla, a skilled Italian confectioner brought to France by Marie de Medici when she married Henri IV. They are usually fruit-flavoured, though there are pastilles made that are soothing for those suffering from a sore throat.

Pastrami
Salted, spiced and smoked beef cut in very thin slices and much eaten in the USA. It is often eaten hot on rye bread and sometimes combined with hot corned beef. Famously served in the New York restaurant Lindy's, where the American comedian Jack Benny ate this as an afternoon snack every day for over thirty years.

Pastry
Made with flour, water and fats, this is the basis for pies, tarts etc. and comes in a variety of forms. Shortcrust pastry varies from very plain to the astoundingly rich in butter and fats. Puff and flaky pastry are made by a different method, in which the fats are left in a more intact form. Puff pastry takes considerable expertise before you get it right (and considerable time as well), and for this reason many people buy ready-made puff pastry (brands such as Jus-Rol abound), and they are of a very high quality. I use the ready mixes simply because I could not achieve such consistency doing it myself. Another reason for this inconsistency on my part might be that, as the

Scottish master baker James Burgess (see **baking**) once told me, my 'hands are too hot'. It is indeed true that cool hands make for light pastry.

Choux pastry uses eggs as well; brioche pastry contains yeast. Necessary for pork pies, game pies and the Scottish mutton pie is hot water crust pastry, which makes for a very strong, crisp and hard durable pastry that will not be saturated by its wet filling.

And then there is the paper-thin filo pastry (known in Hungary as *retes* pastry) used widely in Greece and throughout the Balkans for pastries such as strudels, and for sweet and savoury tarts and pasties. You will occasionally be told how to make this thin pastry in cookery books and TV programmes. In the countries where this pastry is common few home cooks make it today as you can buy ready-made pastry. Filo requires at least two people and a large table to stretch the dough into its required near-transparent slenderness. Throughout most of Europe most pastries and cakes are sensibly left to the specialist *patissiers*: this is most certainly the case with dishes using this delectable pastry.

Pâté

Though in France this is a term for any sort of pastry, elsewhere it now means the filling itself. In France a pâté also means a raised pie – *pâté en croûte*, with the filling encased in pastry – which is usually served hot. To confuse us all further those pâtés, such as those made with liver etc., are eaten cold and can be seen as a sort of meat paste, both smooth and roughly chopped. More confusion: most of these are in fact called terrines by French cooks.

The most famous, and certainly the most expensive, pâté of all is . . .

Pâté de foie gras

This exquisite delicacy has probably excited more passion than any other food. To *aficionados*, of whom I am one, it is an ambrosia: to food fascists it is as fur coats are to animal rights activists. Many people are appalled at the manner of overfeeding the geese, by putting a funnel directly into the birds' throats in order to increase the size of the distended liver. It has to be said, however, that the geese concerned rally round their feeders, desperate to be force-fed.

Pâté de foie gras is a speciality of Strasbourg and is delicately laced with the truffles of the Alsace area. (Two chefs from this area, Clause and Doyen, who had worked for the nobles of the Ancien Régime before the French Revolution and been forced to open a food shop, claimed to be the first to make *pâté de foie gras*.) It is, even in its native Strasbourg, very expensive indeed.

There are a considerable number of dishes that include the pâté, but in my view they are a dreadful waste of what should be eaten very simply with buttered toast and chilled white wine or a glass of **marc**.

Pea

A vegetable grown throughout the world save in tropical climates, it was introduced to the UK as late as the sixteenth century, since when it has become possibly the most widely eaten vegetable in Britain. Apart from **mangetout**, the pods in which peas are carried are inedible. There are a large number of varieties available including the large marrowfat, which can be made into the dish known as mushy peas, much enjoyed in northern England, where it is served either on its own or as an accompaniment to pies. It is said that the former Labour MP Peter Mandelson spied mushy peas on sale in a take-away in some northern city and expressed surprise that a chip shop was serving what he took to be an avocado dip, thus confirming northerners' view that the Labour Party had become impossibly effete. (On that note I recall that the great dandy George 'Beau' Brummel, when asked by a hostess what his favourite vegetable was, laconically replied, 'Madam, I once ate a pea'.)

Peach

I do not care much for peaches: I don't know why for everybody else seems to delight in them. (Though I encountered a dessert in the famous Savini's in Milan that consisted of peaches stuffed with an odd mixture of crushed macaroons – **amaretti** – ground almonds, **marsala** wine, cocoa powder, egg yolk and sugar, lightly sprinkled with white wine and then baked in butter. It was delicious.)

This fruit of a deciduous tree originated in China, though it was introduced to Persia many centuries before Christ. It is now grown mainly in the USA and in Italy. The flesh is very sweet, and the skin possesses a soft down. It is certainly a very beautiful-looking fruit and is often referred to when describing a young girl's lovely complexion. T.S. Eliot's J. Alfred Prufrock asked 'Do I dare to eat a peach?', which does not strike me as such a wanton act of courage at that.

Peach Melba

This dessert consists of a halved peach poached in syrup, then served with ice cream and a raspberry sauce known as Melba sauce (see **ice cream**). It was created and named by the famous chef of the Carlton, Escoffier, in honour of the great Australian operatic soprano. There was an occasion when Dame Nellie ordered the dessert on a trip between Brussels and Vienna on the Orient Express, which prided itself on being able to cater for any tastes. Unfortunately the train had forgotten to take any peaches on board, and an anxious chef served it using a pear instead. It met with Ms Melba's approval, however, and thus was born the delightful *poire Melba*, a much better sweet entirely.

Peanuts

For some reason peanuts seem to have caused an epidemic of allergies among young people in recent years. It is a dangerous allergy too and can cause fatality within an hour or so. One of my god-daughters suffers from it and has to carry a supply of adrenaline to counter the side-effects of any contact with these nuts. As many restaurants, especially Chinese ones, use peanuts and their oil, and any contact, no matter how slight, can cause cause allergy to erupt in seconds, sufferers are often very restricted in their eating-out habits.

Peanuts are also eaten as salted savouries, often as offerings in bars because the saltiness invokes greater thirst, and are used in peanut butter. This purée of the nuts, salt and oil is very popular, particularly in the USA. Peanut butter and jelly (jam) sandwiches were almost a staple diet of the late Elvis Presley. Every American child seems to have been reared on peanut butter, which was good news for former American President Jimmy Carter, who was a millionaire peanut farmer. Peanuts are also known in the UK as monkey nuts and have thus joined the pantheon of faintly risible foods, along with the **coconut** and **banana**.

Pear

This fruit of a deciduous tree is related to the rose family and its origins can be traced to Europe and some parts of western Asia. It has a unique taste and, though it can be used in cooking and for chutneys, its common use is as a dessert fruit. As noted before, it makes the delectable dish known as *poire Melba* and also a classic French dessert using pear halves, ice cream and chocolate sauce called *Poires belle-Hélène*.

I first encountered pears in tins, for fresh fruit, especially one as exotic for the days of rationing after the war as a pear, was often unavailable. I have loved them ever since and, perhaps oddly, still prefer canned pears in sweet syrup to fresh pears. Pears also make a pleasant alcoholic drink called perry, the most famous of which is the brand known as Babycham, which its makers describe, somewhat loosely, as 'sparkling perry'. There are also pear brandies, mostly of German provenance.

Tinned pears mainly come from South Africa and, despite my views on the apartheid system then in force, I could not resist them. Principles do tend to waver when it comes to food.

Pebronata
A sauce which is a speciality in Corsica, made with tomatoes, olives, pimentos, olive oil, garlic, red wine and juniper berries. It is very robust and is often given, spread on bread, to children as a snack. It is very good indeed.

Pecan pie
Made from pecan nuts, which hail from the southern states of the USA, this dessert is sweet and is the traditional pudding for American Thanksgiving dinners. I first saw this at the celebrations held in memory of the Pilgrim Fathers in Hampstead in 1965, where John Lennon, the director Dick Lester, fresh from the triumph of his Beatles film *A Hard Day's Night*, actress Julie Christie and an assortment of American expats enjoying the days of Swinging London, were present. I was not, however, a guest myself. I was employed as a waiter for the beano.

Pepper
Probably the world's most important spice, pepper is now largely imported from India, Indonesia and, in the last hundred

years, Brazil. But why? Virtually every British household has a 'cruet set' and, though the word 'cruet' simply means a vessel for sauces, oils or condiments, the cruet set consisted of a salt cellar and a similarly shaped container for ground pepper. It is almost always ground white pepper: when stale, this tastes medicinal and unpleasant. My discovery of freshly ground pepper was a revelation.

Pepper seeds grow on climbing trees rather like ivy and originally came from India. It became the most important spice in Roman cookery and was very expensive, often equated with gold and silver. A large bale of pepper was sent as a gift to Attila the Hun by the Emperor Theodosius III, and throughout the Middle Ages pepper was taxed and seen as a currency. In short, when you read of the demand for spices in history you are talking of pepper.

Though the use of pepper in the West is almost confined to savoury dishes, it is widely used in sweet dishes in South-East Asia, sprinkled liberally on fruits such as melon, mangoes, peaches etc., and in India is used to flavour **tea**.

White peppercorns are less pungent than black, though I prefer the latter for their flavour. When the waiter comes round, especially in Italian restaurants, with the ubiquitous pepper mill and gives it a few twists, I always demand more because in many pasta sauces the last addition of ground black pepper is as necessary as the **parmesan** cheese, with which too many waiters are equally niggardly. There are also green peppercorns, exported almost exclusively from Madagascar. These unripe berries are marinated in brine or vinegar and are most often used as an accompaniment for steaks. *Steak au poivre* is a favourite dish throughout Europe.

Peppermint

This plant of the **mint** family is cultivated mainly for its aromatic oil, which is used in confectionery and in some liqueurs such as crème de menthe. The oil is also used to flavour the small pungent sweets known as peppermints, reputed by tradition to be sucked all through interminable services in Calvinistic Scottish Presbyterian services as, though they be sweets, they are 'nippy' enough not to be actually enjoyed. Peppermint, usually the spearmint variety, is employed as a flavouring for the disgusting **chewing gum** so much enjoyed by adolescents, footballers, yobs, Americans and others.

Périgord
The cuisine of this region of south-west France has become very famous, not least because one of the most influential, and prolific, writer-chefs of the great days of **haute cuisine**, Marcel Boulestin, wrote his many books in English and championed the cookery of his native Périgord. It is rich cookery, with luscious duck and chicken dishes, cream sauces, elaborate fumets, pâtés and, most important of all, its famous truffles. The black Périgord **truffle** is highly scented and very, very expensive.

Pestle and mortar
A pestle is a sort of thick stick used to grind food into a paste or powder, and a mortar is the bowl in which the paste is ground. Though it is ages old and perhaps could be considered as primitive compared to such technological aids as electric blenders, the old pestle and mortar technique is still usually better as a grinding process. (Pestle and mortar are still the traditional symbol of pharmacies and can yet be seen as hanging signs above their doorways.) Both are often made from marble – especially, if you are as pretentious as myself, from the best Carrara marble.

Pesto
Said to derive its name from the above utensils, this wonderful preparation is made by grinding fresh basil, pine nuts, good

olive oil, garlic and *pecorino sardo* (a sharp ewe's milk cheese) or/and **parmesan** together into a smooth paste. Nuts such as the **walnut** can be substituted for the pine variety. It is a speciality of Genoa and the surrounding area. The sauce is very pungent and rather discordant, and a little goes a long way. It is not, however, for every day and most of us would soon tire of it if it were.

There are a number of proprietary brands on the market: I have never encountered one that is much good and, considering how easy pesto is to make at home, there is little reason to employ them. A similar sauce used in Provence is called *pistou*. There the sauce is used mostly as an addition to soups and stews.

Petits pois
Well, I mean, what's the point of them?

Pheasant
It is in season from late October through to March and when hung properly is very flavoursome. In medieval banquets it was often, as many **game** birds were, presented in its coat of plumes and feathers.

Piccalilli
A type of **chutney** (see also **pickles**). Its ingredients are florets of **cauliflower** and diced vegetable marrow, pickling onions and cucumber, brined then pickled in a mixture of vinegar, sugar, mustard, often turmeric (to give colour) and ginger. It is a condiment much enjoyed in Britain.

Pickles
Items preserved in brine or vinegar. Almost all vegetables can be and are pickled. Pickled onions, usually utilizing the small pearl onions, are a British favourite, as are mixed vegetable

pickles using onions, cauliflower, gherkins (small cucumbers) etc. and a pub favourite in the UK: pickled hard-boiled eggs. Pickles flavoured with dill or dill weed are common in Jewish communities and in Scandinavia. And here's a very outlandish pickle from Iceland: pickled testicles (see **avocado**). Icelanders have some very odd foods (see **hakarl**). Rotted shark meat and pickled testicles in whey do not seem quite what the gourmet is looking for.

Picnic

There are many famous picnics in cultural history. One is the picnic that Charles Dodgson gave for the three little Liddell girls in 1862 when he first unfolded his tale of *Alice in Wonderland*. And in the story Lewis Carroll (for Dodgson was he) has the Mad Hatter's tea party.

Jerome K. Jerome's three men in a boat picknicked memorably by a Thames riverside meadow, and John Betjeman penned a poem on picnics:

Sand in the sandwiches
Wasps in the tea
Sun in our bathing dresses heavy with the wet
Squelch of the bladder-wrack waiting for the sea
Fleas round the tamarisk
An early cigarette.

Every British child has yearned for an invite to the Teddy Bears' Picnic, and the lovely little song invokes childhood innocence to even the most curmudgeonly. And though those French chaps are not the picknickers that the Brits are, was it not Manet who had just that in his famous painting *Le Déjeuner sur l'Herbe*? Mind you, being the salacious French, the female guest was stark naked. Another French note: the attendant, and fully clad, males did not have the decency to remove their hats in the presence of a lady.

Pie

A sweet or savoury filling either covered with or encased in pastry, usually baked in a pie dish. When it is uncovered, it is often referred to as a **tart**. Pie fillings range from the very simple to the elaborate. In rural areas right up until the twentieth century pies, more often than not meatless or containing little flesh, were a staple as the flour from which the dough was made was considerably cheaper than bread flour. For many rustics actual bread was rather a luxury food.

Pigs' trotters

Once an item for the poor, these are now often served as a delicacy and are probably the best-known animals' feet for the table. Often used for their gelatinous qualities in French stews and daubes (see **daube**).

Pilchard

This round-bodied seawater fish of the herring family was once very popular canned, often in a tomato sauce. Though widely respected in Mediterranean countries – sardines (see **sardine**) are young pilchards – it was regarded in Britain as a cheap food-fish, but in Cornwall it was a staple food and there are many traditional Cornish recipes using pilchards. The reason why this should be so is rather shocking. Though the principal industry in the Cornwall of the past was fishing, the more expensive varieties of fish were sold, and the humbler pilchards were left to the Cornish, who thus invented a huge number of dishes from the oily fish. The famous stargazy pie had pilchards in a pastry crust with the heads of the pilchards staring – gazing – upwards. It looks spectacular but is not recommended.

There is a pleasant dish made with pilchards, bacon and hard-boiled eggs covered with pastry which is known in Cornwall as prie hoggitty. The Cornish language, which died out, more or less, in the nineteenth century, is yet retained for its unique cookery terms.

Pineapple

This fruit, native to Brazil (though today the largest exporter is Hawaii), is very exotic-looking and indeed is often used simply for decoration on a platter of other fruits. It is widely canned as chunks or in rings and is used mainly as a dessert. Just after the Second World War it was often made into a cheap and popular **jam**, in the absence of soft fruits, and 1950s' Britain saw canned pineapple, often combined with tinned **cream**, as a common pudding in working-class households. It is often combined with gammon steaks – despite the proletarian reputation of this dish, the combination is very good. Pineapple is also much used in South-East Asian cookery and is necessary to the famed sweet and sour sauce encountered in Chinese restaurants in the West.

Pint

Despite the metrication of the UK nobody, to date at least, has ever suggested going to the pub for a 'litre': they go for a pint. The measurement is 20 fluid ounces. Most Britons also think of milk in terms of pints. Doubtless in years to come the measurement will come to be as archaic as chains and rods and furlongs. But a pint of beer will still be a pint.

Piperade

In the Basque region of France this refers to a dish of scrambled eggs with chopped tomatoes, peppers and ham. In the Spanish Basque area it becomes an **omelette** and is splendidly robust. Basquais cooking is, like the Basques themselves, colourful but rather odd. I used to dine in a lovely cheap little Basque restaurant near the Sorbonne which was a haunt of students in the early 1960s. The food was inexpensive, the wine amazingly coarse and the girls all looked like Juliette Greco. What more could you ask for?

Piroshki

These are small pasties filled with meat, fish or fruit, and sometimes with **caviar** and are popular Russian **hors d'œuvres**. They are sometimes deep-fried rather like the French *boulettes* or such street foods of the Indian subcontinent as **pakoras** or *samosas*.

Pizza

In my childhood there was no such thing as a teenager. That concept grew in the USA, but it was not till the mid-1950s that it was imported to Europe. With the flood of rock'n'roll and teen movies we young Brits discovered teenhood with a vengeance, much to the bewilderment of our parents. What has this got to do with pizza? Well, it was through the importation of the popular comic-strip books starring a crew-cutted character called Archie, and his friends and their bobby-soxer high-school girls, that I discovered what they called pizza pies. I didn't know what they were: I'd never seen a pizza. What is more I didn't realize what the illustration of this pizza was because it didn't look like any pie I knew.

It was to be nearly a decade later that the ordinary Briton first encountered a pizza, and that mainly in London. Today pizza has overtaken hot dogs and possibly even hamburgers as a staple take-away food, certainly among teenagers. Its origins are, of course, in Italy, from where it was taken to America by south Italian immigrants. From Naples to be more precise, where it became, and remains, cheap street food. (Neapolitans would be astonished at the prices demanded for their invention in such outlets as Pizza Hut.) Ironically north Italians did not eat many pizzas either until the dish was brought to them from America.

The pizza consists of a thin bread base (an authentic pizza takes some skill to produce, and it is a splendour to witness pizza cooks in Italy making them in their front windows) and has a covering almost always with a tomato base. The Yanks have, as with everything else, turned this simple bread tart into a riot of over-the-top toppings.

The Neapolitan pizzas are actually very simple, and to my mind very much better. There is the the *pizza napoletana*, with a topping of garlic and tomatoes, and the *alla marinara*, with olives and anchovies, and the famous *margherita*, with **mozzarella**, tomatoes (see **tomato**) and **parsley**, oregano and **basil**. The Pizzeria Piltro in Naples boasts that its original owner, Rafaele Esposito, invented this last-named pizza in honour of Queen Margherita of Savoy, wife of King Umberto, who sent for a pizza when she came to that city to escape a cholera epidemic.

No matter, if you stick to those three above, or a combination of them, you will have a delicious meal and a far cry from those over-rich abominations with tuna and curried chicken, sweetcorn and any old rubbish at all.

There is also the French Provençal version known as *pissaladière*, which uses onions, anchovies, black olives and tomatoes. Sadly this simple and much-loved tart is being corrupted with lavish toppings too.

Ploughman's lunch

This is now said to be traditional and is a pub snack consisting of a slab of, usually tasteless, **cheddar** cheese, a few slices of bread or a bap, **butter** and **pickles**, washed down with a pint of **beer**. It is indeed traditional and was and remains a common snack at midday for many agricultural workers. The use of the term for this little noon-day reviver seems, however, to date from the mid-1960s, when London pubs were wont to offer this, much to the bemusement of bucolic visitors.

Plovers' eggs

The small game birds are rare, and their even smaller eggs are regarded as a gastronomic delicacy. As such no Edwardian hostess could afford to fail to offer them as one of the starters on her menu. This was in fact a sham as, according to *Law's Grocers' Manual* for 1901, 'Gourmets have for years been eating eggs never laid by plovers, and paying fancy prices for them. A large section of the gull family, who are farinaceous rather than fishy in their diet, lay eggs precisely similar to those of the plover. These are collected in hundreds on the small islands in the inland lochs of north Scotland and sent to London. They are ridiculously cheap (to the collectors) and require no dye or artificial flavour to give them artistic verisimilitude.' In an about-turn smart restaurants of today will proudly boast gulls' eggs on their menus.

Plum

Yet another fruit of the rose family, the plum varies from a light amber colour to almost black. Though it is of north European origin, it has become a major ingredient of Chinese cuisine, especially noted in the plum sauce that accompanies the famous Peking duck.

Plums are not as popular a dessert fruit as once they were. But at least they are now known by their own name. It was not always so – in the past in Britain 'plums' were actually raisins, which is why the traditional steamed pudding known throughout every public school and all the British armed forces as 'plum duff' was called exactly that. 'Plum pudding' is a term for the so-called Christmas pudding, an exceedingly rich and rather coarse mixture of raisins and brandy-flavoured, flour-based cornucopia. The English like it. That says enough.

Polenta

This yellow **maize** flour is a staple of northern Italy and is famous in the Veneto region. Though **pasta** is increasing in popularity in northern regions of that country, polenta, bean soups and rice for **risotto** remain the common staples of the north. The maize flour is boiled, made into cakes and fried. Served with tomato or meat sauces, it is very filling, though it is to my mind stodgy and lacking in flavour. It was once a main breakfast food and was believed to cause the old skin disease pellagra because many peasants who suffered from this ate hardly anything else. What too great a reliance on this cereal does cause, however, is the bone disease rickets, a result of a lack of vitamins.

Pollo alla cacciatora

This is an Italian chicken stew made with tomatoes, stock, herbs, especially **basil** or oregano, and **marsala** wine. Though it is largely reserved for special occasions in the land of its origin, it is now a favourite on the menus of American-Italian restaurants. There is also the dish known as *pollo alla Marengo*, named after the Battle of Marengo when, it is said, Napoleon sent his chef off to gather material for a victory lunch. The chef came back with tomatoes, white wine, mushrooms, parsley, black olives and a chicken. Thus a culinary splendour was born.

Pollo is of course Italian for 'chicken'. Until recently Italians regarded chickens as a luxury food, and the fowls were bred mainly in the Tuscany region. Today Italians are delivered of the same flavourless frozen battery chickens as the rest of us, though I know of an Italian restaurant in Leith, near Edinburgh, where the owner, feeling bereft of real chickens, now rears his own for his customers' tables.

Polpette

These are little Italian **hamburgers** flavoured usually with grated lemon peel and **parsley** or **basil**. There is also *polpetonne*, basically a sort of meatloaf. The Italians and the French take as much care over these dishes as they would with the best fillet steak, and just why the Brits see the above as an excuse for cheap ingredients is difficult to understand.

Polyunsaturated fats

The acids found in these come from vegetable oils such as corn, rape, sunflower and soy. They are to be recommended to those who suffer from too high a level of cholesterol. But, it should be noted, too low a cholesterol count is also dangerous to health. It is just sod's law that many people who suffer from high blood pressure also have too low a cholesterol level. Life's a bugger sometimes.

Pomegranates

This rather odd-looking fruit is grown in the Mediterranean area, though it is now also widely grown in South America. The flesh is pink and the juice, which was known in biblical times, is very refreshing: the sweet and lovely liqueur/sirop grenadine derives from this fruit.

Pomme de terre

French for 'potato'. Some classic potato dishes are known by their French names, such as *pommes Anna*, *pommes dauphinois*, *pommes savoyarde*, *pommes duchesse* etc., and are much revered. *Pommes Anna* is a type of potato cake which consists of very thinly sliced potatoes in butter and baked in the oven. *Pommes dauphinois* is a wonderful potato dish which causes much controversy among chefs in that, while there are those who claim that cheese should be involved in it, there are others who believe that the cheese should be omitted and that only cream should be employed. Escoffier insisted on the cream-only version, and I cannot help but agree as this rich and garlicky combination hardly needs another flavour to it. But see **potato**.

Popcorn

This is a comfort food long associated with funfairs, fêtes and especially the cinema, where it is consumed in large bagfuls by plump teenagers. It is made with a special type of maize corn and, when heated, 'pops'. There is little nutritional value, and for myself it is very resistable indeed. There was, however, a very jolly jingle common in cinemas which advertised a particular brand. It went: 'When Master Maize meets Blondie Butter; Wham! It's Butterkist!' The advert showed a long thin chap in the guise of an ear of corn wooing a blonde blowzily bosomed *mädchen* with pigtails. For some reason this ludicrous ad endeared itself to cinema patrons who were wont to chant along with the daft little rhyme. There is an entire history waiting to be written about cinema snacks (see **frankfurters**).

Poppy seeds

These seeds of the lovely red poppies have no narcotic properties whatsoever. Though of Asian origin, they are widely cultivated in Holland and Turkey. They are used much in Jewish cookery, especially in speciality breads (see **challah**). As a child I used to go with my father to Michael Morrison's Jewish bakery in Glasgow's Gorbals, where his son Ian used to give us hot sweet coffee with poppy seeds sprinkled on top. This must have been Ian's own special whim, for I have never seen the practice since in either Jewish or gentile homes.

Pork

This flesh of the pig is used for a great many purposes, from bacons and hams to the huge variety of **charcuterie** in France. Germany and many central European countries possess a large number of recipes for pork-based meals. In Italy and in Spain and Portugal very young suckling pigs are a rare and expensive restaurant speciality. Hungarian cookery uses pork more than any other meats, and the area once known as Transylvania, now part of Romania, has a plethora of pork recipes.

In many parts of Europe, though, and certainly in the UK, pork is regarded as an inferior meat, probably because even up to the beginning of the last century most peasant families and those of the lower agricultural labourers would keep a pig, preserving the pig flesh as hams and bacons, as well as using salted pork throughout the year. In poorer areas, such as Cornwall, or in Ireland especially, few would ever encounter the flesh of cattle or sheep during their entire lives.

Pigs are, however, difficult to herd and are intelligent and independent animals. It is not true that they are hygenically unclean: given their choice, in the wild they do not wallow in their own detritus. Wild pigs are not unknown in parts of middle Europe, and indeed boars and other varieties of swine are much prized for their meat. In parts of France and Italy wild pigs are used to smell out truffles (see **truffle**).

Dietary laws in Muslim countries and among Jewish communities preclude any use whatsoever of the produce of the pig, of course, and pork is virtually unknown to much of the Indian subcontinent. (Though there are pork curries in some of the coastal Indian areas, such as Goa. Sri Lanka also has a famous pork *padre* curry which manages to utilize both pork and alcoholic spirits.)

In some countries pork and pig meats are seen as cheaper, though as pointed out earlier Hungarian cuisine owes much to pork. And Chinese cookery makes great use of pork: the famous *char sui* – pork much marinated – is a very individual feature of many dishes. Literary references include the famous essay by Charles Lamb on the origin of roast pig and, of course, the most famous pig in English literature is P.G. Wodehouse's Empress of Blandings, that fattest of admired sows beloved by Clarence, 9th Earl of Emsworth. The Empress is never likely to end up on any menu at Blandings Castle.

Pork crackling

The crisp and scored skin of roast pork is highly prized by many gourmets. And not only them – it is much beloved of the northern English, who make out of this delicacy what are called 'pork scratchings'. They are now artificially produced in little bags, like **crisps**, and are a feature of many northern pub savoury snacks.

Porkolt

This rich stew made with meats and poultry alike is braised and sautéed and is often confused with the more famous goulash (see **Hungarian food**). The stew usually contains tomatoes, green peppers, onions, paprika and quite often fiery Hungarian liquors or wines. A variant called *tokany* has soured cream added. And of course the ubiquitous little dumplings called *galuskas*. My grandmother, married to a Hungarian, made such dishes regularly, but the best porkolt I ever encountered was not even in Hungary but in a gypsy restaurant in Vienna. Viennese cookery is much drawn from Hungarian food, as one would expect of the capital of the Austro-Hungarian Empire. Even the famous **wiener schnitzel** came from Hungary, though it is almost certainly of Italian origin.

Porridge

Gruels made from any cereal are strictly speaking porridges, though it is Scots porridge oats that are the most famous today. The most well-known brand is Scotts, whose brawny Highland Games competitor has figured on their packets and in their advertising for over a century.

Porridge is usually served with milk or cream and with sugar, though Scots tradition has it that salt is used instead. Another Scottish tradition is that the morning porridge would be emptied into an empty kitchen-table drawer, allowed to set and cool and then cut up into slices for the family. This seems, to say the least, bizarre and I am tempted to doubt the veracity of the legend. Another traditional element is real enough. The wooden stick used to stir the porridge in its cooking is called a **spurtle**, a most splendid and silly word indeed.

Port

This blended and fortified wine from Portugal is mainly proferred as an after-dinner drink. It is especially pleasant with the cheeseboard (particularly with a fine **stilton**) and can be incorporated into soups and sauces. A good vintage port can be very expensive and requires careful handling and decanting (though port and lemon was famously a drink associated with working-class ladies of indeterminate age who were *habituées* of public houses).

Oddly, a large number of the great port firms are of Scottish origin (Grahams, Cockburns etc.), as indeed are the distinguished sherry houses. These companies retain their Scottish links and many of their directors, whose families have long been resident in the Iberian peninsula, are still sent to Scotland for their education. It is rather disconcerting to meet the families in the trade who speak perfect Spanish and Portugese yet who utter their English in Scottish accents. Port is popularly thought to be a tipple that old and grumpy sufferers from gout imbibe. (Dr Johnson claimed that 'claret is the liquor for boys; port for men'. But he added that brandy was the drink for heroes.)

Pot au feu

Literally 'pot on the fire', this meal of meat (in France usually beef) and vegetables is known in every cuisine throughout the world, but the French, as they often do with many another dish, have claimed it as their own. Perhaps the reason is that other cultures regard this recipe of boiled meat preceded by the soup or broth in which the flesh has been cooked as peasant cookery, while the French have elevated it to national renown.

Potato

This remarkable vegetable, discovered by Europeans in the Americas as late as the sixteenth century, when Pedro Cieca, the adjutant of Pizarro, sent some examples of this tuber to his Spanish sovereign. They were at first regarded with considerable suspicion because potatoes are in fact a member of the same family of vegetables (*solanaceae*), as the horribly poisonous mandrake. A nice wee poem has:

> Go and catch a falling star,
> Get with child a mandrake root,
> Tell me where the past years are,
> Or who cleft the Devil's foot.

Of course, this was before the potato became an eatable and John Donne was too early either to eat a potato or to discover that his verse was to become the basis for a number one hit song for the crooner Perry Como in 1958. The potato came into its own in European cuisine with the repeated failure of the cereal crops throughout the periods of unrest of the French Revolution. Antoine-Auguste Parmentier, a French army pharmacist who had first noted this tuber's nutritional qualities when he was fed it as a prisoner of the Prussians during the Seven Years War, saw the potential of the potato as a wide-spread food. On returning to his own country in 1763, he campaigned on behalf of the potato, at first to little avail. The continued famines following the Revolution saw his reasoning vindicated. To this day a great many potato recipes in French cuisine include the name *parmentier*.

But in the British Islands the potato, at first considered with a similar anxiety to that of mainland Europe, had, so to speak, already taken root. Though the land-owning classes did not consume the potato, they welcomed it as fodder for their animals, and that included their peasantry. Agricultural labourers in Cornwall and the north-east of England soon discovered that potatoes could provide sufficient nutrition to enable them to survive failures of wheat and other crops. The Scots and the Irish both came to accept potatoes as a staple of their diet.

In the case of the Irish this became such a staple that – and this may seem incredible to us today – the consumption was 14lb of potatoes a day per head of population. This assertion I first encountered in James Morris's account of the Irish Famine in his *Heaven's Command*. I thought this a publisher's error until I discovered a confirmation in Charles Lever's pamphlet, *History of the Great Famine* (1880). I have to confess that I still don't believe this figure.

But the fact was that the Irish population ate little other than potatoes. When the disease that caused the failure of the potato crop occurred, first partially in 1845, then entirely in 1846, and then again in 1848, the results were disastrous. Situated as the Irish were on the edges not only of Empire but on the last border of Europe, it is difficult to understand how this calamity was not alleviated. In a five-year period between 1846 and 1851 Ireland lost over a third of its population.

POTATO

The Highland population of Scotland did not fare much
better. When Mary Robinson, the former President of Ireland,
visited Scotland, she reminded us all that Ireland and Scotland
shared the same tragedy. Few of us prosperous Scots at the
celebration lunch knew of this circumstance. What was especially poignant was, as Mary told us, that Native American
tribes sent gold and coinage to alleviate the suffering of 'our
brothers in Ireland and Scotland'. The English and the Irish
landowners did little to aid the distress.

But to the potato. It is now common to every cuisine in the
world, in every continent. It can range from simple peasant
dishes to those of *haute cuisine*. In the Anglo-Saxon world it
is the invariable accompaniment to fish or flesh platters. It
has become a dish on its own, and there are hundreds of potato
recipes. And hundreds of varieties. Continental Europeans
prefer, as generally I do myself, the waxy potatoes; UK inhabitants prefer the floury, mealy types, such as Golden Wonder
and Kerr's Pinks (bred originally by James Henry of Banff,
Aberdeenshire, in 1907, and first titled 'Henry's Specials'. The
latter quickly became the most popular variety of this tuber
and is the main potato in Ireland, where it constitutes over
30% of the potato crop), as well as King Edward's and the now
rarely seen Duke of York's.

Currently the Maris Piper is the most common in supermarkets, and pretty tasteless it is. The supermarkets like
Maris Pipers because they are cheap and have regular shapes.
They do not taste as good as they look, but most shoppers are
beguiled by the look rather than what food is for.

Potted hough

A brawn, though usually prepared from shin of beef (hough),
is often known in Scotland as 'potted heid', for it was often
made with a sheep's head. This traditional Scottish preparation is rich, nourishing and very cheap. Every Scottish

butcher once had his own version of it, but it is rarely seen these days. In the wake of the fashion for the old recipes of the Depression of the 1930s I think we can see a return of its popularity.

Pouding Nesselrode

A sweet made famous by the chef Marie-Antoine (Antonin) Carême and named after the Russian Count Nesselrode. It consists of a sweet chestnut purée, maraschino custard, raisins and cream. The somewhat effete writer and journalist Godfrey Winn, who was a keen cook himself, regularly made this for his guests and ever boasted that he, and not Carême, had invented it. When told by one such guest that it was not of his own invention and was named after a count, he swiftly riposted that he made it for 'buggers, not counts'.

Prairie oyster

Though there is indeed an item called this (comprising the fried testicles of an ox), this term is normally used for a so-called hangover cure, a cocktail that includes brandy, vinegar, Tabasco, Worcestershire sauce, ketchup, bitters and an egg yolk. It is presumably a version of this that Jeeves administers to Bertie Wooster on the occasions when the latter has awoken after a strenuous night at The Drones. And Christopher Isherwood's engaging Sally Bowles claims to 'practically live off them'. (This was in fact true of the real-life model for Miss Bowles, Jean Ross, a wealthy Scottish girl who became a cabaret singer in Berlin in the 1930s.)

There is, in my view, only one cure for a hangover: more drink, colloquially 'a hair of the dog'. This is, however, not a wise solution: better just take the hangover. In any case, the guilt's usually worse.

Praline

Most cookery books take this product to consist of crushed or powdered almonds which are then lightly caramelized, and most of them claim they are used chiefly in desserts. Neither assertion is entirely accurate. Praline, especially in France, Belgium and Switzerland, is invariably made with hazelnuts, and sometimes a small addition of almonds, and its major use is in fillings for chocolates. Until recently it was rare to find so-called 'continental' chocolates in the UK and why, considering British companies' ascendancy in chocolate manufacture, there should be such a paucity in imaginative chocs in a box one cannot think. (Few Brits realize that the oddly trianglular-shaped chocolate bar Toblerone is in fact a praline.) But a large proportion of the fillings of Swiss and Belgian chocolates are variants of praline, and very good they are too.

Prandial

Meaning 'relating to dinner' (though the origin of the word is in the Latin *prandium*, meaning a morning or midday meal). The word now usually refers to a drink before dinner and is often used by hearty bourgeois chaps who rub their hands and ask if you want 'a pre-prandial, old boy'. At least they do in the sort of middle-class TV sitcoms that Richard Briers was always in.

Pretzel

There is only one excuse for this, originally German Tirolean, flour-based yeasted and salted baked product, and that is that President George W. Bush once nearly died choking on a pretzel. His father, also President of the USA, notoriously vomited over his Chinese host at a public banquet.

Profiteroles

There was a time when no middle-class dinner party in the UK could escape this dessert of small choux pastry buns filled with whipped cream with a smooth chocolate sauce poured over them. This sweet is an example, like **Black Forest gateau**, which has gone from consumption by the aristocracy to the bourgeoisie and now, with its common presence in super-market frozen food cabinets, to the proletariat. Forget about class though. Profiteroles are, in whatever household, very good indeed.

Proteins
Proteins are essential in the growth, repair and maintenance of the body, and spare protein provides energy. They are found in meat, fish, poultry, game, milk, cheese, eggs, pulses and cereals. An insufficiency of them in the diet leads to mal-nutrition and various bone, intestinal and skin diseases: it can also seriously damage the body's immune system. Thus vege-tarians and vegans can put themselves at serious risk to their health.

Prunes
There must be someone out there who enjoys these wrinkled horrors, which were once liberally given to children by fat dinner ladies along with the nearly as awful **semolina**. See also **dried fruits**.

Pub grub
Though food has always been served in English pubs, and some public houses were and are very celebrated for their food, it is only recently that this term has come to be used, mainly for the chain pub outlets' offerings. Unlike the old pub food, most of the dishes on the menu are pre-prepared and, though cheap, of a low quality. There are, though, still some wonderful pubs that serve food good enough to be mentioned in the *Michelin* and the *Good Food Guide*. I'll mention three – The Dove in Fulham, London, The Philharmonic in Liverpool, and The

Abbotsford in Edinburgh. (That city also has the amazingly ornate Café Royal, which is a public house, but its Oyster Bar and the premises upstairs are actual restaurants, and of an expensive and high-class nature.)

Pumpernickel
A black German rye bread much seen in American Jewish delicatessens and eateries. There are *aficionados* of this. What motivates them one cannot quite grasp.

Pumpkin pie
This is a traditional dessert for the American Thanksgiving celebrations (held on the fourth Thursday each November) and is a pastry tart filled with pumpkin – a vegetable of the **squash** family – and sweetened with molasses, evaporated milk, eggs and spices. It is often paired with pecan pie.

The Thanksgiving dinner has its origins in the first meal that the Pilgrim Fathers are said to have eaten when they landed in the New World. The other courses include the indigenous American **turkey** often stuffed with **wild rice**. It is also a truly splendid feast, and every course and ingredient seems to have been invented by the gods. Besides the Thanksgiving meal mentioned before (see **pecan pie**), at which I waited at table, I have been privileged to be a guest at numerous dinners given by American friends. My pal Todd Garner, a highly sophisticated artist, long European-based, becomes an American backwoodsman on this day every year, and it is a delight to be at his groaning table.

Punch
This libation is traditionally made with rum, water (sometimes tea), sugar, lemons and spice. It is served in large punchbowls, which are often richly ornamental tureens of silver, and ladled into little silver cups or glasses. Still often seen at

balls, it originally became popular at military dances in India in the eighteenth century. The name is said to derive from the Punjabi word *panj* meaning 'five'. Yes, that's the number of ingredients of this refreshing potation.

Putrefaction
The state of decomposition when food rots. The physical appearance and unpleasant odour normally means that it is unfit for consumption. There are numerous exceptions, however, in which the food is intentionally rotted: the South-East Asian **blachan** (also known as *trasi*); a number of cheeses – cheese itself can be said to be a food in a state of decomposing; some truly awful fish dishes such as the Hebridean **guga** and the Icelandic **hakarl**; and, most awesome of all, the saprogenic condiment invented by the Gauls which the Romans prized above all foodstuffs, *garum*, probably the most expensive food the world has ever known. See also **fresh**.

Quail

This small migratory bird is a protected species in Britain, and therefore only birds specially reared for the market are available. Quail's eggs, which are like small versions of hen's eggs, are considered a great delicacy and are indeed very rich and creamy. I once incurred the considerable wrath of a particularly pretentious restaurateur when I wrote of him that he was 'the sort of chef who thought *haute cuisine* was sticking quail's eggs up a plover's arse and boiling the result in Châteauneuf du Pape'. The truth hurt.

Quenelle

This patty is usually finely minced raw fish (though meat or chicken livers are sometimes given this treatment), blended with egg whites or cream, and then lightly poached. They are commonly served with a creamy crayfish sauce. The writer Claudia Roden once wrote that most restaurants seem to think they are just fish cakes, an opinion she shared with Elizabeth David, though Mrs David also assured us that when properly made they are exquisite.

Quiche

Who it was who thought up the aphorism 'Real men don't eat quiche'? I do not know, but for many years I heartily agreed with it. Wedges of bland, soggy, heavy, open tarts were ever-present at finger buffets and were, like many foods offered at such party meals, much to be avoided. And then I discovered a real quiche in a modest little café in Geneva. This is a French-speaking city, and the cookery is essentially of that country. The owner explained that his mother hailed from Alsace-Lorraine, so famous for its onion and cream tarts and, of course, the internationally famous quiche Lorraine. Baked with sharp and pungent onions and heavily peppered, it was delicious. So too were other tarts he made: with prawns, with mushrooms and one, especially, with asparagus. I was converted at last to quiche.

Quince

This relation to the apple and the pear is used in most world cuisines almost exclusively as a preserve, especially as jelly (see **marmalade**). But in South America quince is very popular and is used in extraordinary recipes. The favourite dessert in Argentina, for instance, is what they call 'Policeman's Pudding', which consists of slices of quince-flavoured cheese and quince butter. In Colombia there is a stew of beef which includes quinces, and in Brazil no apple pie comes without a few slices of this fruit.

Quinine

Manufactured from the bark of a tropical evergreen tree, the *chinchona*, this is used medicinally and is the basis of what the British call Indian Tonic Water. Quinine helps relieve malaria – thus the tonic water, which is indeed very pleasant mixed with **gin**.

Quorn

This is a meat substitute (see **soya bean**), made from a myco-protein deriving from a plant that is a distant relative of the mushroom. It is fermented in a similar process to the way yoghurt is made. As a substitute for meat or poultry it does not fool anybody: it is truly, deeply, awful.

R

Rabbit

There was a time when rabbit was a favourite game animal for cooking. In legend it is rabbits that poachers are ever looking for, and in many country areas it was almost the only meat the peasantry were able to procure. It became popular among the middle classes in the nineteenth century because of its rich, gamey flavour and was often made into terrines. The agricultural classes and the urban poor had a high regard for rabbit, and even in my childhood in the 1940s and '50s rabbits were more often eaten than the then expensive chickens.

Rabbit pie was a favourite dish. (Such a pie was one of the comestibles that Fagin, Charley Bates and the Artful Dodger brought the convalescing burglar Bill Sykes in *Oliver Twist*. I cannot resist giving you the menu on that occasion. ' "Sitch a rabbit pie," exclaimed Charley, "that the wery bones melt in your mouth; half a pound of seven-and-sixpenny green, so strong it'll blow the lid off the teapot; two quarten brans; pound of best fresh; and a piece of double Glo'ster".' The criminal classes of the London slums of the day lived, in comparison to the law-abiding poor, uncommon well.)

But the days of the popularity of this small and charming furry little woodland creature immortalized by Beatrix Potter were suddenly ended by a dreadful disease called myxomatosis, which had been introduced into the rabbit population of Australia – the rabbit itself was not native to that continent and had been introduced by misguided British agrarians – in order to control it. It was also used as a means of control by British farmers, and the rabbit has ever since been largely eschewed by the British public. But it still makes sitch a rabbit pie as the wery bones . . .

Raccoon
This small carnivorous rodent of North America is a speciality of Cajun cookery in the Louisiana Bayou region and is, too, often eaten by the indigenous Amerindians of Canada. The pelt was used back in the Jazz Age for the fashionable ankle-length fur coats beloved of the male dandies of the Roaring Twenties.

Radish
This root vegetable of the mustard family can be quite peppery and hot (though not as much as **horseradish**, which, despite its name, is no relation, being of the cabbage group) and is eaten raw, mainly in salads. It was once more common in such salads than today, paradoxically in an age when salads are increasingly a feature of dishes for the table.

Ragoût
Another French term for a rich meat or poultry stew. There are ragoûts in every language, but oddly the Italian term *ragù* is used to describe the world-famous meat sauce for **spaghetti** (see **bolognese sauce**).

Railways

There was a time when a railway journey was an adventure. This was even in my lifetime. The great gleaming, foaming beasts of steam locomotives were hugely romantic. For the even moderately well-off there were porters to take your luggage on board, conductors and guards to look after your every whim, first-class compartments, glossy wood-panelled buffet cars and, of course, the magnificent dining-cars which one could find on any train with even a fairly short journey. The London train from Glasgow and Edinburgh was a journey that was made a luxury by its dining-car, with its snowy napery, gleaming silver, deferential waiters and often very high-quality food and wines. All of this has almost entirely gone in the Britain of today.

On the Continent there is still high-quality food in railway dining-cars. (As indeed there is still a high-quality rail service available.) I once ordered a splendid lunch on a train between Milan and Paris. The meal was superb and the cost, I thought, not unreasonable. It was only when I came to pay the bill that the waiter told me that the price was not, as I had thought, in French currency but in *Swiss* francs. I arrived at the Gare de Lyon literally without a *sou*.

The highest point of intercontinental railway cookery has got to be that once enjoyed by the patrons of the *Orient Express* (see **peach Melba**). Not only did every conceivable luxurious and exotic food find itself in the legendary train's pantries, but the chefs were of world-class renown. Indeed the *Compagnie* regularly engaged the most famous chefs of the age, such as Escoffier, as guest chefs and charged their passengers accordingly.

The famous train, which shuddered along for many years after the Second World War, was finally discontinued in 1977, by now a ragged and shabby shadow, a pale ghost of its former splendour. In the late 1980s the cars were revived, though as more of a novelty than anything else, the passengers being invited to dress up in 1920s' style *à la* Agatha Christie's novel *Murder on the Orient Express*. The food is as magnificent as it was in the train's glory days, but the journey ends at Venice unlike in the days when it went far into the Balkans and the Russias and elsewhere. The cost of the fare is suitably exorbitant.

But the demise of the once magnificent dining-cars in the railway system – in Britain at any rate – is not the only aspect of railway catering services to be deplored. For over sixty years the major area of training cooks, chefs and waiting personnel lay in the great railway hotels. Demolished, sold on or virtually empty today, the hotels of which every large British city once boasted are gone. So has any idea of having a pleasant railway journey.

Raisins

As a child I could easily differentiate between the three main varieties of dried grapes. I didn't like currants, and I still don't. Made from black grapes, to my taste they were nasty black, hard, bitter things. Unlike sultanas, which are soft and juicy and made from white muscat grapes. I perceived raisins as somewhat in-between. They are used in the making of many fruit cakes, and other desserts. Also of course in the Scottish speciality **black bun** etc. and in a flat fruit slice once often seen in commercial bakers' shops which consisted of impacted currants and raisins sandwiched between two layers of a thick flaky pastry. It was known as a 'flies' cemetery' because it did indeed look like the corpses of dead insects.

Raisins were once given to children as sweets, and a company, I think called Sun-Pat, sold them in sachets as confectionery, often chocolate-coated.

Raita

The custom of handing round **yoghurt** and **cream**, both fresh and soured, with meat and poultry dishes, is common in the cuisines of the Balkans and the Russias, and in north African cookery. It can be seen in Indian food, often as this sambal, made with yoghurt and diced cucumber with spices such as **coriander** and chilli pepper. Raita sometimes contains other vegetables as well as cucumber. There is also a Provençal dish called *raito*, which has nothing in common with the above: it is a ragoût with tomatoes, walnuts, red wine, herbs and spices, and is traditionally served with veal escalopes on Christmas Eve in that area of France.

Ramekins

These small, individual, tightly lidded pots are used to bake, or boil, eggs and sometimes pâtés. They are usually made of vitreous china and can be beautifully decorated.

Rape

A vegetable of the cabbage family which is grown even more widely these days than before, as it makes good animal fodder, and its seeds yield a great deal of edible oil. Its flowers are a bright and bilious yellow, and many farmers now grow it because, while they can still maintain that they are growing the crop as a fertilizer when fields are lying fallow and thus claim government grants, they can then sell on the produce. Hay fever sufferers (such as myself) have come to hate it because of the amount of pollen the crop produces.

Raspberry

A good few years ago, when I was writing a series on Scottish castles for a German magazine, I stopped off for the night in the small town of Blairgowrie in Perthshire, that rather wealthy part of what is a poor country. Coincidentally I got talking to a

German visitor in the hotel bar. I took him for a tourist, albeit an unusual one, for he was expensively dressed in a lounge suit and tie. He turned out to be in Scotland to buy raspberries for his conserves company. For what he, a German, knew and I, a Scot, didn't was that the largest growers of raspberries in the world are in Scotland, with the Blairgowrie area yielding three-quarters of the Western world's commercial crop.

This ignorance on my part can be excused a little, for it was not until the beginning of the twentieth century that a group of market gardeners from nearby Angus decided to move from the traditional strawberry to the production of its relative (both are of the rose family), and it was as late as 1946 that the Scottish Raspberry Investigation was set up at Dundee University.

Raspberries are very sweet and give off a rose-like perfume. They are sold fresh but can also be found as frozen, canned and puréed, though there has in recent years been a very great increase in both fresh and frozen.

Raspberries also make a pleasant wine, some fine liqueurs and a marvellous vinegar, much used lately by the more imaginative chefs. And also, of course, the wonderful jam from this lovely fruit: in my view the nicest jam of all. (And on that point, there is a short story, by English writer Angus Wilson titled just that – 'Raspberry Jam'. It is one of the most chilling stories I have ever read. See also **strawberry**.)

Ratafia

This liqueur, rather similar to the Italian **amaretto** and also made from almonds, was once very popular in Britain. Georgette Heyer's Regency romantic novels have their characters constantly quaffing this stuff. The taste for sweet wines and liqueurs has rather fallen into desuetude in the last fifty years. There are also ratafias, little macaroon biscuits that are almost identical to the **amaretti** of Italy.

Ratatouille

In Provence this vegetable stew made with aubergines, tomatoes, onions, peppers, garlic, courgettes and olive oil is as common as HP Sauce is in Britain. (There is also a Turkish version, **imam bayeldi**).

Back in the mid-1960s, at the height of Swinging London, I remember that every Chelsea trattoria had this on the menu. Ratatouille seems to have lost its novelty value, however, and is sadly rarely seen as anything other than a sort of side-dish used to mask inferior steaks in cheap British bistros. But it is still very good indeed.

Ravioli

To anyone who has only ever encountered these small cushions of meat-filled pasta in tins, with terrible so-called tomato sauce, real ravioli will come as a taste revelation. Filled pasta parcels exist throughout many world cuisines. You will find **kreplach** in Jewish cookery, *manti* in Turkey, *pierogi* in Poland, *vareniki* in the Ukraine, and *pel'meni* in Siberia, not to mention the huge varieties of the little snacks seen throughout China and called wontons, usually in the West served in clear soup: this is common with many of these stuffed pasta parcels. Fillings can be meat, poultry or vegetable (in Italy many ravioli are filled with **spinach** and ricotta cheese), and there are sweet fillings too.

Such parcels come in many shapes and sizes, especially in Italy, and outside that country you no longer need to be aghast at the tinned rubbish that once was ravioli. There are a number of commercial brands of similar products now available in the UK and elsewhere (*tortellini*, *capellini* etc.): they are of a high quality.

Recipe
Just when this word took over from 'receipt', and why the latter came to mean in the English language a written acknowledgement of goods received and the former remains firmly a list of ingredients or instructions for some food or drink one cannot tell, but they were once one and the same. What is certainly true is that the practice of ladies giving each other little handwritten notes – 'That was delicious; you simply *must* give me the recipe for it!' – has long since died out. After my mother died, I came across hundreds of such little notes tucked into numerous books and handbags. I was unaware before of the levels of hypocrisy to which my mother, like other mothers, could stoop.

Red herring
This old-fashioned method of steeping whole herrings in brine and then smoking them for two weeks produces a very strong flavour and aroma, and it exists in reality as well as being a metaphor. The origin of the figurative use is also in fact: hunt rivals would draw a red herring across a fox course to confound the hounds with its smell, and thus divert them away from their own hunting courses.

Red kidney bean
Also known as the Mexican bean. This is widely used in the famous Tex-Mex dish *chilli con carne*. The beans must be boiled beforehand to destroy harmful toxins (see **beans**). Red kidney beans are available pre-cooked in cans. A very good idea too.

Reindeer
This speciality meat is common enough in some Scandinavian countries. Reindeer tongues are considered a great delicacy. I doubt if today's Britons would consider eating little Rudolph though.

Rennet
See **junket**.

Restaurant
Until the French Revolution there was no such establishment, as we know it today, as a restaurant. There were inns and taverns where food would sometimes be provided. The standard for the main part would not be high, unlike that of the large and aristocratic households, which would have their array of cooks and chefs, *patissiers*, bread-makers and other specialists.

After the fall of the Ancien Régime some chefs, as mentioned elsewhere (see **chef** and **French cuisine**), fled to other countries, especially England, but others were moved to open up shops selling street food. There is considerable historical dispute as to who it was who opened the first restaurant in Paris, but it is widely held that the title of 'restaurant' was derived from the shop opened by Marcel Boulanger in Paris in 1756, where he sold soups and rich broths as restoratives or *ristoratifs* – not as fine food at all, but as health products for people exhausted by the daily grind of work and business. He called his shop 'La Ristorante'. The word became *restaurant*, though the Italians, who later opened up similar establishments, maintained the word as *ristorante*.

M. Boulanger, despite the fact that his name means 'baker', was a pharmacist. You shouldn't be surprised that so many French food innovators, such as Antoine-Auguste Parmentier (see **potato**), were pharmacists, for in the Middle Ages pharmacists were also spice merchants and grocers. (Though not the other way round: Louis XII stated that grocers could not purvey pharmaceutics. The French Revolutionary law of 21 Germinal forbade grocers to sell medical products and the law is still in force, much ignored, in France today.)

By the early Victorian age restaurant eating became fashionable throughout France, and later was transported to London and other large cities. In the continent of Europe restaurants grew in status and came to be as socially acceptable as private dining. Indeed as the reputation of the chefs in the smarter establishments developed, even the upper classes soon regarded eating 'out' as *de rigueur*. It took much longer in the Anglo-speaking world. London had some discreet little restaurants which had some private dining rooms, though it was the gentlemen's clubs that initially had the best food. The Reform Club had the trail-blazing Alexis Soyer in the 1850s (Soyer was trail-blazing enough to be able to sell some of his recipes to Crosse & Blackwell for bottling, a commercial notion that the later Escoffier was to exploit in canned soups), but the restaurant explosion did not occur in the UK until much later in the century.

Though there were still many small restaurants in London, as well as various chop houses and such, it was probably the opening in 1867 of the Café Royal by Daniel Nicols (real name Daniel Nicolas Thevenon) and his wife, Celestine, that first set out the idea of restaurant eating as a fashionable sport.

Later in the 1880s César Ritz set up his restaurant in Richard D'Oyly Carte's Savoy Hotel, and brought the young Auguste Escoffier as chef with him. At first the Savoy provided their patrons with private supper rooms, but Ritz soon realized that a public restaurant gave an opportunity to see and be seen and, as Escoffier himself stated, it 'allowed ladies to show off their magnificent dresses'.

By the 1890s restaurants were a very major part of the social whirl indeed, as much as the theatre, opera, ballet or art gallery openings. The Savoy and the Café Royal were glittering palaces but so, on a smaller, and sometimes even more exclusive, scale were restaurants such as Kettner's, Pagani's, The Florence or

Romano's in the Strand. These were restaurants for the well-off, not to say rich. There were few outlets in London for the middle class until John Pearce, an ex-barrow boy, opened his first restaurants in 1892, where City clerks and their sweethearts could dine in some splendour at a reasonable cost. The 'Pearce and Plenty' shops were very successful, as were the later Lyons Corner Houses (see **tea shop**).

But it is to the exclusive end of the restaurant market that you have to go in order to experience the highest quality. Though burger bars are today's version of the Dickensian chop houses, they are not what patrons would think of as part of what could be called the Restaurant Experience. Even up to the early 1960s restaurants of the first quality were exclusive (in my childhood no working-class people ever visited a top-class venue, and would have felt uncomfortable if they had), and the 'little place in Soho' where Agatha Christie's characters would be greeted by a deferential Luigi or a plump, motherly Maria, still existed, for the majority of Britons, only between the covers of fiction. Yet every Brit has heard of Maxim's in Paris. He has just never eaten there.

Retsina

I was introduced to this odd resin-flavoured Greek wine in a little Greek restaurant, little more really than a café, in Glasgow. (The restaurant, The Golden Kebab, is still there and still fairly basic. But still very good.) I didn't like it at first but was strangely drawn to its flavour. It is one of those tastes that you either cannot abide or demand more of.

Rhubarb

This vegetable, a member of the dock family, is used as a fruit and has become, surprisingly, very fashionable in up-market restaurants throughout Europe. Surprisingly, I say, because probably every Briton brought up during and just after the

Second World War detests it: in the absence of fresh fruits we were given endless amounts of this prolific weed.

Rice

When I told my schoolmates at my primary school that we sometimes had rice instead of potatoes, they were frankly incredulous: to Scottish children of the 1950s rice could only furnish a pudding. They asked our teacher to test the veracity of my claim. Mr Kidd told them that rice as a basis for many savoury dishes was common throughout Asia and that the Chinese especially consumed it. The result was several months of being taunted with the nickname 'Chinky'. Not for the first time was I put into distress by my father's taste for culinary exotica.

But rice is indeed the staple of China and all of the countries of South-East Asia. In India too, though in the far north of the Indian subcontinent breads such as **chapati** and *naan* are more common than rice.

There is a large variety of rice grown, including long-grain, short-grain, polished, Carolina, **basmati**, patna, **arborio**, brown, white and **wild rice** (though this is not, in fact, a rice at all), and rice can be made into flour, flakes and even edible paper. It can also be fermented, and the Chinese rice wine, which when sweetened tastes rather like sherry, can be extremely potent.

Though rice is not so common in Anglo-Saxon countries, it is widely eaten in the Balkans, Spain, Africa and northern Italy (see **risotto**).

Rice pudding

After some consideration (during which mental exercise I thought of **mince**, **tripe** and **prunes**) I have decided that there is no more disgusting dish than this. Sometimes it is, God forbid, combined with the aforementioned prunes. But rice pudding has given rise to a lovely metaphor, as in 'he couldn't kick the skin off a rice pudding'. Enough said.

Risi e bisi

This delectable dish is very economical, consisting as it does of a simple **risotto** with green peas (they must be fresh) and sometimes a little diced ham. With added butter and some grated **parmesan**, it is very good indeed. It is a little different from the traditional risottos in that more liquid is used, and more of it at a time. Also, unlike the Milanese version, it is not to be stirred. North Italian mums feed their bambinos on *risi e bisi* many a lunchtime. North Italian children lap it up.

Risotto

If I have boasted before of my culinary achievements (see, for example, **lasagne**), they are as nothing to my risotto. My brother Brian is so mystified by the recipes he insists on following from cookery books that nowadays he simply asks me to cook it for him. I have tried to show him how simple this magnificent dish is to make, but he, and many others, somehow cannot grasp the secret.

The secret is there in front of his and their eyes. First, you need the very best-quality **arborio** rice, from Tuscany. You will find packets of this in supermarkets, but such products are merely adequate. Go instead to an Italian deli and ensure you obtain the real thing. The second secret is **saffron**, without which no real risotto can be made. (Though it is not used in vegetable risottos: this spice would tend to overpower the delicacy of such lovely risottos as that made with, for example, **asparagus**.) Do not use powdered saffron if you can help it. Use the genuine article, the expensive filaments of this remarkable ingredient. And the third secret is: do not take your eye off it as you cook.

Risotto is a rice dish that, as Elizabeth David observed, breaks all the rules of rice cookery. The rice is slightly sautéed in butter or oil, and then the liquor (stock, white wine) is added little by little until the rice absorbs it. Stir from time to time using a wooden fork.

The classic *risotto milanese* was said to have been invented when an apprentice stained-glass worker, asked to prepare lunch for the artists, had not washed his hands of the residue of saffron used for colouring the glass. The result was this risotto, which is often served with **osso bucco**, slices of shin of veal. All other risottos are made with the fish or meat or vegetables cooked along with the rice. It is a sumptuous dish, and if you make more than enough (and you should), the leftover risotto can then be made into *supplì alla telefono* (see **leftovers**).

Despite Milan's (and the Lombardy region's) pre-eminence in the matter of risotto, the best I have ever tasted was in Turin in Piedmont, at an extraordinary restaurant called Del Cambio, where one of the architects of the unification of Italy, Camillo Cavour, was wont to dine. The décor looks quite unchanged from his dining days of the 1850s, but the prices surely have risen because the risotto with sweetbreads was by no means cheap. But it was nearly as good as the risotto I make myself.

Roast beef

Though other joints of meat, such as **lamb** or **pork**, are also roasted, it is the Roast Beef of Olde England that has gone down in legend. For most English people throughout the centuries the legend would be more of a myth, for meat, especially beef, would rarely have crossed a peasant's table. The legend of *le rosbif* has crossed the English Channel, and the French are particularly convinced that every Briton consumes this daily. J.K. Huysmans (see **English cookery**) wrote of this.

Traditionally roast beef comes with **horseradish** sauce, **roast potatoes**, and Yorkshire pudding. In reality most Brits overcook the beef beyond belief, especially the belief of the French and other Europeans who, quite rightly, prefer to roast their joints of beef rare, with the middle pink and even, like myself, bloody. Bloody right too.

Roast potatoes

I include this as a heading because it is one of my favourite dishes of all time and I could eat them, alone, with perhaps a little gravy, and nothing else. But there are so many cooks out there who do not know how to cook this delectable food that here I must explain how to make perfect roast potatoes.

First you should parboil the potatoes (and get the right variety of potatoes: the otherwise splendid new potatoes, for instance, are not suitable for roasting). Incidentally, you can deep-fry boiled potatoes. This will not have the same result as roasting but is still a grand item on your plate. For roasting try to obtain the Golden Wonder, Kerr's Pinks or King Edward varieties: they have a lower water content and lend a crisp finish with a wonderfully floury interior. Next, use dripping or, if you prefer, a mix of good oil and butter, to roast. By all means put the potatoes in a roasting pan beneath your roast meat to catch the fat, but do not put the potatoes alongside the meat – the spuds will become soggy. And last, do not roast too long as the over-hard bullets that are too often put on your plate as roast potatoes are a travesty of one of the most majestic of baked delights.

Rogan josh

A rich lamb curry from the North-West Frontier which uses tomatoes. Though tomato purée is much included in many of today's curries, rogan josh has a strong element of the fruit included and is subsequently a deep red colour. Tomatoes were late in being introduced to the subcontinent, and a curry with their presence is still considered as bestowing prestige in rural India.

Roll

Though this describes any food item that is rolled, such as meat or even fish (the **herring** rollmop), in my childhood a roll was a bread roll. Though bread rolls are seen in every restaurant with every meal, they were, in Scotland, essential to every breakfast. These mini loaves are as popular in Scotland today as they were when I was young, and their popularity has never waned. Most Scots prefer sandwiches made with bread rolls to those made with slices of bread. Thus a cheese roll, salad roll, bacon roll and, most dear of all to the urban Scot's heart – and it is not good for the heart either – a roll and sausage, not at all the same thing as that sausage roll which is made with puff or flaky pastry. And one last thing on rolls. Burnt ones – so-called 'well-fired' rolls – are much liked in Caledonian households.

Roly-poly pudding

While normally I largely eschew puddings, I make an exception for this piece of suet pastry spread with jam and then rolled up and baked. In fact, I do more: I make room for it and would gladly forego the main course to ensure my full enjoyment of this British favourite. Children and servicemen love it. Why it should have been such a morale booster to British troops in the Second World War I do not fully comprehend, but it was. Even the snobbish Evelyn Waugh wrote in his wartime diary that 'jam roly-poly day' was looked forward to 'nearly as much as weekend leave'.

Romertopf

This is the brand name for a highly decorative German version of the chicken brick and is a porous earthenware pot capable of holding an entire chicken or joint of meat. It is made of terracotta and, like the chicken brick, will retain the flavours and juices of the meat cooked inside it. No additional fat is needed. It is a highly effective way of cooking healthily, and potatoes and vegetables are also excellent cooked in this manner.

Roquefort

This blue-veined ewe's milk cheese is protected by French law. It is ripened in caves in the Périgord region. Astonishingly, given the Chauvinism of most French cooks and gourmets, the English **stilton** has recently been considered by them to be a superior blue-veined cheese to their native product. There are even those who prefer the Italian gorgonzola.

Rose water

An ingredient of many sweets and desserts in Balkan, Arab and Indian cuisines, this is distilled from the petals of roses, which grow widely in Iran and throughout the Balkans. The essence is used in such confectionery as *loukoumi* (**Turkish delight**). It is also used in the perfume industry (see **attar**).

Rosemary

This herb, rather like seeds really, is most often used with **lamb**, but I must admit I do not like it much, though I enjoy its aroma. The flowers of the rosemary bush were said to have been originally white, but were changed to blue when the Virgin Mary hung her clothes up to dry on a bush.

Rosti

This is a Swiss dish made from grated potatoes and chopped onion and fried in fat. There are variants of it elsewhere, perhaps the closest relative being the American **hash browns**. Other dishes made with grated potatoes are the Irish **boxty** and the Jewish favourite potato latkes (fried pancakes), which in turn are similar to the German **kartoffelpuffer**. Latkes are usually served with salt beef and pickles and were a common afternoon snack in the legendary Lindy's restaurant in New York.

Swiss cookery has few speciality dishes of its own (though see **fondue**), and the food of this beautiful Alpine country is based on whatever region you are in – French-, German- or Italian-speaking. But rosti makes a welcome change from the ubiquitous French fries.

Rotisserie

Until I first travelled to Europe at the age of twenty-one, the only time I ever saw food roasted on a spit was in films set in medieval times, with the likes of Errol Flynn jouking about kitchens and stabbing folk. In France I met roasting on a spit when I encountered it in little bistros with suckling pig. Years later it was introduced to Britain in supermarkets and such, with whole chickens threaded through an iron rod. The result, especially when the chickens or other meats are of good quality, is very flavoursome indeed. Probably the most common example of rotisserie cooking in the UK today is the doner kebab. But do not dismiss the rotisserie-cooked whole chicken in a quality supermarket/delicatessen.

Rowanberry

The bright orange berries of the ornamental rowan tree are very bitter, but when blended with apples and sugar they furnish an excellent jelly accompaniment for **venison**.

Traditional in Scotland, there are a great many poems and songs (including a famous one by Rabbie Burns) featuring this tree and its fruit. In Scotland the Rowan Tree is a popular name for tea shops and pubs, of which one, The Rowantree Inn, Uddingston, near Glasgow, is not to be missed. It is unique and looks like an elaborate Art Nouveau church. It does not, sadly, serve venison or rowanberry jelly.

Rum

When writer and jazz singer George Melly titled his autobiography *Rum, Bum and Concertina* he was paraphrasing the old Royal Navy dictum concerning life aboard ship 'Rum, Sodomy, and the Lash'. Rum indeed was the drink below ship: the officers drank **gin**. The daily rum ration tot became rum with added hot water and was called 'grog': it was abandoned by the Senior Service only in 1979. (The practice of adding hot water was introduced about 1740 by a famous Royal Navy sea dog, Admiral Vernon, who was known throughout the fleet as 'Old Grog' because of his coat made of a weatherproof cloth known as 'grogram'.) But rum still continues to be a favourite tipple for mariners throughout the world.

The spirit is made from fermented cane sugar and is produced mainly in the Caribbean, where it is the major drink. Its distinctive flavour makes it a common ingredient of cocktails and, of course, **punch**. It is also used in sweets and desserts such as rum baba, a **savarin**-style baked **yeast** pudding served with cream and rum syrup. And it is often included in meat and fish dishes from the West Indies, and also in Creole cookery in Louisiana. Elsewhere in the USA, however, rum is viewed as cheap alcohol fit only for alcoholics. Thus bootleggers were often referred to as 'rum-runners' and writers such as Raymond Chandler and Ernest Hemingway would describe habitual drunkards as 'rumpots'. Both of them would know all about that too.

Rump steak

Though in the south of England this cut from the rear end of beef cattle is considered a prime cut and expensive, it is often the preferred beef cut in Scotland for stews, and many Scots consider this high-quality cut not quite correct for grilling or frying, though it is equal to that treatment. Scottish butchery differs from that of England and is more akin to that of the Continent. Beef is therefore generally more expensive in Scotland than it is south of the border. Thus a certain snobbish attitude to cheaper cuts of beef.

Rutabaga

This is the American name for the yellow-fleshed swede or **turnip**. I love this melodious word (which I first encountered in the list of ingredients in proprietary brands of fruit chutney). It sounds like an especially rumbustious pavane at a barn dance in the Blue Ridge mountains. This turns out to be quite logical. Rutabaga is also American slang for a rustic or hayseed.

Rye

A cereal popular in Scandinavia and parts of northern Europe, where it is used to make 'black' breads such as the German pumpernickel, which is loved in both German taverns and in New York Jewish eateries such as Lindy's. In North America it is the basis for their rye whiskey, while bourbon is made from maize (see **whisky**).

S

Saccharine
This horribly sweet sugar substitute, which is useful to diabetics, is made from coal tar and is today often used, as a word, to denote a sickly sweetness in films or especially lachrymose novels etc. and is thus usually a pejorative term.

Sachertorte
This rich chocolate cake was created by Frau Sacher in her restaurant, which stills exists to this day, in Vienna. (It was not in fact the creation of the pastry cooks in the famous Hotel Sacher in Vienna, as is commonly thought.) The gateau is covered with a heavy, thick, crisp chocolate icing and is derived from the *tortas* of Hungarian patisseries. I have indeed eaten this in Vienna but not in Sacher's: to eat there you have to book well in advance.

Saffron
This member of the crocus family, *crocus sativus*, grows in the wild on hillsides from Italy to Kurdistan, but the cultivated variety is mainly produced in the Valencia area of Spain.

The three stamens of each flower produce the most expensive spice in the world, and the reason for its high price is simple: it takes between 70,000 and 80,000 stamens to produce a pound of saffron, and each flower has to be picked by hand.

As well as being a food spice, saffron was and still is used as a colourant dye. (The name comes from the Arabic *za' faran*, meaning 'yellow'. Today the saffron robes of Buddhist monks are coloured by the saffron substitute **turmeric**, which is often used in curries as well, though of course the flavour is very different indeed.)

As to the flavour of saffron, it is unique and there is no substitute at all for it. The *risotto milanese* cannot do without it, nor can a proper Spanish **paella** be produced in its absence. Luckily a very little of it goes a long way. The proper method is to infuse a few threads in a small amount of hot water. (There is powdered saffron, though this is never as effective as the original stamens.) Arab cuisine also uses it.

In Britain it is today rarely used save in Cornwall, where it features in a number of savoury dishes but is especially used in the Cornish saffron cake. This seems unusual in such a poor part of the UK until you realize that saffron was brought to their rocky shores by Spanish fishermen. Yet at one time it was a popular spice in Britain: indeed it was such a common crop in Essex that a town is named after it, Saffron Walden. It is a kingly spice and seems an unlikely source for this douce, prosperous and bourgeois, bloody awful little town. One other oddity. It is hardly ever employed in French cuisine. But you will find that the above chaps, while depending much on the use of herbs, do not use spices so readily.

Sago

Once a staple of **school dinners**, like **rice pudding** and **semolina**, this is truly vile and generations of schoolchildren have called it 'frogspawn', which it does indeed resemble in appearance. And in taste.

(A literary reference here: in Noel Coward's *The Swiss Family Whittelbot* revue (1923), a splendidly spiteful spoof of the Sitwells' pretentious *Façade*, he renamed Osbert, Edith and Sacheverell Sitwell as, respectively, Gob, Hernia and . . . Sago.)

Salads

I do not appreciate salads, any of them. In Edinburgh there was a vegetarian restaurant, Henderson's, which sold nothing but salads. I occasionally ate there because very silly girls opted for boring salads instead of proper food, and if you wanted to get the knickers off them there was indeed a culinary price to pay.

I also resent the side portion of bits of lettuce and slivers of tasteless beef tomatoes that frequently comes with perfectly respectable meat dishes. Salads can be slightly enlivened with dressing of oil and vinegar and mustard (French dressing, otherwise known as vinaigrette), or with **mayonnaise** or even salad cream. There are a great many different salads, however, from the American invention of Caesar salad (created in 1924 by Caeser Cardini in his Tijuana kitchen when he had a sudden rush of guests and a nearly empty larder), to that which I do enjoy: potato salad. I will not burden you with more mentions of the many salads that exist: it is damn near as boring writing about them as it is eating them. Lots of women like them.

Salami

There is much confusion in the British mind concerning these usually hard preserved meats which are almost always served thinly sliced. The confusion arises because many Britons do not realize that every Italian province has its own traditions and recipes. The salami most commonly seen in British super-markets is the famous *crespone*, usually known as *salami milano*, which is made with beef, pork and slabs of pork fat. There are a great many such meats, and some are rather bland, such as **mortadella**, and some highly spiced and peppery, such as the rarely found *salami ungherese*, originally a Hungarian recipe, which uses pork meat, garlic, peppercorns and paprika, and is flavoured with white wine. But there is seemingly an endless supply of different salamis. They are common as **hors d'œuvres** and make up a major part of the *antipasti* that are the usual start to a meal in Italian households and restaurants.

Though such a style of eating was uncommon in my child-hood, I remember the first time that, as a young man in my early twenties and moving in more sophisticated circles, I first had a repast of *antipasti* – salamis, several types of con-tinental cheese, olives, tomatoes, pickles, crusty bread and chilled white wine. We ate **al fresco** in the rambling back garden of a house in Hampstead. I remember this very well because a young girl who was studying at the Royal College of Music came out with a marvellously pretentious request. Knotting her eyebrows and clearly wishing to be thought to be entertaining her muse, she asked the assembled company if any of us had manuscript paper on our persons. One of them did.

Salmagundi

There are conflicting descriptions of this old-fashioned dish. Some claim that it is made with vegetables, pickled herring, beef and chicken, and vinegar and oil. So suggest many newer cookery books, but Eliza Acton in her *Modern Cooking for Private Families*, first published in 1845, gives a recipe for a hotch-potch using minced veal, eggs, anchovies, olives and vinegar. It sounds very discordant, and I have never actually seen it on any menu, unlike its Scottish cousin **gallimaufry**, which has made a cautious return to some native-style restaurants in that country.

There is, however, a dish popular in Nova Scotia in Canada called Solomon Gundy, which consists of pickled herrings, onions and spices. And then there is of course the rather nasty nursery rhyme which goes as follows:

> Solomon Grundy
> Born on a Monday
> Christened on Tuesday
> Married on Wednesday
> Took ill on Thursday
> Worse on Friday
> Died on Saturday
> Buried on Sunday
> This is the end
> Of Solomon Grundy.

Nursery rhymes fair cheer you up.

Salmon

Until recently this was regarded as very much a luxury fish: a rarity seen only on the table of gastronomes. It is an anadromous fish. (It is born in fresh water, spends most of its life in the sea and returns to its native river to spawn. This is the opposite of such sealife as **eels**, which see the light of day in the sea, spend their lives in fresh water and end their lives back in the oceans. They are known as catadromous fish.) Since about 1969 there has been a spectacular development of salmon farming, for good or ill. Those who argue the ill side claim that farmed salmon are grossly inferior; those for farming point out that it is now affordable and that a good, well-kept farmed fish is as well flavoured, or nearly, as the wild, river-caught salmon of the salmon beats in the Spey or the Tay rivers of Scotland. What is true is that about 130,000 tonnes of salmon produced each year are farmed, and perhaps 600 tonnes of wild salmon legitimately caught. (It is estimated that around 200 tonnes of the wild variety are illegally caught or poached.)

But that is the Atlantic salmon, of which variety the Scottish is the most highly prized. The Pacific salmon is a different story. The varieties of this larger and oilier fish come as sockeye, coho, red or king salmon or the commonest, the pink, and the chum, the latter two varieties being usually used for canning. (There are other names for the above, such as chinook.)

The Pacific salmon is coarser in taste, though some, including myself, actually prefer it to the costlier Atlantic. To be frank, I find the delicate flavour of salmon rather bland, especially as it is more often than not overcooked and can become dry as it loses its slight fattiness when thus presented.

But smoked salmon is a different matter entirely. If of the highest quality, Scottish smoked salmon is majestic. Thinly sliced and eaten with thin wholemeal bread, fresh unsalted butter and a little lemon juice, and perhaps a sprinkling of coarse-ground black pepper, this is a meal in itself and it joins, to my mind, beluga **caviar** and **pâté de foie gras** as foods that are even more magnificent than their just reputations.

Salmonella

This bacteria is the most common cause of food poisoning and, though it is rarely fatal (except among the very elderly or very young infants), it is extremely unpleasant. Symptoms of such food poisoning are severe headaches, diarrhoea and vomiting. These can take several days, occasionally up to a fortnight, to subside. Care should be taken to ensure basic personal and kitchen hygiene and freshness of food ingredients. What I can tell you is that food poisoning is not the same as an 'upset stomach' and is not very cheery at all, though I did manage to write a column on the subject when I was suffering myself. I did it whilst undergoing all the symptoms. It is amazing what you can achieve when you are a freelance writer and need the money.

Salsa verde
A famous and delicious Italian vinaigrette sauce which includes **capers**, **garlic**, **olive oil**, anchovies (see **anchovy**) and lots of **parsley**. Though its most common use is with cold meats, I like it with delicate fish such as whiting and lemon sole.

Salt
This mineral, sodium chloride, is essential for life. There is much concern these days about the presence of too much salt in many diets, especially its overuse in 'junk' foods. It is certainly true that most natural foods contain sufficient salt for little addition to be needed (though vegetarians and vegans are often required to supplement their appalling diet by adding salt). Mammals excrete salt through their urine and sweat, and thus in hot countries more salt is consumed.

Salt is indeed so necessary that at some time or other every culture has come to prize it, so much that entire economies grew up around it. The Romans paid their soldiers in salt and from this the word 'salary' (from the Latin *salarium* – 'pertaining to salt') is derived. 'Salami', 'salad', even 'sausage', have their roots in the Latin for this product, *sal*. During the Indian Mutiny (Indians refer to the conflict more accurately as the 'War for Indian Independence') the Sikh soldiers were said to be 'true to their salt', meaning that they remained loyal to the British because they had taken an oath of allegiance, as well as a salary, which was therefore sacred to Sikhs.

Yet seventy years later salt became the biggest issue in the struggle for an independent India. On 5 April 1930 Mahatma

Gandhi arrived at a beach in Dandi after a march – joined by thousands of followers – of 240 miles. There he picked up a handful of salt crystallized by the evaporation of the sea-water. The British did not permit the manufacture or sale of salt without a licence, and the salt tax was a symbol of their rule. Gandhi's salt march was symbolic too, but potently so. It led indeed to independence.

Saltimbocca

The literal meaning of this Italian dish is 'jump in the mouth'. It consists of small rolls of thinly flattened veal tied up with sage leaves and simmered in **marsala** or sometimes white wine. In restaurants it is generally a starter, an *antipasto*. As with many other *antipasto* dishes, often I just have this instead of a full meal. And then lots of wine.

Sambals

These are condiments common to India and South-East Asian cuisine. They can be chutneys, flavoured yoghurts or sometimes coconut-based pickles. They are indispensable to Malaysian food. The famous Raffles Hotel in Singapore (named after the merchant adventurer Sir Stamford Raffles, who founded Singapore) lists fifty-two sambals on its lunch menu.

(A side-note on the great hotels of the British Raj. Though the food was rarely particularly distinguished, consisting mainly of British dishes such as roast beef etc. and often British versions of indigenous food such as curries for the colonial patrons, it was considerably better than that which now graces the less grand and largely anodyne hotels of today's American imperialists. The great hotels of the heyday of the British Empire, such as Raffles, Shepheard's in Cairo, where General Gordon stayed prior to his disastrous foray into Khartoum and his death, The Crescent Hotel in Aden, the Grand Oriental in Colombo in the then Ceylon, now Sri Lanka – these were all seats of Empire and a very far cry indeed from the Holiday Inns and hamburgers of today's American world hegemony.)

Sambuca

See **zambuca**.

Sandwich

When the 4th Earl of Sandwich (1718–92) was reluctant to leave the gaming table, he called for his meat to be inserted between two slices of bread and thus created this universal snack. Today children everywhere are sent to school with sandwiches, workers have them for their midday break, housewives traditionally (though in the West there can be few housewives around to be traditional at all) have 'just a sandwich' for lunch, and sandwich bars abound, having first been popularized in Britain just after the First World War. London's first sandwich bar opened in 1919, when the travel writer Bassett Digby (most improbably, it was in fact genuinely his name) sold sandwiches with fillings of reindeer tongue, sheep's milk cheese, tuna and other delicacies opposite the *New Statesman* offices in Great Queen Street. The good earl should have patented his invention.

Sandwiches can be very simple – **cheese** or **ham** for instance – or very elaborate indeed. The famous Lindy's restaurant in New York has many bizarre and fanciful sandwiches. I will cite one example, said to be a favourite of the Marx brothers: 'corned beef, pastrami, roast turkey and Swiss cheese quarter-deck with coleslaw and Russian dressing on rye bread'. Such a feast would surely have put the earl right off his game.

Sardine

A young **pilchard** of the **herring** family commonly eaten fresh in Mediterranean countries, especially in Spain and Portugal, where it is almost a staple. Elsewhere, in the UK and North America, sardines are usually canned with added oil. In Britain, though, the small tins of fish known as sardines by almost everyone contain not this fish at all but brisling, a small sprat that is fished mainly in Norway, though it is sometimes known as 'Swedish anchovy'. I recollect, as a small boy after the war, that an advert ran: 'Skippers are back!' This was a brand name for the brisling. It is a measure of just how austere Austerity was that the humble wee tin of sardines should then have been considered a luxury.

Sarsaparilla

Once a popular soft drink in the USA, this is now regarded as old-fashioned and belonging to the America of Norman Rockwell's lovely illustrations. It is produced from the dried root of a climbing plant native to Central and South America. I have never come across it, but I do remember a gag about it in *Son of Paleface*, in which Bob Hope, playing the part of a cowardly innocent in a tough frontier town, orders a sarsaparilla in a saloon, much to the disgust of the other gunslinger customers, then quickly adds 'in a dirty glass'.

Sashimi

A famous Japanese speciality, this is a style of presenting various pieces of thinly sliced raw fish, which must therefore be very fresh. (In Japanese cuisine presentation is absolutely integral.) Sashimi is a starter course and is usually accompanied by a small glass of rice wine. It is now, like **sushi**, becoming increasingly popular in Britain.

Saskatoon

I can't resist listing this: it is too good a word to miss. It is the fruit of the shad bush, sometimes known as the juneberry, and is used as an infusion for nerve tonics and **tisanes**.

Sauce

There was a time when every Briton thought that sauce was either 'brown' or 'red' (see **ketchup** for both). Otherwise in Britain most sauces were condiments such as **horseradish** sauce or **tartare sauce**. Some toffs used the term for gravy. But to many cuisines, especially that of France, sauces are essential. The great classic sauces of French cookery, the glazes and *fumets* based on long-simmered stocks, were largely evolved in the eighteenth and nineteenth centuries, in the châteaux of the great houses, in the grand restaurants and later hotels. But through them the sauces of even bourgeois households came to a considerable sophistication.

Such basic sauces as *espagnole* and *béchamel* came to have such variants in quite humble French cookery that, until quite recent years, most Frenchwomen, and not a few Frenchmen, could and did make sauces that were fit for the raw material, and many possessed a large repertoire in their kitchens. Many Anglo-Americans, cooking in their own homes, are both confused and unconfident when faced with this *éclat* in food.

But do not worry unduly: it is all very well to have vast pots of splendid stock bubbling away in huge saucepans in restaurant kitchens, but this can hardly be achieved in the average home. It is no disgrace to resort to commercial bouillon, or stock, cubes, certainly if you can get good-quality products. (I find the brand Maggi and a kosher stock cube known as Kosher Telma are relatively free from oversalting and are quite effective.) Butter and cream sauces are easy enough, but it has to be admitted that hot egg-yolk ones can be tricky at first. But one thing above all. No sauce, no matter how elegant, should ever be used to mask inferior meats or fish or anything else.

Sauceboat

I mention this, usually porcelain, piece of table crockery for only one reason: it is invariably of a splendidly elegant design, to use that word again.

Sauerbraten

A German speciality, this is a meat stew which includes vinegar and either **ginger** cake or biscuits. It has a unique, somewhat discordant, flavour, a little like sweet and sour, and is usually accompanied by **kartoffelpuffer**. I ate this in a beautiful little town in Bavaria called Bad Wumffen, washed down with German pilsner lager. I did not like it very much. To be honest, I don't much like German food at all: it goes a long way to explaining Teutonic chaps such as Wagner, Goethe and even the vegetarian Hitler. That is, of course, a disgraceful statement to make but, to hell with it, I've made it.

Sauerkraut

Och – or 'ach', if you are German – I am not one bit sorry about the burst of anti-Germanic sentiment above: after all, I was brought up in the era of commando comics and there was sod-all comic about Germans in my childhood. It wasn't very comic for Germans, either, especially those in the East part.

But this food item, much considered to be German, is not. Sauerkraut courses through Mittel-European cookery, and very good this pickled cabbage is too. When I used to eat at Schmidt's restaurant in King Street in London, I often had this with real and genuine **frankfurters** and slices of horseradish: the reason was that it was the cheapest and most filling item on the menu.

Schmidt's had the rudest waiters anywhere in the world but was much patronized by the Communist Party of Great Britain because the headquarters of this steadfastly dated organization were across the road. It was somehow rather satisfying to see the comrades being insulted by East German refugees in grubby aprons. Schmidt's was also a hotbed of British government spies and *agents provocateurs*. They were often rather noticeable, which added to the fun.

Sausage

There was a rhyme in my childhood which celebrated a nearby pork butcher's product: 'McKellar's sausages are the worst/ In your belly they do burst.' In those days sausages were on every household's menu several times a week. Even middle-class families had sausages as a main course. The better-off, of course, had them for breakfast.

Sausage, and sausages, are a staple of many European countries and Germany and Austria are the sausage capitals of the world, but in Britain sausages are confined, almost to so-called 'link' sausages, of varying quality, and are regarded as fodder for the British working class. (Which holds the humble 'banger' in great affection: the traditional proletarian dish known as 'bangers and mash', i.e. mashed potatoes, has now, like **bread and butter pudding**, penetrated some of the most distinguished restaurants.)

Though there are stringent regulations concerning sausages, the regulations cannot produce a consistency, and many sausages are a mixture of gristle and cereals, often over-spiced to hide the inferior meat, usually **pork**. There are specialist sausages, however, such as the rather grandly named Cumberland sausage, a large pork sausage that does not come in links but in a roll and which contains a high amount of pepper and nutmeg. It is traditionally eaten with Cumberland sauce, made with port and oranges and lemons. There are gourmets who prize this stodgy dish from northern England: I am not one of them.

The Scots and the Northern Irish have a sausage loaf which is very popular in those communities. And then there is the perennial favourite known as sausage rolls: sausage meat encased in short or flaky pastry. Hardly a finger buffet goes by without them, and here I confess it: I love them, just like every other Brit.

Savarin

A yeasted pudding moulded in a ring often, like the rum babas, steeped in a rum-based syrup, sometimes with fruit conserves added. It became popular in England in the late 1950s and early '60s in the aftermath of the Cyprus crisis, when many Cypriots elected to emigrate to the UK: what was once a rather exotic dessert confined mainly to select little Soho restaurants catering for slumming nobs, became a staple of every coffee bar.

A note on coffee bars here: for the young of the late 1950s the new 'invention' of coffee bars was a godsend. Teenagers flocked to these cafés, bedecked in retina-shattering bright *moderne* décor, Formica-topped tables, moulded plastic seats, and overseen by the ubiquitous Gaggia *expresso* (actually not **espresso** but *cappuccino*) coffee machines, jukeboxes and, usually, Italian, Cypriot or Maltese owners. Such establishments were held in horror by older generations, and much criticism was directed by churchmen, teachers and the Older Generation at large. Rock'n'roll, boys in drainpipe trousers and sideburns, girls in ponytails and sticky-out dresses swigging Cokes and frothy coffee out of glass cups while listening to Elvis or Ricky Nelson records, were all held up to be harbingers of the end of the Empire, if not civilization. Viewed today, in the light of a teenage drug culture, the teenagers of the past would seem to be remarkably healthy and innocent. Hindsight would also suggest that those same teenagers were a damned sight more pleasant and even responsible than the adults of the day who so condemned them. The foregoing has little to do, I admit, with savarin, but I just thought I'd have a nice wee rant.

Saveloy

Originally made from minced brains (the French version is known as *cervelas*, from the Latin for brain, *cerebellum*), this is now a large sausage rather like a frankfurter and, like that sausage, usually smoked. It was a popular cheap filler in snack bars in south-east England. The English writer Thomas (not Samuel) Smiles has a character in his then bestselling book, *Life and Labour* (1887), stop at a stall in the Haymarket in London to buy a penny saveloy. As the character is described as a gourmet, it can be seen that this sausage was once well considered as a delicacy. But it is little seen these days.

Schmaltz

This splendid Yiddish word, meaning in common parlance showy and cheap sentimentality, originally was the term for cooking fat, often in *Yiddisher* households meaning rendered-down chicken fat.

Schnapps

A colourless strong spirit of German origin but also drunk in many Balkan countries. It is usually flavoured with **caraway seeds** or juniper berries, though there are fruit-flavoured versions. In today's Germany few young people drink it regularly: it is considered an 'old man's drink'. Certainly when I visited Frankfurt a few years back when I was writing some articles for *Geo* magazine, a kind of German version of *Time* magazine, Wolfgang, the editor, was astonished when I ordered schnapps in a tavern. 'Why,' he asked in amazement, 'when we've got your wonderful Scotch whisky in the bar?'

School dinners

Boarding schools, including the English public schools, were of course obliged to provide food for their charges, but why this should be required of the ordinary state school does seem rather odd. Not as peculiar as the food itself, it seems, for school dinners are a synonym for very nasty grub indeed – stale overcooked cabbage, grey and watery mutton stews, steamed puddings such as **spotted dick**, **sago** and **prunes**, the list of horrors stretches far.

Yet I once was given lunch at a school in Normandy in which the simple fare consisted of a large plate of creamy *pommes dauphinois*, a slice of Norman *jambon* with a Grey Poupon mustard sauce, and an open apple tart topped with a dollop of crème fraîche to follow. This was in their school dining hall, and we ate what the children had. The older pupils also had a glass of wine and water with their meal, and the older girls waited table on the dominies. It was extraordinarily civilized.

But school dinners are a different matter in Britain. Today, of course, a school dinner is largely made up of chips, hamburgers and fish fingers, despite occasional and highly publicized attempts at 'healthy' alternatives. Indeed, as far as I can see, most schoolchildren bugger off to nearby fast-food establishments and feast upon fried rubbish. Yet the traditional awfulness of school dinners still attracts many. There was, for instance, a restaurant in London called School Dinners, in which the food was the mutton and boiled cabbage, sago etc., and as a bonus for nostalgic former public schoolboys, waitresses clad in short skirts and suspenders and nylons would administer a caning to the trouser seats of the entirely male guests upon request. It would seem that what the French call *le vice anglais*, that is, flagellation, applies to both the inner and the outer English appetite.

There is a splendid book titled *School Dinners*, by a Linda Sontaag, with wonderfully salacious drawings, pastiches of

1920s' school story illustrations, by Tim Earnshaw, with such surreal captions as: 'The girls began to regret their curry powder prank at the staff luncheon.' The illustrations have schoolgirls in gym tunics and navy-blue school knickers. Only in Britain could any of this make sense.

Scoff

Following on from school, we have this lovely word meaning to eat greedily. Billy Bunter, 'The Fat Owl of the Remove', a character created by the prolific writer Frank Richards, was forever scoffing. 'I say you chaps, Bunter's scoffed the lot' was a common cry from his fellow pupils at Greyfriars School.

Scone

For some reason highly genteel English people pronounce this as 'scoon', probably because the town of Scone in Scotland, once the seat of the Scottish kings, is pronounced thus. This now sleepy little Perthshire town plays no part in the derivation of the word, though. You will readily find these small flat cakes made with flour, raising agent, sugar or salt and a little fat in every baker's and every home in Scotland.

Just why 'tea and scones' should have become a byword for middle-class gentility is anybody's guess, for throughout the UK scones transcend all class distinctions.

Scotch broth

I once encountered a *potage* with this name in a fashionable Chelsea restaurant: it was a clear consommé with a few corns of barley, some julienne strips of carrots and swedes, and some delicately braised pieces of beef. It was very nice, but it was never Scotch broth. I told the owner and he summoned the (French) chef. Then I told him about this speciality of my native land. When I explained that it is not really a soup, more like a **pot au feu** but with added barley as a thickener, he understood. The restaurant was called Daphne's and I am glad to report that the broth, made rather more to its traditional recipe, was on offer the last time I dined there.

And as with *pot au feu*, there are no hard and fast recipes: what is used is simply what is available. Onions, carrots, cabbage, beef or ham or mutton, butter and pearl barley, (barley with the husks removed) are the major ingredients. The other is long and slow cooking. A really good Scotch broth is a meal in itself. A common variant is made with a ham hough (the joint behind the knee and the fetlock) and red lentils.

This is a superb, cheap and very filling soup. (It could be made even more cheaply. In my childhood my mother made it with ham bones, which could be obtained from the local butcher's for a few pence.) Scotch broth is no effete delicacy, and all households once made it each week. Every Scot, male and female, could make a broth of some kind. Today few Scots know what it is really; a great pity.

Scotch eggs

Hard-boiled eggs wrapped round with pork sausage meat, then coated in egg and breadcrumbs and deep-fried. There is nothing Scottish about them, and they are most often seen in English pubs as a delightful snack. The name derives from the verb to *scotch*, meaning 'to chop up'.

Scottish food

I have titled this 'food' rather than 'cookery' for there isn't much cookery in my native land, though once there was. Indeed in the days when Scotland had more in common with the continent of Europe than with its neighbour England, the cuisine of the Scottish court and its aristocracy was elegant in comparison to that of the then rather boorish

English. When Mary Stuart – Mary, Queen of Scots – came to take her throne, she brought with her French chefs and pastry cooks. But French cuisine was already there in the households of rich merchant adventurers in the Lowlands. The Scottish chieftains of the Highland clans kept a lavish table, and many of them possessed wine cellars of a magnificence that would be the envy of wine connoisseurs of today. It was later, when famine struck again and again throughout the late eighteenth and nineteenth centuries (following on from the disastrous rebellion of the '45, when 'Bonnie Prince Charlie' brought romance and calamity to Scotland) that Scotland lost its cooking skills.

Today Scottish cookery is improving greatly, but it is not the cooking of which Scotland can be most proud: it is the Scottish larder itself. No other country can be said to be so well endowed with such ingredients. Scotch salmon, Angus beef, soft fruit such as raspberries and strawberries, Ayrshire potatoes, the huge variety of fish and shellfish, the dairy produce from the herds of Galloway cattle, the magnificent **venison** of the populous deer herds – all of them are regarded by chefs and gourmets alike as among the finest ingredients of all. Sadly most Scots know little of the above and prefer fried foods and ready-prepared meals. Though there are a number of restaurants now attempting to serve more traditional Scottish dishes, such as cock-a-leekie soup or the superb dessert cranachan (whipped cream, oatmeal, brambles or sometimes raspberries, honey and a little whisky), there are still too many customers for Burger King or Kentucky Fried Chicken.

Scouse

Just as the seaweed called **laver** gave its name to the seaport of Liverpool, so the inhabitants are named after a foodstuff. Scousers are so called because it was believed by southerners that Liverpudlians lived entirely on a diet of this cheap stew originally known as 'lobscouse' (still popular in the Baltic regions of Germany and Scandinavia and called *labskaus*: it is a speciality of another seaport, Hamburg, which is where of course the Liverpudlian Beatles learned their musical trade – a lovely serendipity at that). The dish is made of meat, vegetables and ship's biscuit. It was a staple meal for mariners.

Scrambled eggs

The writer and theatre director Dr Jonathan Miller once said that the most important thing he learned from his fellow *Beyond the Fringe* performer, and later Hollywood star, Dudley Moore, was to add a little water to the eggs when scrambling them.

What I also learned came from an Edinburgh chum, Martin Currie, a noted trencherman himself though, apart from this recipe, no cook. He added cheese to the dish. Years later I was to encounter the same scrambled eggs with cheese and cream in Italy, where it goes under the sonorous title *uove stracciate al formaggio*.

Scrambled eggs must not be overcooked as they then separate into a solid pudding surrounded by a disgusting liquid, rather as do curds and whey.

Scraps

Pieces of leftover and discarded food. Perhaps the most famous scraps in English literature are those fed to Oliver Twist on his first meal in the undertaker Sowersby's kitchen. They had been intended for Trip, the dog.

Sea pie

A beef or mutton stew topped with suet pastry. It is a filling dish and was popular in the poorer districts of south-east

England. During the years of the Depression of the 1930s a common phrase was 'sea pie today, see sod-all tomorrow'.

Sea urchin
This repellent creature is highly thought of by many gourmets, especially for the female's roe. French diners like them, as of course do those of Japan.

Seasoning
Added to dishes to enhance the flavour are such ingredients as salt, spices, herbs, condiments etc., and most cuisines deem them necessary. Indeed there is a well-known fairy story of the little princess who displeased her father, the king, because when asked how much she loved her papa, she replied that she loved him as she did 'salt in her food'. It was only when a sympathetic cook served his monarch his victuals without seasoning that the daft old king realized that his daughter was paying him a great compliment.

Sediment
The dregs at the bottom of a bottle of liquid such as wine. Good **port** is very susceptible to this and normally must be decanted as a result. A bottle of vintage port should be disturbed as little as possible to ensure that this residue, the 'lees', does not diffuse in the wine. Lord Peter Wimsey's obsequious manservant, Bunter, goes doollally in one of Dorothy L. Sayers's novels when a charwoman gives all the cases of port a good dusting. One is inclined to give both Wimsey and Bunter a right good dusting too. With a poker.

Seed cake
This rather old-fashioned lemony-rich cake, which is similar to madeira cake, contains, like Abernethy biscuits, caraway seeds (see **Abernethy biscuit**). Agatha Christie has her

dreadful old harridan Miss Marple (the novelist disliked her creation) shoving this down her gob at every mention of **tea**. And her constant complaint in the tea shops she frequents as much as Dylan Thomas did pubs, is always that 'You cannot get a really good seed cake these days'. The weary tearoom waitresses must have felt like choking the aged horror. With seed cake.

Self-service restaurants

Self-service still exists in school dining halls and student refectories and in the canteens that a few larger companies maintain. (Many firms have closed such facilities on the strength of their accountants' advice, to save time of course. Even journalists are today tied to their desks. Some companies have ghastly automats purveying tired filled rolls and ersatz coffee etc.)

The self-service fashion has rather disappeared as a restaurant set-up in recent years, save for the buffet service seen in some hotel restaurants. The Edinburgh academic librarian Annette Hope claims in her splendid history of food in the UK capital, *London's Larder*, that the first London self-service outlet was opened in 1921. This may be so, but the first self-service restaurant to be opened in Britain (and even before the USA took the idea on board) was in fact Langs, which opened in 1898 in my native Glasgow. It was a large public house which had an extensive range of excellent luncheon and dinner dishes. You paid at a cashpoint only after you'd finished your meal. It was a godsend to the students of the College of Music and Drama across the way and cheating was commonplace among the young aspiring artistes. Sadly it was swept away, along with its magnificent dark-panelled interior, in the late 1960s.

Sell-by date

This can be seen emblazoned on many foodstuffs and refers to the point by which the product should be sold. It is not the same as shelf life, which indicates the point after which the food should not be consumed at all. It is, for instance, perfectly safe to take a foodstuff at its sell-by date and freeze it for later use.

My brother Brian once found my freezer full of food which had a sell-by date later than he thought appropriate. Because of his abysmal ignorance he threw out over £100 worth of perfectly edible grub. I have since discovered that this fate is encountered by many others who have similar idjits in their families.

Semolina

Yet another horror of the school dinner, this is made from a cereal milled from durum wheat. Usually it was served with a spoonful of cheap jam in the centre. Occasionally the sadists who were in charge of the school kitchens would add **prunes**.

Serviettes

When Nancy Mitford ventured to burlesque the speech and tones of the upper middle class (she was herself irretrievably aristocratic) in an article concerning 'U' and 'Non-U' words and phrases (later, in 1954, to become a book, *Noblesse Oblige*), among other words was 'serviette' because it was definitely non-U: the 'proper' word is 'napkin'. Sir John Betjeman, later the poet laureate, immediately gently lampooned the lampoon of Ms Mitford's book in the poem 'How to Get On in the World', in which he wrote of a *nouveau riche* lady:

Phone for the fish knives Norman,
As Cook is a little unnerved;

327

> You kiddies have crumpled the serviettes
> And I must have things daintily served.

A good restaurant will have proper linen napkins: I once advised a restaurateur who had opened a modest yet excellent eatery to have linen napery, tablecloth and napkins instead of paper materials because, though the cost of the laundry was indeed expensive, he could put the prices of his fare up as the napery made his place look classy enough to charge more.

There is nothing as splendid as a table clad in snow-white tablecloths, refulgent silver cutlery and good, if simple, crockery, to establish the idea that you are bound to encounter a good meal – even if you aren't. Thus reasoned the once magnificent British railway dining cars. Oh, and if you ask me, the European habit of tucking your napkin, or serviette if you prefer, into your collar is extremely sensible, if frowned upon by U people.

Shallot
A member of the onion family, this is similar to **garlic** in that it comes in cloves. It is milder than garlic, however, and is highly prized, especially in French cuisine. The largest grower is Syria.

Shark
Until recently the edible variety of this fish was almost unknown in Britain, though it is common enough in the Iberian peninsula. Shark steaks are now seen in many restaurants and smarter fishmongers.

Shark's fin soup
This is a speciality of Chinese cookery and consists of thin pieces of the fish's fins combined with strips of chicken and

ham and Chinese mushrooms, simmered in chicken broth and highly seasoned. Cans of it can be purchased in some specialist delicatessens and are very expensive.

Shashlik
This lamb kebab, marinated in oil and lemon juice, is originally of Russian origin but coursed through Armenia and then on to Turkey and thus to Cyprus. On the odd occasion when I visit a kebab **take-away** it is always this that I order, with salad and spicy sauce wrapped in pitta bread. Though such kebabs are often put into the junk-food category, this is, in fact, a very healthy item, consisting as it does of lean lamb meat, salad, a pleasant chilli or **yoghurt** sauce and pitta bread.

Sheep's head
Though there is indeed a fish named 'sheepshead', this usually refers to a whole sheep's head, a dish once eaten mainly by the poor. The once popular **mock turtle soup** is made from this rather appalling ingredient.

Sherbet
For British children during much of the twentieth century this was a yellow lemon and sugar compound which, mixed with water, constituted a lemony drink. (The most famous brand, which also contained a soda nitrate, was Creamola Foam.) It also came as a dry powder in small bags, along with a **liquorice** straw. None of these rather innocent children was aware that the original sherbet meant a cooling alcoholic drink from Arab cultures (Arabic *za arbat*), which eventually became the iced refreshments referred to by European as sorbets.

Sherry
This grape wine of the Jerez region of Spain is fortified by brandy and has become both, at the cheap end of the market,

inexpensive and, at the other end, very, very exclusive indeed. The cheapest is what was once popular when I was a student, Cyprus sherry (some Cyprus sherries are quite palatable, some horribly sweet, though they cannot properly be called sherries), and the expensive sherries are superb.

Sherry is more often than not taken as an aperitif, or else in mid-afternoon. The most popular styles known outside Spain are Fino, Amontillado, Oloroso and Brown, but in Spain itself if you were to ask for an Amontillado or a Fino in a bar they would hardly know what you meant. The term for such would be *seco*, that is a dry sherry; *dulce* would be a sweet sherry such as Oloroso or Brown.

Sherry is also used in cooking, in the West nearly always in desserts, such as for instance **trifle**, though it was once often added to vegetable soups. In Chinese and South-East Asian cookery it is a different matter entirely, where it is used in a vast number of savoury recipes. One of them is an astonishing sherry dish called Drunken Chicken, in which a chicken is simmered in water with fresh ginger and spring onions, cooled, sliced and marinated for two days in a surprisingly large amount of sherry wine. It has a sumptuous flavour. While the Chinese make their own wine, these days they also import a considerable amount of sherry from Spain.

As with **port** producers, a good many of the great sherry companies are owned by Scottish families. I was once given a sherry by the Scottish war hero Sir Fitzroy MacLean (who had helped to organize the Yugoslav partisans during the Second World War) – a Findlater's sherry which he told me was 'really rather old'. The ancient bottle was dated 1944: it tasted of old Italian lace, sweet dates, a young girl's first ball and, somehow, nutmeg. It reminded me of biblical times. If the above sounds pretentious – and it most certainly should – it was indeed what it tasted like.

Shortbread

This is a Scottish speciality, but it has travelled the world. Only Scotch **whisky** can be said to be as famous a product from this country. There are a good many recipes, but all include butter. When I was a child, our 'lollipop man' old Willie Rae, a Highland chiel, made his own shortbread and presented my father with about a ton of it every Christmas. Along with a bottle of his own whisky (poteen). They were, I may say, a heady mixture.

The shortbread cut delicately into rounds and known as petticoat tails is said to have been so named either after the French *petites galettes* (as the early Scottish version of Mrs Beeton, Meg Dods, had it in her 1826 book *The Cook and Housewife's Manual*) or, more probably, because it resembles old-fashioned petticoats. Either way, shortbread can be robust or very fine and is always delicious. The American jazz pianist and gourmet Thomas 'Fats' Waller immortalized the confection in the song 'Shortnin' Bread' (lyrics by Andy Razaf, real name Andreamata Razafkeriefo). You can't get much more information than that.

Shpinatnie shchci

An extraordinary soup from the Russias which I was once served by a Ukrainian couple who own the Galoski Gallery in Edinburgh. It is a spinach and sorrel soup heavily flavoured with onions and accompanied by hard-boiled eggs and sour cream. It is a main course and is traditionally eaten at Easter. Follow it with the equally traditional Easter cake **pashka** and Stolichnaya vodka and you will feed with kings. Or at least tsars.

Shredded wheat

This breakfast cereal made of cooked dried wheat is highly nutritious and, like other breakfast cereals such as Puffed

Wheat ('shot from guns', as the legend said) and Rice Krispies, Weetabix, **Cornflakes** etc., was once universal, especially for small children. Recent surveys show that fewer than 30% of schoolchildren between the ages of ten and sixteen take any breakfast at all. And that a quarter of the same age group is obese.

Singin' hinnies

These small round cakes filled with raisins, currants and mixed spice have such a high fat content that they emit a loud hissing sound when being cooked on a griddle. Thus the name. They hail from Lancashire. This led the late John Lennon to describe his favourite girl group, the Shirelles, as 'the Singin' Hinnies'.

Sinistral

This, of course, is the term for 'leaning to the left'. A left-handed person is called a sinistral (and in heraldry the word denotes an illegitimate lineage). But a grand surreal note concerns some species of flatfish which have their two eyes situated on the one side of their heads. Though the fish are born with the eyes on both sides, one eye soon migrates towards the other. If the left eye goes towards the right, it is known as a 'dextral' flatfish; if the other way round, you get sinistral. This should be the world of Señor Dalí, but it is real enough.

Sirloin

Legend has it that this prime cut of beef from the loin was so enjoyed by Henry VIII that he knighted it, thus 'Sir loin'. Sadly there is no substance in this at all. It is a corruption of the French term *surlonge*, from *sur* meaning 'over' and *longe*, 'loin'. There are times when reality is tiresome. But a sirloin steak is magnificent with or without legends.

Skate

This flatfish is often despised by English diners because of its cheapness. It is not so in the Normandy region of France, where a famous dish is made of the wings of the fish simmered in cider and shallots. One other distinction: the male fish possesses an almost exact replica of the human penis and testicles. In Normandy the fishmongers coyly place a little frilled paper cap over the offending genitals.

Skillet

'Sally-Annie easy, make the skillet good and greasy'. So goes a traditional Appalachian Bluegrass folk song. A skillet is the American term for a frying pan.

Sloe

This small member of the plum family, a fruit of the blackthorn bush, is rather bitter but can be used as a flavouring with **gin** to make a country potation called, of course, sloe gin.

An old friend of mine, the late Betty Galt, a great-great-great-niece of the Scottish poet John Galt, used to offer me small glasses of this, despite the fact that she rather disapproved of strong drink. I rarely got home sober.

Smoking

This ancient method of preserving food also provides a distinctive taste and, though some commercial companies try to simulate it with dyes (see **herring**), there is really no substitute for the proper smoking process, whether it be with wood, peat or turf. A great many fishes are smoked, and very good they are too, but nothing can touch smoked **salmon**.

Smorgasbord

There was a brief fashion for this in Britain in the late 1960s: it is a famous buffet tableful of Scandinavian food including fish (especially herring dishes), meats, poultry, cheeses, condiments and assorted desserts. It is surprising that these countries with such cold climates should choose cold food as their national meal; perhaps not – it can't be easy keeping food hot in such temperatures. If you glance at the entry on **fricadelles** you will note that a famous Danish dish is *frikadeller* and that I was offered this by a Danish art student. The art college of which I am a graduate (Edinburgh) had a relationship with Scandinavian architectural schools, and thus we Scottish art students discovered Scandinavian food.

What we found was that Danes often liked their food hot, and that it consisted mainly of pigmeat and potatoes, that Norwegians ate endless amounts of fish, and that Swedes survived on a diet of cold food and salads. What we Scots boys also discovered was that their womenfolk did not share our Calvinistic sexual morality, which fairly spiced up our lives, if not their grub.

Smorrebrod are Danish open sandwiches, of which it is said there are over 600 varieties. This suggests that the Earl of Sandwich has a lot to answer for.

Snails

Disgusting gastropod molluscs (see **escargots**). Incidentally there is a restaurant in Soho in London called L'Escargot which is justly famous. The carpets are decorated with snails, and the walls have pictures of snails. It does not serve snails.

Snoek

To anyone over sixty this is nearly the worst word in the English language. Even I myself (who have not attained that age) know about this fish. It is a barracuda, and the name is from the Afrikaans language of South Africa. During the Second World War it was introduced to a fish-starved Britain in cans and became a byword for the privations suffered by civilians. It was, quite simply, bloody awful. The public rejected it and it ended up as cat food. (For a slight sketch on this see **Wartime food**.)

Soda

Though this is common enough as a carbonated water used as an additive to Scotch **whisky** (the origin of adding soda water to whisky lies in the fact that London water is too hard for whisky, which requires the softness of Highland **water** and thus London clubmen discovered soda water), a soda in America is an ice-cream concoction and is necessary to teenage American innocents (see **ice cream soda**).

Soda bread

No Irish breakfast could be complete without this bread, which is made without yeast but contains bicarbonate of soda. Another ingredient is **buttermilk**. Soda scones, common in Scotland, are made with the same mixture but often include cream of tartar in the recipe.

But to soda bread: I recollect a memorable breakfast in a magnificent small restaurant (it also possesses a few bedrooms) in Anagragh, Co. Donegal, called The Killinbarrach, though locally known as 'Danny Minnies'. It was the morning after a concert in which the celebrated Irish popular singers Philomena Begley and Daniel O'Donnell had starred and I had played the harmonica. Daniel is almost teetotal, but Philomena and myself had partaken of the water of life up till the wee sma' hours. Daniel could not eat breakfast, but myself and the aforesaid songbird took a gargantuan breakfast of **bacon**, **eggs**, **colcannon** and the best soda bread (fried in goose fat) you could find in the world.

Soffritto

This slowly cooked mixture of onions, capsicums, garlic and often ham or salt pork is the base for many Roman stews and soups, and is also known as a *battuto*. For some reason it has transferred itself to Latin American countries and to the Caribbean, though it is indeed peculiar to Ligurian cookery and not to that of the Iberian peninsula.

Sole

This flatfish is the basis for many classic French fish dishes. The famous Dover sole is larger than other soles and is usually served plainly, though breaded, as *Sole Colbert*, with the spine removed at the table and the resulting space filled with a *maître d'hotel* butter (softened and whipped butter with lemon juice and chopped garlic). I once had this magnificent fish along with Lord Fitt in one of the many splendid dining rooms in the House of Lords when I was doing an interview with him. The reason I mention this is that Lord Fitt hails from a very working-class, and deprived, area of Belfast, and from his earliest days in first the House of Commons as an extremely energetic MP and later as a still energetic Lord, astounded many of his aristocratic, well, peers, by his knowledge and appreciation of fine food. This was considered highly unusual in a working-class Belfast chap. What the noble lords didn't know was that the young Gerry Fitt had learned his **aristology** at source: he once worked as a waiter.

But to sole. *Sole Bercy* is a French dish of sole cooked in white wine and shallots. *Sole dugléré* has white wine and tomatoes. Another French classic, *Sole Waleska*, created for one of Napoleon's mistresses, Comtesse Waleska, has a mornay sauce, truffles and diced lobster. Though all the various soles are relatively expensive to buy, they are also worth the money, and not just for the wonderful flavour of them: they are amazingly filling.

Sommelier

I am very, very ashamed to admit this: I do not appreciate, indeed I do not much like, **wine** and I am too old to learn (though I must have wine with Italian food). But what I do know is that gourmets insist that a first-class restaurant will always have a sommelier, a wine waiter, a chap – or today often a woman – who is truly knowledgeable about wine, and will be able to guide the patrons as to which wine goes with which dish.

The sommelier Terry Ashe (see **diner**) once told me that the art of it was subtle. 'You don't just balance the wine with the dish, you do it with all of the courses which make up the eating experience. You have to be able to tell if your guests' – note he called his customers 'guests' – 'are experienced or not, if they know about wine, what they can afford, how much they are able to drink. And it is a delight to teach the young people about wine'.

In a good French restaurant the sommelier is more than a waiter: it will be he, or she, who advises the *patron* which wines to buy and when, and who oversees the conditions of the cellar. And once again I am ashamed to admit my ignorance of what all my gourmet friends tell me is essential to eating.

Sorbet

This water ice is usually served today as a dessert but is also occasionally served between courses to refresh the palate. Though its origin lies in Arab cuisine (see **sherbet**), this iced fruit pulp seem to have been introduced to France and thus European cookery by the Italians. (An Italian, one Buontalenti, first enchanted the court of Henri IV in the late sixteenth century with his ices when he came with the entourage of Henri's bride, Marie de Medici. Later a Signor de Mirra brought ices to the court of Charles I of England.)

Though sorbets were once thought to be rather posh, every ordinary British child has unknowingly consumed them. They are, after all, much the same as an ice lolly.

Sorrel

A herb of the dock family, this is common enough in French cookery and also loved by Russians. It is rather like **spinach**, though it has a higher acid content and is much used in soups. It also makes a wonderful filling for an **omelette**.

Soufflé

One thing I can tell you about this light dish, which can be sweet or savoury, and consists of egg yolks and whites beaten and incorporated into a thick sauce with other ingredients, is that it takes considerable expertise to make. Even the most experienced chef approaches a soufflé with a certain trepidation. But when it is done well, it is spectacular. A rather large and clumsy girl I knew, a fellow student at Edinburgh College of Art, was a superb cook and made the most wonderful soufflés. It was no surprise, then, when I discovered that she had been taught to cook by her *grand-mère*, a Parisienne. What was surprising was that Helen (that was the girl's name) had as a grandmother the cousin of General de Gaulle.

Sour

Anything that tastes the opposite of sweet is often described pejoratively, but this is not so in the world of food, for the flavour is often encountered in dishes in most cuisines. The use, for instance, of soured cream in the cookery of Mittel-Europa, throughout the Balkans, the Middle East, the Indian subcontinent, the Russias, even North America, is a testament to this. **Hungarian cookery** relies upon it.

Southern fried chicken

In the southern states of the USA this is almost a national dish. The floured pieces of chicken are fried in butter and served with corn fritters, gravy, bananas and mashed potatoes, and are then known as Maryland chicken. There is no escaping this in the Deep South. You will find it at every picnic, and in every home, from a poor white shack to a Good Ol' Boy's pilastered mansion: a Ku-Klux-Klanner will have this as readily as a militant Black activist. It is omnipresent at political rallies and fundamentalist Christian gatherings. It is also the dish most often asked for as a last meal by prisoners on death row, the majority of whom are southerners.

Soya bean

This legume of the pea family is a staple of South-East Asian food, especially that of China and Japan. Ubiquitous as the bean is in that area, in the West it is best known in the form of the condiment soy sauce, which can be either dark or light: it is essential to Chinese cookery. The soya bean also makes many appalling meat substitutes. And is the basis for the Japanese bean curd tofu.

Spaghetti

When I was a very small child, this type of **pasta** only came as a canned convenience food. Later I was to discover it in the Italian delicatessens my father patronized. In the 1960s there was a famous April Fool spoof on the popular BBC television programme *Tonight*, then presented by the avuncular Cliff Michelmore, which presented the nation with spaghetti trees. Forty years on, at a birthday party for my great-niece, the chef in the Italian restaurant we had booked took her and the other little girls round the kitchen to inspect the spaghetti trees (he had draped the pasta round artificial bushes). They were enchanted.

But spaghetti is now an almost universal food, especially with **bolognese sauce** (for which you can discover my own recipe under that heading). The one basic point that must be emphazised about spaghetti bolognese is that there should not be very much sauce at all – it should merely coat the pasta.

About the best dish of this I ever encountered was in a small transport café in Glasgow, owned by an Italian couple called Umberto and Dorina Pelosi, now long since retired to their native Tuscany. I used to eat there on a Sunday and had wine with the meal, which was unusual in that in those days the sale of any liquor, and its consumption, were forbidden on a Scottish Sabbath. It was round the corner from the local police station and we were often joined by a variety of high-ranking *gendarmes*. Umberto got round the licensing laws by the simple expedient of overcharging for the food on Sundays. The boys in blue saw no problem in this stratagem and tucked in with alacrity.

But there are other sauces to go with this marvellous pabulum. One of the best is possibly a simple sauce of garlic and olive oil, but there is also any tomato sauce and of course the *carbonara* sauce, which has finely chopped bacon, herbs, garlic and cream (it is supposed to have eggs as well, but I leave them out myself). No matter – spaghetti is a wonder to us all. And where would *The Godfather* be without it?

Spam
The *incroyable* Marguerite Patten, who worked as a government food adviser during the Second World War and whose food writing now spans seven decades, says that this canned cooked pork meat, now almost an eponym, is a version of 'shoulder of pork and ham' and that the name was suggested by the brother of the vice-president of the canning firm Hormel, which first produced this food item. In fact it is an

acronym of SPiced hAM, and was suggested by readers in a magazine poll.

Ms Patten's book on Spam, which was written for the company, is of little culinary interest – the product is, after all, just a canned convenience food – but it has sociological merit. No child of the immediate post-war years can forget the wonder of Spam fritters in the school dining hall.

Spare ribs

These ribs of pork can be cooked either in a barbecue sauce – an American favourite – or in Chinese style. Spare ribs once were cheap and eaten by poorer families: they are now almost a delicacy.

Spatchcock chicken

The chicken is split open and flattened out, then grilled. Some smaller game birds are treated the same way. It allows a short cooking time. Some caterers garnish the flattened chicken with two slices of hard-boiled egg and a little slice of truffle in the centre of each to make 'eyes' for it; this looks deeply macabre.

Spices

It was James Joyce who wrote in *Stephen Hero* that while God created food, the Devil was responsible for spices, but then many of his opinions were as odd as his last novel. In fact spices have been associated with God and religion since prehistoric days. In the days of the Pharaohs they were used for embalming and mummification, and this has continued throughout subsequent centuries. Both frankincense, a resin from the spruce tree, and myrrh, another Arab tree resin, which were costly gifts allegedly bestowed upon the infant Jesus by the Three Wise Men from the East, were regarded as spices, though strictly speaking, they are herbs.

The commercial importance of spices, though, was for preserving foods. The Romans used a bewildering number of spices, as did the gastronomy of the Middle Ages. So important were they that, as every schoolchild knows, Christopher Columbus went on his travels to find an alternative to the Spice Route, in the process unfortunately discovering America.

In today's European cookery spices are less used, but they are fundamental to North African and Indian cuisine. (Indeed so important are spices to Indian cookery that there are legions of books written on them, including a very odd novel, *The Mistress of Spices*, by an Indian lady now domiciled in the USA, Chita Banerjee Divakaruni, in which the story is woven around spices.) In Arab and Indian cookery their use is based upon medicinal practices. It is untrue, as many Westerners would have it, that 'spicy' foods are injurious to digestion: in fact, the opposite is true. Many of the so-called 'hot' spices help to break down food in the intestinal tract and actually aid digestion.

Spinach

This vegetable, imported from Persia to Europe some time in the sixteenth century, is best known as the very substance of strength for the magnificent cartoon character Popeye. Though such a gourmet as Brillat-Savarin extolled spinach, and his good friend the Abbé Chevrier produced an absurd recipe that required five days' cooking, frankly this vegetable is best used as an ingredient of little cheese **ravioli** or in some Indian curries: as a vegetable on its own, it is no wonder that Olive Oyl was so frequently attracted to the villain Bluto.

Spirits

Virtually any product that contains sugar – from grape or grain to tubers such as the potato and fruits such as the banana –

can be fermented, and the resulting liquid distilled to produce a spirit. Paradoxically it was the Muslim Arabs who first discovered the art of distilling. The injunction against any alcohol at all (the very word derives from the Arabic *alcool*) is now endemic throughout the Islamic world, which suggests that Arabs have somehow got things the wrong way round and are now inflamed by religion rather than by such an admittedly potentially dangerous substance as the Demon Drink. Spirits include **brandy**, calvados, **gin**, **rum** and **whisky**, as well as arrack, a spirit distilled illegally throughout the Arab world.

Sponge
Though there are edible varieties of this sea creature, this is also, of course, the name of a cake mixture. In my childhood much was made of those who could make 'a really light sponge', without which no tea party was complete. Some hostesses cheated and obtained sponges from a local bakery, thus a jibe was that a rival lady's cake was 'shop-bought'. A more subtle stratagem was to buy ready-made cake mixes such as the American Betty Crocker brand.

Spotted dick
This steamed suet pudding is a British favourite and contains sultanas and raisins. It was ubiquitous in school dining halls and an established feature of English public school fare. There is a splendid paragraph in which one of the Greyfriars Remove complains about Billy Bunter: 'I say, chaps, Bunter's made my dick all sticky'. In this case the scholar was referring to his dictionary.

Sprat
An oily fish of the herring family. It is much smaller than the herring, growing to, at most, perhaps five inches, and is a term

of contempt for anybody of little consequence. Actually, sprats are rather good to eat. See **sardine**.

Spread

Apart from the obvious use of the word as a verb, this is also a now probably obsolete noun meaning a lavish display of food on the table in someone's house, as in 'I must say, Hoskins gave us a jolly good spread'. If there is anybody out there who today utters such an encomium I shall be very surprised indeed but somehow grateful for his archaism.

Spring chicken

Now this is really a delightful archaism at that, and probably only on the lips of old and sometimes malevolent people. In reality it is a small chicken, a little larger than a poussin. Its use as a metaphor, as in 'I'll tell you this: she's no spring chicken', is to be admired.

Spring onion

This immature and highly (but delicately) flavoured onion is widely used in Chinese and South-East Asian cookery but also in European countries such as Ireland, where it is known as a scallion (see **champ**), and in Scotland, where it is known as a syboe. In North America spring onions are called green onions, which is the title of one of the most famous blues songs of all time, written by John Lee Hooker and in the repertoire of every R&B musician – including myself.

Spring roll

Known in the USA as egg roll, this comes in a kind of filo pastry casing and usually has a filling of bean sprouts, Chinese pork and prawns. I have never known even the humblest Chinese take-away to do anything other than a very good spring roll. One of the nicest street foods ever.

Spritzer

Just when the young of Britain started calling a fruit drink, often with alcohol (often in large quantities), mixed with soda water a spritzer I cannot tell, but it has certainly been in use for over a decade now. I suspect it is a misuse of the word 'seltzer', as in Oscar Wilde's characters endlessly shoving hock and 'seltzer' down their *soigné* throats. The commercial products of this are often known as 'alcopops'.

Spurtle

A wooden stick, sometimes elaborately carved, traditionally used in Scotland to stir **porridge**. For some reason it is argued that the porridge should always be stirred clockwise with a spurtle. Presumably the direction is reversed below the equator.

Squash

Though this is a generic term for such vegetables as marrows, pumpkins and courgettes, it is also used for soft drinks made usually from orange or lemon juice which have a high fruit content.

Squid

Nothing will induce me to countenance this visual horror. It is, despite what its adherents say, rubbery, with little flavour. See **cephalopod**.

Squirrel

Like the **raccoon**, this is a speciality of Cajun cookery from the Bayou region of Louisiana in North America. For once I admit a certain sentimentality here: I would no more think of eating this delightful little bushy-tailed creature than I would of cooking a favourite cat, drowned in a tub of goldfishes or not. I might eat the goldfish (a species of carp), though.

Starch

This carbohydrate is found in cereals, grain products, such as wheat and rice, and in potatoes and other tubers. It has good nutritional value and is what helps to make rice, pasta, potatoes etc. not only palatable but filling as well. Too great a reliance on starchy food, however, makes for an unhealthy diet.

Steak

A generic term for certain cuts of meat, also of fish. Generally, though, a steak is thought of as a thick slice of beef such as **fillet** or **sirloin** or rib etc., and is one of the most popular meat dishes ordered in restaurants throughout the Western world. The French have their *bifteck* with *frites* (chips), and the Italians have a massive steak known as *bistecca alla fiorentina*, which can be seen in restaurants all over Tuscany. It is so large that special plates are used.

In the USA steaks are so ubiquitous that they talk about 'a steak dinner' when they mean going to a restaurant. Erle Stanley Gardner always has his Perry Mason concluding his adventures with steak dinners for himself, Della Street and Paul Drake playing gooseberry, which is doubtless why in over forty Perry Mason mysteries the ever-victorious lawyer never gets to shag the delectable Della.

I rarely order a steak myself when eating out – it is so easy to cook it yourself at home at a quarter of the cost, I cannot see the point of ordering it in an eatery. There are a number of different steak recipes, however. Steak Diane is a dish of thin steaks cooked in butter and **Worcestershire sauce**, then flambéed with brandy; sometimes cream is added. Steak tartare is a classic made with raw minced fillet steak mixed with egg yolks, chopped onions, capers and parsley. (There are versions of this throughout the Far East; see **yang-hoe**.) There is also *steak au poivre*, in which unripe 'green' peppercorns are used.

There is really no need for all this tarting up. A good steak cooked lightly in butter with a little red wine and shallots can hardly be beaten. I once preferred my steak cooked *bleu*, that is, hardly cooked at all and very rare, but no longer digest it well, and thus have it cooked rare or medium rare. There are those who have it 'well done', which is to say burnt. This is for idiots and footballers and their wives.

Steak and kidney pie

The late Jack House, a famous journalist in his day (see **grappa**), often described himself as an aristologist and indeed he was, among other things, a restaurant critic. He had a splendid idiosyncrasy which more restaurant foodies would do well to adopt. He extolled what he called 'the steak pie test'. As he was by no means sophisticated in his culinary tastes, he would always want to know if a restaurant made 'a good steak pie'. By this he meant none of that stew with a silly little square of loose puff pastry. Though he ate in many expensive restaurants in his long career, his favourite for steak pie was the Boulevard Hotel in the very working-class Scottish shipbuilding town of Clydebank. He ate there so often that they kept a table reserved for him. And he always had steak pie.

Originally the steak was tempered by the then cheap oysters, and in later years cheaper versions were made (and still are) with stewed beef link sausages. The best recipe, however, includes only kidney, as this provides a subtle richness to the gravy (see **kidneys**). The real glory of a good steak pie is the splendidly soggy underbelly of the pastry lid, which the flakiness of the top helps to counter. This is the traditional meal for the Scottish New Year, Hogmanay, but is common throughout the year. To this day in Scotland it is made in every decent butcher's – not, as one would expect, by bakers. And there is no skimping on the quality of the ingredients.

Teamed with very creamy, almost puréed, mashed potatoes and green peas I can think of no greater comfort food than this. Followed by a jelly trifle, and then a few drams of whisky, I could die happy.

Steak and kidney pudding

The same mixture of good rump or chuck steak and kidneys is the filling for this excellent and very English pudding, which is made by lining a large bowl with **suet** pastry, adding a lid of the pastry and then steaming. It is traditionally served in its bowl, with a snowy white napkin tied round it. I once had this in the somewhat ornate upstairs restaurant of the very ornate Philharmonic Bar in Liverpool. It was a variation of the usual pudding because the steak filling had been braised in Guinness **stout**. I washed it down with a chilled white wine. Even the most discerning and snobbish gourmet would have been ecstatic.

Stew

To most Britons of my age group (I confess to my late fifties) this word has an ominous ring to it. My generation knew a stew to be a cooked-to-rags concoction of cheap cuts of meat and root vegetables with a gravy supplemented by such corn-flour-based commercial products as the infamous Bisto.

But in defence of stew I must admit that this is exactly what the magnificent **daube**, meat simmered in wine or, in the case of the Belgian **carbonnade**, in **beer**, has as its cooking method.

Stifado

A Greek term for a **stew**. In Italian it is a *stufatino*, in France and elsewhere in Europe an *estouffade*. But still a stew at that. Why the UK should have turned this splendid creation into such a horror is difficult to fathom.

Stilton

As mentioned before, no blue-veined cheese – not the **roque-fort** of France, the gorgonzola of Italy or the Danish blue of Scandinavia – can compare with this product from Britain, this King of Cheeses. Said to have been invented by a Mrs Elizabeth Scarbrow, a housekeeper to Lady Beaumont at Quenby Hall in Leicestershire, it was subsequently passed on to a daughter called Mrs Paulet, who provided this cheese for her customers in her coaching inn, The Bell, in the village of Stilton in the county.

This regal cheese is today a registered product and, like **champagne**, for instance, is *appellation contrôlée*, which means that Stilton can only be called such if it hails from Leicestershire or the shires of Nottingham and Derby. It matures at about six months old, though there are those, and I am among such connoisseurs, who maintain that it should be consumed at a later age. Traditionally eaten at the end of a meal with a glass or two of **port**, this is a taste sensation that doesn't actually need a preceding meal at all. Stilton is, of course, expensive: it is worth the money.

Stout

> When your health is bad and your heart feels strange
> And your face is pale and wan,
> When Doctors say that you need a change
> *A pint of plain is your only man.*
> When your larder's bare and there's nothing there
> And no rashers grease your pan,
> *A pint of plain is your only man.*

So wrote Flann O'Brien (real name Brian O'Nualláin) in his novel *At Swim Two Birds*. He was referring to plain porter, a version of stout, the most famous example of which is, of course, Guinness. The success of this proprietary brand outside Ireland was much due to a remarkable campaign in the 1920s by the advertising agency S.H. Benson, one of whose copywriters was the detective story novelist Dorothy L. Sayers. It is said that it was she who coined the slogans 'My Goodness, My Guinness' and 'Guinness Gives You Strength'. Certainly Guinness stout came to be so associated with health that expecting mothers were often prescribed a bottle of it a day by their doctors.

Stovies

I only mention this dish, made with leftover meat and potatoes and gravy and traditionally served on Mondays, because it is one of the few national dishes of my native Scotland. It is no longer common in most Scottish households, though many good restaurants that specialize in traditional Scottish fare offer this cheap and filling meal.

There are versions of this dish throughout Europe (see **krumpli**). And there is an especially sumptuous version of stovies in the traditional Tirolean dish *Tiroler G'Rosti*, in which potatoes, herbs, sliced pork, ham and frankfurters are cooked together, topped with a fried egg. I had this in a little restaurant in Innsbruck, washed down with strong local beer.

Stracciatella

A clear consommé which has beaten eggs introduced to it, producing little threads. Originating from Liguria, it is now popular in Roman restaurants. My friend Derek (Dericci) Rafaelli often adds a small glass of **strega** to your bowl. It is discordant but brisk.

Straits Chinese cooking

I know this curious but delicious amalgam of Chinese and Malay cookery because my Uncle Tom had spent thirty years in Malaya and was so addicted to this style of cuisine that even when he had retired to the UK he would often fly off to his former haunts in Penang and Singapore just to eat the food he missed so much. He and my aunt would come back laden with the special spices and herbs needed for the Straits Chinese style. There are very few Straits restaurants in the UK but a very good one in the Grande Place in Brussels, where just about every cuisine in the world can be found.

Strawberry

The most famous strawberries are in the film *The Caine Mutiny*, from the novel of that name by Herman Wouk, in which Humphrey Bogart gets into a fearful wax concerning these fruits. But there is an earlier literary reference by Saki (H.H. Munro) in his chilling story 'The Lumber Room'. Munro was brought up, like many another child of the British Raj (another famous example was Kipling), by a despotic aunt and took his revenge in his later stories.

Strawberries have a conical shape and consist of a cluster of globules. To write that is to say nothing, for it is difficult to express the sheer poetry of the strawberry. Wimbledon fortnight would be impossible to imagine without one of the greatest desserts of all, strawberries and cream. The fruit varies from the small and delicious wild forest variety to the splendid cultivated varieties grown in Scotland to a white strawberry that is grown in the Isle of Man. In my childhood summer started when strawberries were in the shops, displayed in little straw baskets called punnets. Summer had girls with long legs in print dresses, and cherry blossom, and hot days, and strawberries.

Streaky bacon

This cheaper cut of bacon is widely used to line terrines and pâtés, but many people, including myself, enjoy the rashers as an accompaniment to fried eggs for the classic bacon and eggs.

Street food

In many cultures the street is a major food source. Indeed in the nineteenth century for many of the poor in the Victorian cities of Britain it was the only source of hot food. Fried fish (later **fish and chips**), baked potatoes, pies, jellied eels, hot chestnuts etc. were widely consumed in the street by all classes. Italy had and has its pizzas (see **pizza**), Greece and the Balkans pitta bread and a variety of kebabs, Russia proffers piroshkis (see **piroshki**), and the Indian subcontinent a lather of cheap foods to be eaten outside the home, for few urban homes had anything other than the most basic cooking facilities.

Strega

A strong viscous yellow Italian liqueur which is very sweet, some think sickeningly so, with an aniseed flavour. It usually comes in long elegant bottles. Actually I rather enjoy a small liqueur glass of it with an **espresso** at the conclusion of a meal. My brother Brian once drank a half bottle of it late one night in my house. The next morning he thought his teeth were welded together. He has never touched a drop of strega since.

Strudel

This wafer-thin pastry is the case for the famous Austrian and Hungarian *apfelstrudel* (in Hungary known as *retes*). I have had it in the cafés of Vienna and Budapest, but the best I have ever encountered was in a patisserie called Schenk's in London's Kilburn High Road. The thin pastry had a filling of apples, sultanas, cinnamon and rum. It was back in the early 1960s and for me as a young Scot was the most exotic thing I had ever tasted.

Stuffing

All sorts of comestibles are stuffed with all sorts of stuffings. Sausage meat (or forcemeat), breadcrumbs and herbs (see

chicken), rice and diced mushrooms, as well as the famous chestnut stuffing for **turkey** (see **chestnuts**) and other poultry, are all used to stuff, and complement, meat, poultry, sometimes fish and vegetables. (It was the English journalist Shirley 'Superwoman' Conran who wrote that 'Life is too short to stuff a mushroom'. In fact mushrooms, stuffed with a *duxelle* of shallots and herbs, then breaded and baked, make a very good **hors d'œuvres**, as do stuffed tomatoes.)

An especially good little snack is a stuffed pimento. Popular throughout Europe (for once I prefer the young, green, capsicum), this has a stuffing of cooked rice, onions, parsley and diced ham. In the tavernas of Athens it is a staple. And then, of course, roast chicken would not be complete without the British favourite: sage and onion stuffing.

Succotash
This native American dish of lima beans and sweetcorn in a cream sauce is sometimes seen at Thanksgiving dinners.

Suckling pig
Though this young unweaned porker is common throughout Europe, split and roasted, it is especially popular in Spain and also in Roman and Umbrian restaurants, where indeed some restaurants serve only this delectable meat. (An English girl I travelled with in Rome was appalled to see these animals roasted whole on a spit with a large skewer stuck through from arse to mouth. She thought it barbaric. She also was astonished to discover that the Roast Beef of Olde England, in the guise of whole roast cow, started this way in Italy as well. Tender-hearted English girls are inclined to enjoy cooked bits of animals only if they don't look like the animal in the first place.)

The suckling pig meat is tender and juicy, and the crackling of its skin is a great delicacy. In the streets of Madrid suckling pig is often sold as slivers of meat and a piece of the crispy skin wrapped round it: a sort of sandwich.

Suet

A rendered meat fat, usually beef, and best when taken from the area surrounding the kidneys, this is used extensively in many meat dishes but is also the constituent of suet pastry which is used for **steak and kidney pudding**, and a number of sweet steamed puddings such as **roly-poly pudding**.

Sugar

Because the bulk of cane sugar today comes from the Americas and the Caribbean, many people are inclined to think that this was yet another import from the New World. In fact sugar originated in the Indus valley (indeed the Chinese called it 'Indian salt'), and the wild grasses that provided the sugar cane were grown widely in the Ganges delta. An enterprising fellow called Pedro d'Arranca took it with him on his journey with Christopher Columbus and in 1506 planted it in the island of Hispaniola (now divided between Haiti and the Dominican Republic). By 1618 there were eight sugar plantations there.

But it was over a century before these plantations became profitable. That they did become so was entirely due, as was the case with cotton, to the importation of African slaves. And by the middle of the eighteenth century the taste for sweetened coffee and chocolate had trebled the consumption of sugar cane: the result was that the sugar merchants, like their contemporaries of the tobacco trade, had become fabulously wealthy. And so too had the slave traders. (All the emergent great British industrial cities were developed as a result of this merchandise in human flesh from the Dark Continent. Glasgow was tobacco, Manchester cotton, and Liverpool sugar. The fortune of the Gladstone family was based on sugar: when slavery was abolished, the great liberal William Ewart Gladstone was compensated by the British government to the tune of what would today be £15 million.)

But in the early nineteenth century came the production of the carbohydrate from sugar beet. No longer was the cane sugar industry in a position where it could dictate the price of its product. This, appallingly, increased the use of slave labour in the West Indies, for as prices had fallen it was no longer possible to pay wages to a workforce.

Sugar beet was first noted as a potential major source of sugar by the German chemist Margraf in 1745, and was first commercially developed by his disciple Aschard, who built a refinery at Silesia in 1786. Sugar beet refining swiftly passed to Britain.

Sugar beet struck an even heavier blow to the West Indian economy, and is now commonplace throughout the world. Many other sources of sugar are available, such as grapes, or even the sap of the maple tree, but there is now a glut of sugar which has lowered the price to an extent unimaginable just over one and a half centuries ago, even in the developed West. Some of that abundance is now used for the manufacture of alcohol (there is even a fuel made from sugar which can be translated into a substitute for automobile fuel).

The refined white sugars are the most popular, though many prefer the less refined brown sugars such as demerara and muscovado. What I can tell you is that had the Rolling Stones titled their song 'Brown Sugar' as 'White Sugar' it would be a different song altogether. 'White sugar' is a slang term for pure heroin. It suggests therefore that Mick Jagger wrote the lyrics and not Keith Richards.

In many diets there is too great a sugar content, and junk foods are stuffed with it, as they often are with **salt**. I do not myself possess what is often called 'a sweet tooth', but a great many people do, and sugar intake in the Western world is high. It is a curious fact that, as chocolate and confectionery manufacturers are well aware, those who are breast-fed as infants are less likely to develop a taste for highly sweetened foods, owing to the natural sugar content of mother's milk. Research also shows that in the West the consumption of sugar is higher among the poorer classes than among the better-off. And that the better-off are more likely to breast-feed their young than mothers from the lower orders. Well, well, well. It's the rich what gets the pleasure, it's the poor what gets the blame.

Sukiyaki

This is perhaps the most famous Japanese dish of all, and consists of thinly sliced vegetables and even thinner slices of beef, along with cubes of tofu, fried in a mixture of soy sauce, rice wine, water and often, in Western restaurants, sesame oil. It is the oriental origin of the Swiss *fondue chinoise* (see **fondue**) and, far from being unique to Japan, is a common dish throughout South-East Asia. Probably the only Japanese words known to Westerners and certainly Americans are *hara-kiri*, *banzai* and *sukiyaki*.

Supper

This is today the toff's term for **dinner**, but to most people it means a late meal; for children it is a light repast administered just before bedtime. This is not only a very good idea for little ones, it is an excellent notion for grown-ups too, if the meal is light, as the gastric juices work during the hours of sleep. A heavy meal just before retiring is a very bad idea indeed, though one which I admit to entertaining, especially if I have been drinking solidly, as one's appetite is enhanced by alcohol.

Not only does a large meal late at night frequently produce indigestion, it can even lead to heart attacks. Elvis Presley was said to have consumed a large meal of peanut butter and jelly sandwiches late at night prior to his fatal attack. There is something horribly gruesome about what was once the most beautiful of young men dying, obese, drugged and with his pyjama bottoms around his ankles – truly a king croaking it on his throne.

Surati paneer

A famous Indian cheese made from buffalo milk and matured for some time, thus giving it a much stronger flavour than the Italian **mozzarella**. The European practice of having cheese and biscuits at the conclusion of a meal is not seen in the sub-continent save in the Punjab in the north. This is a poor part of India, so it is all the more surprising that the cuisine of the North-West Frontier is astoundingly rich. Dairy produce such as butter, cream and cheese are in abundance. The Sikhs of this area, as they are less inclined to a strict observance of dietary laws than their Muslim and Hindu neighbours, have produced an especially lush style of cookery derived from the great traditions of the Mogul emperors' tastes.

Sushi

A famous Japanese food which has become popular through-out Europe in recent years through the rise of sushi bars, this is a rice-based dish in which a variety of foods, though mainly raw fish or shellfish, is served with vinegared rice. Why this has become quite so fashionable among the young, when the more robust *sashimi* (raw fish with a pungent horseradish paste called *wasami* and strong dipping sauces) is not so common I do not quite fathom. Perhaps the way the delicate flavours of the fish contrast with the accompaniments is the reason. In Japan *sushi* is common enough and is attended by strong rice wine.

Sweet

Though this, of course, is a taste deriving from sugar or honey or their substitutes, it also refers to confectionery such as boiled sweets, and also to the **dessert** or pudding at the end of a meal.

Sweet and sour

Though Europeans have come to regard this splendid flavour conundrum as the province of oriental cookery, it goes back in Europe to the Romans, who widely used honey and sweet wines as well as fruits in combination with sour vinegars and strong game and meat. Yet the sweet and sour pork and prawns which have become a major feature of every occidental Chinese restaurant are what we think of when this phrase is used.

Such dishes are easy to make in your own home. The sauce is made usually with **pineapple**, soy sauce, **sherry** and **vinegar**. Two Jewish friends of mine, Aharon and Melanie, who introduced me to a wonderful book called the *Chinese-Kosher Cookbook*, by Ruth and Bob Grossman (see **Chinese restaurants**), often cook a roast duck for me in a sweet and sour sauce. They call it 'duck chutzpah'; basically a very cheeky duck.

Sweet potato

When the British troops during the North Africa campaign in the Second World War were introduced to this, they detested it. The Catering Corps had mistaken the name and tried making fried chips with this tuber. Though it is, in fact, a different botanical genus from the **yam**, it is often confused with it. Actually if the British Tommy had persevered with unusual foods, he would have eaten rather better than he did, for sweet potatoes are excellent both as a dessert vegetable and as . . . chips.

Sweetcorn
See **corn on the cob** and **popcorn**. There is simply no excuse for this type of maize. Especially in a salad.

Swiss roll
A sponge cake filled with jam and rolled up. It is sometimes covered with chocolate and then becomes a Christmas dessert called a **yule log**.

Syllabub
This ancient English dessert is made with wine, sugar, lemon juice and cream and is a sort of version of the Italian **zabaglione**. My Cornish grandmother used to make this with her home-made elderberry wine. It was about all her home-made elderberry wine was fit for.

Syrup
Though this is the generic term for any liquor that derives from poaching fruits in sugar and water, to most Britons syrup means the childhood favourite produced by the sugar company Tate and Lyle from a concentrated and wonderfully sticky cane sugar concentrate. North America, of course, has its magnificent **maple syrup**.

T

Tabasco

In a recent survey ten leading chefs were asked what were essentials for every larder. All of them demanded this fiery sauce, made from fierce red peppers, from Louisiana. It is, of course, indispensable with **oysters**. And no Bloody Mary cocktail can exist without it.

Though the name is now in common usage, it is actually a registered trade name. Tabasco was created by E. McIlhenny in 1868, in Avery Island, Louisiana, and is long matured in oak casks. It can long mature in your larder too, as only a few drops of it are ever necessary. I have had my bottle of Tabasco in my pantry for nearly twenty years and there is still a little left.

Tagliatelle

These ribbon strips of **pasta** are also called, in the south of Italy, *fettuccine*. They are the most common form of pasta eaten in that country. Like the large sheets of **lasagne**, the pasta is often coloured and flavoured with **spinach**, which gives a pleasant green colour to it; the strips are then known as *tagliatelle verdi*.

Here I must point out that Italy's favourite composer of operas was Giuseppe Verdi – that is, in English, Joe Green, which is not exactly romantic. But what was romantic was the meal of *tagliatelle verdi* with ham and cream (*col prosciutto*) I had in the restaurant of Milan's famous La Scala opera house over twenty years ago. I was sharing the meal with a lovely girl called Elissa when an astounding thunderstorm broke out over the canopy above us in the balcony restaurant. The electric lamps failed and a waiter brought candles for his customers as the storm raged and the lightning tore the skies. That's enough to have you eating *tagliatelle col prosciutto* for the rest of your life.

Take-away

In the UK, in particular, the concept of a ready-made meal from a restaurant, usually modest and unpretentious, literally taken away and consumed at home, has become so ingrained that it is now part of the native culture. Although **fish and chips** is an obvious example of this, most Britons think of Chinese and Indian restaurants when they talk of take-aways.

Tamarind

Widely used in Indian cookery, this pod, the fruit of a tropical tree native to Africa as well as the subcontinent, gives an acid taste to dishes, and is used rather as one would use **lemon**. It is usually sold as a pulp in solid form and also has medicinal properties: it helps to break down body acids and aids the reduction of high blood pressure.

Tandoori

A *tandoor* is a clay oven utilized in Indian cuisine. It imparts a special flavour to food, especially meats such as lamb and chicken. Introduced to Britain only in the last two decades, food cooked in this way is now ubiquitous in the form of tikka masala (see **curry**), although the tandoori method is now sadly much misused. Proper tandoori cooking requires consider-able expertise, and the traditional spices, which must be very fresh, include garlic, ginger, cardamom, nutmeg, chillies, cumin and coriander. My friend Nav Basi, who owns the mag-nificent Dhabba restaurant in Glasgow, employs a specialist chef just for tandoori.

Tangerine

This little orange originates in China: hence the alternative name mandarin orange. The name 'tangerine' originates from Tangier, from where the fruit was imported. It is very sweet-tasting and has the extra benefit of being easy to peel. Widely available as canned. I am addicted to this lovely little fruit, fresh or tinned and am capable of consuming a large can of them with great dollops of ice cream at one sitting, especially for breakfast. I can think of few better treats. The dried tangerine peel is used as a condiment in many Chinese dishes.

Tannin

A strong chemical found in many foods but most particularly in **tea**, this has an astringency that affects both the taste and aroma of tea. It also reduces the effects of caffeine. (Many medical experts claim that tea contains a higher element of caffeine than **coffee** and say that it is the presence of tannin in tea which means that the insomnia which caffeine in coffee can induce will not occur with tea. And it has properties that can help those suffering from a bout of diarrhoea.)

Tea drinkers in the Far East mostly prefer the green teas in which the tannin content is high, and it is said that the chem-ical has an addictive quality. In many parts of the world the tannin is reduced by adding milk or some other dairy product, as the proteins in milk reduce the astringency of the tannin.

But if you think the Chinese and Japanese are addicted to tea and tannin you should see the British.

Tapas

These **hors d'œuvres** can be found in virtually every Spanish bar. When British holidaymakers first travelled to Spain in the 1950s, they were suspicious at being offered these little snacks (which can range from a simple dish of olives or meats and pâtés), not realizing that the Spaniards were offering them free to go with the wine or sherry they were purchasing, as was the custom with the natives. You will not get tapas free in many bars of today's Spain, however.

Some Spanish gourmets claim that the cooking of Andalucía has been spoiled because many Spanish people now have their midday meal made up entirely of tapas.

Today in Britain there are a large number of tapas bars, and this is A Good Thing because it helps to reduce both the amount of alcohol being drunk and also the effects of the excess of it. It has to be said that this does not seem to affect many British holidaymakers in Spain, especially young ones, as they get, to the bewilderment of the Spanish natives, horribly drunk. In Spain, as in all Mediterranean countries, to be seen inebriated in public would be a disgrace. Soaking up alcohol with food is a dashed good idea. See **tightener**.

Tapioca

Much the same as **sago**, once much utilized in school dining halls and quite as disgusting.

Taramasalata

I first encountered this Greek dip, which is made from fish roe, potatoes, olive oil, lemon juice and vinegar, in a little family-run restaurant in Glasgow which I have mentioned before (see **retsina**) called, rather ludicrously, The Golden

Kebab. It is more of a sort of café actually and is situated incongruously in a pleasant leafy suburb. Despite the existence of very smart Greek restaurants in the city, this little eatery is still the best Greek place in Scotland. Fortunately few know this, so I can dine there without booking.

Taramasalata comes as a smooth paste and is eaten with hot pitta bread. It is common in the cheap tavernas you will find throughout Greece.

Tarragon

This herb hails from Asia and is a major commercial product of Siberia. It is not much used in British or American cuisine but is widely employed in French cooking, where it is most associated with poultry. I add it myself to almost every chicken dish: it has a comforting, cosy, almost sleepy flavour. (Like thousands of others, I was alerted to the combination of tarragon and chicken by a famous remark of Elizabeth David's that this herb has 'a special affinity' with chicken. She was, as ever, right.)

For some reason tarragon reminds me of a warm bed and fresh cotton sheets and, somehow, childhood. There is also tarragon vinegar, which is good with shellfish.

Tart

The same as a pie, but with no pastry lid. The famous tarts, besides quiches (see **quiche**) are of course **jam** tarts, the ones the Queen of Hearts baked and which the rascally Knave of the same suit stole.

Tartare sauce

This is a **mayonnaise** sauce flavoured with parsley, chopped gherkins and capers, and is served with fish, especially fried fish. I myself add a pinch of dried English **mustard** and a few drops of lemon juice. Though I did indeed invent this out of my own head, I later discovered that others had invented the additions out of their own heads before me. Michel Guérard, the chef credited with creating *cuisine minceur*, had created the same years before. The sauce is essential with scampi but the awful little sachets that often go with the above in pubs are to be avoided.

Tartrazine
A synthetic colouring agent once much used in ready-made meals, it is said to cause allergies to which children are especially susceptible. It is now less common in food and drink.

T-bone steak
During the food scare of the 1990s, when Mad Cow Disease was devastating British agriculture, humans were said to contract the human form of the disease from beef on the bone. T-bone steaks were thus banned. My local master butcher went on television to prove that you could have a T-bone steak without the bone.

The steak is cut from the rump end of the **sirloin**. (Porterhouse steaks are cut from the rib end of the sirloin.) The ban was regarded with incredulity by Americans in the UK, as T-bone steak is a favourite cut in the USA.

Tea
Though there are Chinese texts describing tea-drinking in the first century BC, it was not until the Tang dynasty of the eighth century AD that the first philosophical and technical treatise on the subject appeared, the *Cha-sing* or *Classic Art of Tea*, by the Taoist poet Lu-Yu. He was immortalized by becoming, according to legend, the tea genie Chazu on his death, and his effigy is honoured to this day by all tea merchants from Hong Kong to Singapore.

Tea did not become common in China until about the sixth century, when it was still chewed in small pressed cakes, rather as tobacco was at one time in the Americas. The way of making tea as an infusion became common during the Ming dynasty and spread in the ninth century to Japan, where tea-drinking became even more ritualistic and ceremonial than in China. In both countries tea houses are of very great importance, much as cafés became and remain in Europe.

Talking of Europe, tea did not figure there until the mid-seventeenth century, when it was imported by Dutch and French traders in Macao. It was, like **coffee** and **chocolate**, at first denounced as an intoxicant but gradually became considered as of medical use. The spread of tea was sporadic, as it remains to this day, in Latin countries, but in Holland and especially Britain it soon became a drink for rich and poor alike. After Thomas Garaway had opened the first tearoom in England in 1640, Oliver Cromwell, always on the look-out for extra revenue, put a special tax on it. In this he erred for, far from people drinking less tea or paying tax, tea became a major item for smugglers. In this activity, also in the smuggling of brandy, silk, spices and other highly taxed products, it was clergymen who played a considerable role. Militia were reluctant to raid church premises such as crypts, where the tombs were emptied of human remains that had lain there for centuries and filled with the precious tea, which had now become a necessity for aristocrats and farm labourers alike.

Tea-drinking in the British Isles is well recorded and is not mere legend. Today instant coffee has made inroads into tea-drinking in Britain, but tea is still the national drink. There is a sort of ceremony about it among the gentrified (see **afternoon tea**), but also among the humbler orders (see **char**), and more than that – when disaster looms there is always, for the British, 'a nice cup of tea'.

Tea had become a British obsession by the late eighteenth century, and the era of the great tea clipper races had begun. Tea had increasingly been grown and imported from India and

Ceylon, rather than China, and now the race to bring the millions of pounds of tea in ship after ship produced races upon which a great deal of money was bet. And by the early twentieth century it was even incorporated in the entire tea trade and developed into yacht racing when Sir Thomas Lipton, a colourful Glasgow tea merchant who was the first entrepreneur to develop what we would now describe as chain grocery shops, competed for many years in the Atlantic yacht race. He never won, but he afforded much amusement to Britons and Americans alike.

Tea became a major trade for the British Empire, focused in India and Ceylon and cutting a large part of the China tea trade (though Russia and Arab countries still import much of their tea from China). Famous teas such as Darjeeling and Assam are the ones most frequently used in British blends, though the Chinese Oolong is often included too. The European countries have little taste for tea – the French average one and a half cups of tea a month, and the Italians three cups of tea a year, which are probably accounted for by British tourists. Since the Boston Tea Party Americans have been coffee rather than tea-drinkers, though in New England – oddly, considering it was in Boston that the dumping of tea into the harbour occurred – tea is taken by the older and more genteel families. Arabs are, however, avid tea jennies and consume their hot boiling tea in glasses held in ornamental holders called zanfs (see **zanf**). Russians are also great tea-drinkers and consume the beverage with a spoonful of jam and lemon. They brew their tea in silver samovars and dilute with water to taste.

Many tea-drinkers add milk or dairy products such as butter or yoghurt. On the subject of milk there is a heated debate on milk in tea among the British. The middle classes insist on milk in first, the lower orders on adding it afterwards.

Tea boy

I note that this term virtually no longer exists in British offices, for reasons explained in the following entry on the **tea break**. Yet at one time it was a term of considerable abuse for one who claimed a status to which he was not entitled. 'He's just a bloody tea boy' was a phrase used to deflate such a pretension.

Tea break

This was once common in every office in the UK, a period when employees would stop work for ten or fifteen minutes each morning and afternoon for a cup of tea. It was, of course, replaced by a skivvy with a trolley who brought it to the clerk's desk. This was later replaced by nothing at all, or perhaps a bloody awful automatic machine which dispensed tea, coffee or an ersatz soup: each of which tasted of the others.

It should be noted that in Italy and France and other Mediterranean countries employees have their mid-morning break in nearby cafés. The workplaces there are thus more civilized, although not noticeably less efficient.

Tea jenny

A term for an avid drinker of tea which, when used of a male, is invariably a pejorative, rather as is 'milksop'. Famous tea jennies include Dr Johnson, who drank several pints of the brew at a time, and the British politician Tony Benn, who used to consume over sixty cups of it each day. Both eventually made themselves ill because of their compulsive behaviour. Both were barking mad.

Tea shop

Agatha Christie's Miss Marple (see **seed cake**) was forever nipping into tea shops. In this she was not alone, even in real life. For many spinster ladies of her generation this would be one of the few circumstances in which social contact could be made outside church committees and such.

Though the first tea shop in London, established in 1707 by the tea merchant Thomas Twining, had tea drunk as a process of sampling, it was not until 1717 that Twining opened his first actual tearooms. Excluded as they were from the coffee houses, the ladies were delighted. (Later a craze for tea gardens took over for a while.)

But from the first tearooms and tea shops were female-orientated and often derided by men. From the later years of the nineteenth century up till the early 1960s, tea shops abounded throughout every city, town and village, most of them virtually exclusively for female customers. (Indeed most men would have felt seriously out of place in such an environment.) There were, of course, places such as the Lyons Corner Houses, where the sexes would mix and meet, but the tea shops were mainly for female patronage.

In Scotland, however, where there was a strong temperance movement, there grew a phenomenon by which the tearooms and tea shops became highly fashionable establishments. Stuart Cranston, a teetotal tea merchant, opened his first tearoom in Glasgow in 1875, and his sister Kate established Miss Cranston's Crown Tearooms three years later. They were intended as an alternative to public houses, for heavy drinking was indeed a significant problem in all Britain's cities.

It was in 1903, however, that Kate Cranston's world-famous Willow Tearooms opened. 'World-famous' because everything at the Willow, from exterior to interior to furniture, even down to cutlery, was designed by the now legendary Charles Rennie Mackintosh, who also designed, of course, that city's art school. Art lovers and architects came from all over the world to view the work of this most innovative architect and, with many more tearooms opening in this most industrial city, it became known as the tearoom capital of the world.

The great years for tearooms and tea shops lasted from about the turn of the twentieth century till the mid 1960s. A lack of cheap female labour plus changing attitudes among the young saw to that. This was the case throughout the country, though the tea 'shoppe' never entirely went away from the more genteel villages.

But just as coffee houses have made a dramatic return in recent years, so I suspect you will see tea shops reappear in the future. Indeed after many years Cranston's Willow Tearooms were recreated right down to the crockery and cutlery. In fact, a few years ago I was interviewed on a radio programme in the new tea shop and a farrago ensued in which I was supposed to be a regular of such establishments. How my friends did laugh. I would no more think of becoming a *habitué* of tea shops than I would of giving out religious tracts in a night-club.

Textured vegetable protein

This is widely used as an ingredient of many ready-made meals, and also in the catering industry. Known in such trades as TVP, it is derived from plant proteins, especially soya beans, and is used as a meat substitute, usually as a supplement in the manufacturing business, but it is also sometimes used by catering establishments to lengthen out pie fillings or hamburgers or even stews. I can taste its presence immediately and dislike it intensely. And there is worse: just one mouthful of a dish containing this horror will find you waking the next morning with an absolutely foul taste in your mouth.

Thousand island dressing

In North America this salad dressing is made with **mayonnaise**, chopped onions and gherkins and **Tabasco** sauce, and sometimes hard-boiled eggs. In the UK it is *always* made with sieved hard-boiled eggs and, according to Ceserani and Kinton's *Practical Cookery* (that ubiquitous textbook in all British catering colleges), oil and vinegar rather than mayonnaise is employed.

Thyme

There is a lovely Irish ballad with a haunting melody called 'Once I Had a Leaf of Thyme'. Though it is sung by men and women alike, it is in fact a girl's song about a sailor lad who 'steals away' her thyme. It made no sense to me at all until I discovered that in Celtic folklore this herb is the symbol of virginity. (Yet in what was once a little manual owned by every middle-class lady, *The Language of Flowers*, the plant denotes activity, and the Greeks thought the herb promoted vigour.)

But then, herbs are often symbols of grace, purity, goodness and so on in many cultures throughout the world. In the case of thyme it must be a very sturdy virginity at that, because it is a strong herb and is used widely in French cuisine. It is one of the principal herbs in a **bouquet garni**. It can be utilized in the delicate lemon, parsley and thyme stuffing for poultry as an alternative to the more robust sage and onion which is common in British cooking. In southern France farmed rabbits are fed on thyme to enhance their flavour.

Tightener

I do not know if this term for a snack organized to counter the effects of much alcohol is widespread in the UK, but it is, like the habit of **tapas** in Spain and Portugal, a good idea. Much of the binge-drinking pursued by so many Britons would be much alleviated by the business of eating between drinks. And I do not mean those bloody awful crisps or an olive or two. When I have guests back to my house for late drinks I will serve an omelette or perhaps some thick slices of ham and pickles or, quite often, a **welsh rarebit**.

Tikka

A style of cooking meat and poultry that involves marinating the ingredients in yoghurt and **tandoori** spices. It comes from the north of India, from the Punjab. An Indian restaurateur friend of mine won't have it on his menu because he says that British diners are so used to the corrupted versions in the UK that they would not appreciate what is intended to be a delicate and subtle flavour. He says almost all tikkas he has tasted in British Asian eateries are over-salted, over-spiced and about as authentic as British curry powders.

Timpana

This is Malta's national dish and consists of a pastry pie filled with **macaroni**, a meat sauce like the *bolognese*, with eggs and chicken livers. It was once popular in the little Maltese cafés that abounded in London in the 1950s and '60s, where it was often called Valetta pie, after Malta's capital.

Tipsy cake

I only mention this sponge cake, laced with sherry and covered with pink marzipan, because it was a friend of my childhood. I haven't seen it in years.

Tisanes

Hercule Poirot is much addicted to a variety of these herbal teas, and certainly they are much enjoyed by the French and Belgians alike. They consume more of these herbal, sometimes fruit-based, infusions than they do actual teas, and do so often for medicinal purposes. Few Britons drink them, partly because they are already addicted to tea, and partly because those who sip herbal teas are considered to be loony nut-cutleters.

Toad in the hole

When I was a child, my family made an occasional – a very occasional – visit to an aunt and uncle who lived in a very bourgeois part of rural Ayrshire. My aunt was a Domestic Science teacher and one of the worst cooks I have ever encountered, which is of course why the visits were very sparse indeed. She invariably made this atrocity of link sausages cooked in an egg batter. Somehow she managed to make the batter watery. This was a time when parents made you eat everything on your plate, especially in the house of a hostess. The ordeal of trying hard not to actually throw up was worse than the ordeal of consuming this disgusting dish.

Toast

It was Mary Poppins who smelled of 'the flavour of toast which always hung about her so deliciously'. (P.L. Travers, who invented the character back in 1934, was a former actress and dancer who worked for the British Ministry of Information in the USA during the war. Her private life was about as far away from that of Mary Poppins as you can possibly get.)

There is T.S. Eliot going on about 'the taking of a toast and tea' in 'The Love Song of J. Alfred Prufrock' and there remains another literary reference to what is simply slices of bread grilled on both sides, in Saki's chilling story *Sredni Vashtar*. In this tale the little boy Conradin celebrates the demise of his truly appalling aunt and guardian by making the hitherto forbidden toast. Our protagonist has a little rhyme which I have sometimes repeated to myself ever since I first read the story at the age of twelve. It goes:

> Sredni Vashtar went forth,
> His thoughts were red thoughts and his teeth were white,
> His enemies called for peace, but he brought them death,
> Sredni Vashtar the Beautiful.

Sredni Vashtar is the name Conradin gave his illicit pet polecat–ferret. This will doubtless leave you somewhat bemused. You will just have to read the story for yourself. But one thing is true. No toast smells or tastes as good as that produced with a toasting-fork in front of an open fire. With lots of butter and Seville **marmalade**. And it helps to be a child.

Tobacco

Though this solanaceous plant native to America can hardly be considered as a food, it is most definitely a food substitute, as many young girls and women have unfortunately discovered. Smoking the weed diminishes appetite and keeps you thin.

The plant is addictive, as I know well. In writing this book (and everything else I have written), I have spent more on tobacco in the form of cigarettes than I shall actually earn on its publication. Yet I would not be without tobacco. And despite what anti-smoking fascists say, I still find the smell of it heavenly.

Toffee apple

Once astoundingly popular in my childhood, this was a dessert apple impaled upon a stick and covered with a hard shell of toffee (a mixture of syrup, sugar, water, butter and a small amount of vinegar). Though this sweetmeat is rarely seen in today's Britain, you will still find it throughout Europe and Asia.

Tomato

Just how Italians managed to survive at all before this little fruit was introduced from the Americas is a wonder to us all, for the cuisine of modern Italy is virtually dependent on it. The South American Indians explained to the first Spanish colonists that tomatoes, combined with chillies (see **chilli**), made a fine and piquant sauce, and a certain Father de Acosta had the fruit exported to the Old World.

The tomato first entered Italy in the sixteenth century by way of Naples, then a Spanish possession, and after great suspicion – as was the case with the **potato** – came to be perhaps the most important fruit in Italian cooking. The Italians called it *pomodoro*, 'golden apple'. And the French *pomme d'amour*, 'love apple', which was also the term used by the English.

But it was not until the early nineteenth century that tomatoes became common eating outside southern Europe. Indeed the gourmet writer Brillat-Savarin first discovered the fruit – it is not, in fact, a vegetable – in the famous Trois Frères Provençal restaurant in the Rue Sainte-Anne in Paris about 1786. He recorded in his diaries fifteen years later that he wondered how he could have done without it in his youth.

Tomatoes come in various forms, and canned Italian plum tomatoes, as well as tomato paste or purée, are suitable not just for use in Italian dishes but everywhere else as well (see, for example, **rogan josh**). And as a fresh fruit they are wonderful. As a small boy I used to visit a tomato grower in Ayrshire with a gift of clotted **cream** from my Grandma and was rewarded with bags of small Scottish cherry tomatoes: they were sweet and delicious. Scottish tomatoes are highly regarded, and the Lanarkshire region is world famous for its little sweet tomatoes – so much so that smart French restaurants import them in their tons. And where would we be without tomato juice for our Bloody Marys?

Tongue

It was once the practice of butchers to display a whole ox tongue in their front windows. Rarely seen whole these days it always looked healthily gruesome to me. Boiled tongue, sliced very thinly, is, or was, a major sandwich filler. Frankly I don't like it. Not just because of its taste or texture. For a quite irrational reason I cannot quite get it out of my head that this product resided for some time in an animal's mouth.

Tonic water

A carbonated water with a small amount of quinine added. It was introduced to Europeans as an antidote to fevers occurring with malaria, though its major use today is as a mixer with **gin**. My father, who had contracted malaria as a young soldier in China in the 1920s, didn't like gin: he combined tonic water with an Islay malt **whisky**. (He liked most of all an especially astringent Islay malt called Laphraoig.) He was right too. With ice it is a bracing combination which can be very refreshing on a rare hot summer's day in the Hebridean Isles of Scotland. Or anywhere else, if it comes to that.

Tortillas

Mexican food has become very popular in the UK in recent years, especially among the young. Why, I don't quite grasp, for it is very limited in its flavours, which in any case can be found in many European cuisines. Tortilla bars are now fairly common in most British cities and these filled pancakes certainly help, rather as **tapas** do, to soak up alcohol. Considering that British youth now seems to feel that a good night out means getting pissed out of your brains, I am rather in favour of both tapas and tortillas.

Trattorias

There used to be a small diner in my native city of Glasgow called the Trattoria Marida, run by two Italian brothers and their families. As is the way with Italian brothers, there was a falling out and the eatery was reopened as the Ristorante Marida. This increase in status ruined what was, until then, one of the best outlets for Italian food in the city. For in Italy the small trattorias often provide excellent food, much as the Indian dhabbas and French bistros and *routiers* do (see **bistro**). What is more, in many trattorias throughout Italy you will find local specialities not seen so readily in the more expensive *ristoranti*.

Treacle

Known in the USA as molasses, and sometimes in the UK as 'black treacle', this is a by-product of the sugar cane refining process. It is thick and unrefined, unlike the so-called 'golden syrup'. Tins of it have a shelf-life which will outlive yours. Rarely seen these days, it is used in baking and confectionery. A speciality of Scottish baking used to be treacle scones, also now uncommon, and there is of course the treacle tart, which in fact uses the aforementioned golden syrup rather than treacle.

But there was once a traditional game, played at Halloween, in which a large scone, coated in black treacle, was suspended from a string in the ceiling and then little boys and girls had to try and . . . to hell with it: the game is both innocent and inexplicable.

Trencherman

On a newspaper I once worked for there was a restaurant critic called Raymond Gardner who was cited as *Trencherman*. This is a name for a keen and prodigious eater, which Raymond most certainly was despite his slender frame. But the term derives from the word 'trencher', which was originally a thick slice of bread used as a plate upon which meat and other foods was served. In medieval times the poor would congregate outside their lordships' houses when they feasted and the trenchers would be thrown to them. It was the poet Matthew Prior (1664–1721), with Rabelaisian wit, who wrote of the aristocracy:

> Their beer was strong; their wine was port;
> Their meal was large; their grace was short;
> They gave the poor the remnant-meat;
> Just when it grew not fit to eat.

Just like the trencher-throwers of yore. Not much has changed.

Trifle

To make this splendid traditional British dessert you have to start with lining a nice big crystal bowl that your mother inherited from her grandmother with fingers of late sponge, drench them with **sherry** and perhaps a few drops of rum essence, strew slices of tinned pears over this, pour over it all a thinned-down and hot amount of fruit juice **jelly** from Jello cubes, let it set, then over this spread a coating of Bird's **custard**. And later a topping of greatly whipped **cream**, and a little grated chocolate, or perhaps some hundreds and thousands: do all this and then you have a genuine trifle.

Though I rarely have dessert in a restaurant myself, preferring cheese and biscuits, I do make this for my godchildren and nephews and nieces and other people when I give a wee party for them. My own sainted mother did the same.

The British are, in fact, very good indeed at desserts, just as they are pretty dreadful at other foods; paradoxically they are wonderful at the last course, so much so that continental Europeans do indeed copy, often inadequately, British puddings and desserts. This is certainly true of trifle. The Italians, for instance, have a lovely travesty of the above called **zuppa inglese** (why Italians name this 'English soup' is rather beyond me), which is made with macaroons and other exotica. The French make it too and use orange liqueurs such as Cointreau. Americans top this with ice cream.

When in 1986 the chef Tom Vernon made a series of television programmes on world food for the BBC, he included this as a British product and was later bemused when he encountered Islamic fans of his shows in north Africa who made a trifle according to his recipe and included the forbidden alcohol of sherry. His Muslim followers admitted that the sherry was indeed necessary.

Tripe

There is no excuse for this save actual starvation. It is the stomach lining of the ox and was once horribly popular among the masses of Britain, where it came in the form of tripe and onions cooked in milk. It retains a certain popularity in Europe. You will find it on offer in many Florentine restaurants, and there is the famous tripe of Caen in Normandy.

Tripe is visually repellent, tastes like ordure and smells – and its aroma will permeate a house for days – like diarrhoea.

Trout

This member of the **salmon** family is to my mind more flavoursome than its more expensive cousin, especially the colourful rainbow variety, despite the fact that this is largely a freshwater fish. And here is a singularity. Trout tastes best when bought whole before gutting and before the head is removed. Even when your fishmonger fillets it an hour before you cook this magnificent fish, it is still preferable to delay evisceration until cooking and serving. Sadly many Anglo-Americans get squeamish when they see what a fish actually looks like as a corpse – they don't like to see the skin or the head or even the wee swishy tail which once propelled it through water. This is, of course, ridiculous as the creatures of the sea themselves have no such aesthetic notions and eat each other with an avid will.

Truffle

It is an enigma, this curious and costly fungus. It is notoriously difficult to find – in the famous truffle region of Périgord in France and the equally legendary truffle grounds of Piedmont in Italy trained dogs and pigs are used to find these elusive fungi. In Italy the white truffle, which has a powerful scent and flavour, is the most sought-after and is used raw often as a slight shaving over pasta dishes, some types of **risotto** or veal. (In Italy dogs are used to sniff out truffles. In France, in the Périgord region, pigs. The difference? Pigs have a keen sense of smell and love truffles: the problem is that they also eat them, whereas dogs will simply locate them.)

The classic French truffle is the black variety. It is less flavoursome than the Italian white (actually a muddy brown colour), but it is prized for the aroma it lends to the recipes in which it is used. Colette was an avid fan of the black Périgord truffle, but in Italy the most famous *aficionado* of the Italian white truffle was the composer Rossini, a noted gourmet, who loved the white truffles in the cafés and *ristoranti* of his native city Bologna so much that all over the world you will find dishes utilizing truffles and given his name.

Truffles are expensive and do not keep for much more than a week. You can obtain tinned truffles, but they hardly seem worth the effort let alone the cost, though vacuum-bottled ones are reasonably effective.

Truffles

Very different from the above, these are a type of sweetmeat made from a chocolate base and often flavoured with alcohol and made into little spheres, then dipped in cocoa powder or sometimes chocolate vermicelli. In expensive confectioners these can cost damned nearly as much as the fungi from which they take their name.

Tuck

A British term once primarily used in boarding schools to describe sweetmeats and pastries in the unfortunate student's tuck box. A tuck shop would be the premises of a nearby confectioner or pastry cook. Today virtually every British state school has a so-called tuck shop open at morning break which sells, to aid school funds, fizzy drinks, potato crisps, chocolate bars and such. Considering that obesity among children is now an epidemic, this practice is not only inexplicable but also deeply dangerous.

Turbot

A close relation of the **halibut**, this member of the flatfish family is regarded as a luxury fish and is expensive. (But then, ludicrously, all fishes in the UK are now very expensive in the shops.) I am not saying that this medium-oily fish is over-rated, for it makes for good eating, but it is horribly over-priced.

Turkey

I recently saw a description of this large fowl, native to North America, as a flightless bird: well, it's not – in the wild they roost high in trees. Not that you will find many wild turkeys these days, for they are prodigiously farmed – and battery-farmed at that. Thus what was once a rather gamey flesh is bloody blotting paper and usually tough.

It was not always so, and in fact once turkey was not only an excellent fowl but also a relatively rare food bird in Europe. The Christmas turkey is thus of fairly recent date in most British households: for those who could afford a Christmas dinner the traditional main item was **goose**.

A turkey is a large bird which can indeed grow to over 40lb in weight and is high in protein whilst being low in fat. And despite what I have mentioned above, a non-battery turkey makes for good eating. It is, of course, essential for the Thanksgiving dinner in the USA, when the roasted bird is served with potatoes and **wild rice**, corn fritters and gravy. These allegedly were the only ingredients the Pilgrim Fathers could find and the meal has been celebrated ever since.

Turkish coffee

In every coffee house in every bazaar in every city, town and village in Turkey you will be offered their version of coffee: a thick, sludgy and incredibly sweet potation. In fact you will find this throughout the Arab world and all over North Africa. What is astonishing is how refreshing it is in a hot climate.

Though **coffee** is not grown in Turkey, it was indeed the Ottoman empire that introduced it to the West and ritualized the taking of it. Turkish coffee throughout the Islamic world is very much a substitute for alcohol, which is of course forbidden to Muslims, though this does not deter Arab sheikhs from getting pissed out of their heads when they visit Europe – as I discovered when I worked as a barman in London back in the early 1960s.

Paradoxically Turkey, which is a secular state, not only serves coffee but also alcohol in its cafés and bars. And here I simply must name-drop. I once had lunch with the great-grandson of Kemal Atatürk, the founder of modern Turkey, and we drank whisky. He told me his great grandfather was renowned for his ability to drink everybody else under the table. 'Except your Winston Churchill', said Amnir. 'My father said he drank more than anybody and still talked.' Heavens, I felt somehow proud of being British.

Turkish delight
A confection much travestied in the UK, where it is often a slab of synthetic-flavoured gelatine covered in milk chocolate, this is widespread throughout the Middle East. You can find real Turkish delight in Europe, however: it usually comes in little round wooden boxes and is relatively expensive. (It is, however, a favourite gift that I bring to the hostess of a house to which I have been invited for dinner. The boxes look spectacular, and this confection is still cheaper than Belgian chocolates.) Turkish delight comes as square cubes covered in a film of icing sugar. Known as *loukoumi*, it is usually flavoured with **rose water** and **vanilla**. There are a great many variations of the sweet in Indian confectionery shops.

Turmeric
A spice made from a root of the **ginger** family, this is mild-tasting and is more often used as a colouring agent. (Some use it as a substitute for **saffron**. There is, however, no substitute for saffron.) Turmeric is an ingredient of most versions of **curry powder**. On its own it tastes rather medicinal.

Turnip
This is the north British term for a swede or, in America, a **rutabaga**. In Scotland it is rather endearingly known as a 'neep' (see **haggis**). It is a root vegetable, globular in shape, and the flesh is generally creamy in colour and is almost sweet.

When boiled and mashed, it is especially good with strong ground black pepper. Like **cabbage**, however, it has long been associated with cattle fodder. And the famous lamb dish *navarin printanier* would be the sadder without its presence.

Tutti-frutti

'Awop-bop-a-loo-mop-a-lop-bam-boom. Tutti-frutti.' Thus started the classic rock disc by Richard Penniman. He was of course Little Richard, a diminutive but very wild piano-playing rock'n'roller, who transmuted this song long known to the American homosexual community (Little Richard had every drawback a teen performer could manage – he was tiny, black, a hot-gospeller with a deeply religious background, and he was gay), but with sort of cleaned-up lyrics by writer Dorothy La Bostrie he cut the record in five minutes. Originally it was titled 'good booty', which was gay slang for, well, the act of sodomy itself. And what has this to do with tutti-frutti? Nothing at all except that in every American drugstore and juke joint you could both hear the record and buy and consume this ice cream, topped with chopped glacé fruits.

Tzimmes

Traditionally made at the Jewish New Year, this is a kosher dish made of braised brisket of beef with root vegetables and sweetened with honey. It is simply dreadful.

U

Ugli

This is a very nasty name for what is a very nice fruit indeed, a sort of hybrid of a grapefruit and a tangerine. It grows in North America, but I first discovered it in the West Indian grocers of Notting Hill in London back in the early 1960s.

Ulster fry

This is made in Northern Ireland from a bacon joint sometimes known as 'Ulster roll', and is a canned product of bacon rubbed with saltpetre, salt and sodium nitrate, rather as is the way with **corned beef**. It is then salt-cured and smoked. Sliced thinly and fried with eggs, it is odd but delicious. It used to be quite common in the west of Scotland, but I haven't seen it in some years. But you will indeed find it in Ulster. The splendid Crown Bar in Belfast – the only bar on the National Trust list in the United Kingdom – always has this on its breakfast menu.

Unleavened bread

Necessary, of course, to Jewish cookery, this is bread (unleavened biscuits also exist) that has no raising agent such as yeast. Where would Passover be without it? In fact, in very religious Jewish households even the tablecloths must be unstarched during the six days of Passover as the starch is made from wheat or barley, which might have fermented. This injunction against fermentation makes it a right bugger for Jews who like a spot of whisky and soda.

Upside-down cake

When Beth in Louisa May Alcott's horribly saccharine *Little Women* recovers from a fever (she croaks it in the next chapter, though, and the scene has one in tears of mirth), the March family celebrates by baking an upside-down cake, which is a sponge mixture with fruit placed at the bottom. When turned out, the fruit is at the top. There is also a pudding made in much the same way.

V

Vacuum flask

This container, usually cylindrical, possesses a vacuum between an inner and an outer shell and is used to keep soup or tea or coffee hot (or indeed cold) for a considerable amount of time. The trade name Thermos is now synonymous with it, rather as Hoover is now with – what else? – a vacuum cleaner. (Incidentally the Thermos flask was introduced to the USA by the father of the American painter, and friend of F. Scott Fitzgerald, Gerald Murphy. I will bet you didn't know that.)

Vanilla

It was stout Cortez who, with eagle eyes, spotted that the Aztecs were using vanilla to flavour their chocolate drinks. The same Spaniard brought it back to Europe, where it became an important item in, especially, confectionery and ice creams. The pod of this member of the orchid family has a unique flavour and scent but is now more often produced artificially. And a vanilla ice cream still has most of us moved to ecstatic silence, upon a peak in Darien.

Veal

I have mentioned before the distressing circumstance when calves' liver became difficult to come by, and there was a period in the late twentieth century when there was a ludicrous campaign against veal: veggies and soppy-eyed women didn't like to have cuddly little baby cows slaughtered for their delicious flesh. During this time I was forced to obtain veal from Italian friends who own one of my favourite restaurants.

Italian restaurants, and indeed Italian cuisine, could not do without veal. Though the French have a great many veal dishes, among which is the famous *blanquette de veau*, a white stew with a cream sauce which I find myself a little too bland, and a splendid dish of veal escalopes in a vermouth sauce, it is in Italian cookery that veal reaches its greatest heights. Some gourmets claim that the ever-present breaded veal escalopes in Italian places are boring (some people find veal, with its delicate flavour, boring in itself), but I never find these delectable dishes so. One of the most enjoyable dishes is *vitello alla marsala*, veal in a marsala sauce, and I serve it to my dinner guests regularly. It is a simple dish, cooked in minutes, and has a considerable advantage in that it is almost impossible to spoil. The pickiest of children like it too. And then there is **wiener schnitzel**. Try also a roast joint of veal with a caper sauce. It is not only exquisite; it looks more expensive than it actually is and impresses horribly. See also **vitello tonnato**.

Veal cordon bleu

There are those who will tell you that this 'sandwich' of two slices of veal containing soft cheese and ham and then coated in egg and breadcrumbs is a Swiss dish, but it is not: it is an old Italian recipe cooked in a thin mix of broth and marsala wine. It is a rich and filling dish. Often chicken breasts are substituted for veal, usually without the breadcrumbs.

Vegetarianism

There was a fad in the late twentieth century among many young people for this diet, in which meat is not eaten. It takes various forms. There are those who will eat poultry, and those who do not allow poultry but will permit fish. Some vegetarians eschew eggs, as these are embryos, and some others will not drink milk or allow any dairy products. A vegetarian diet is very unhealthy, no matter what such nut-cutleters say, and many on a vegetarian regime are forced to take vitamin supplements (see **vitamins**).

You will find throughout this volume my deep contempt for vegetarianism. The fact is that, despite what such cranks like to maintain, human animals are omnivores. Some, probably most, faddists make their children follow their beliefs, and a great many GPs have cause to worry about this. Look at it rationally: a cat or dog will not follow a vegetarian diet. While it is wrong to feed, as many farmers did, herbivores such as cattle with meat products, it is just as idiotic to insist on a lack of the necessary foods among meat-eating animals such as humans.

That being said, it is certainly true that too many people in the developed world eat far too much meat and ingest too little fruit and vegetables. There is even a newish diet, and as silly a one as that of vegans, called the Atkins diet, in which an intensive diet of red meat and dairy produce is all that is permitted. It is true that this can produce a slimmer figure, but at a dreadful cost to the liver and other bodily organs. In short, common sense should prevail. Common sense, when it comes to diet is, however, not all that common at all.

Venison

It is bizarre that in my country of origin, Scotland, this meat of the deer is so seldom seen, let alone eaten, for Scotland has such a sizeable deer population that they have now actually become a pest, threatening forestry, plants and wildlife. Thus deer have to be heavily culled in the Highlands, not least for their own good, as too large a deer population leads to their starvation. (There are roughly 40,000 wild red deer alone culled each year in Scotland.) The vast bulk of venison meat is exported abroad, especially to Germany, though both France and Italy are considerable consumers of Scottish venison.

The three varieties of deer are red deer (the largest), fallow deer (of medium weight) and roe deer (the smallest). The extraordinary absence of venison from British menus is strange in that Scotland in particular has a large number of recipes for the meat. In Margaret Fraser's *Highland Cookery* (1930), for instance, out of ninety recipes there are sixty-six on cooking deer meat, from antlers to feet. There is even one that utilizes the velvet from the antlers. I suspect that there are those who, when they think of deer, imagine either little Bambi or the Monarch of the Glen.

Vermouth

This is a classic Italian *apéritif*, the most famous brands being Cinzano and Martini. It is flavoured with herbs and spices and also, in its original form, with wormwood. It can be used in cookery and makes an effective and rather odd sauce (see **veal**).

Victoria sandwich

Nothing to do with the Earl of Sandwich's creation, this is a sponge mixture usually filled with jam or cream and used to be the standard test for schoolgirls in their exams in what was then called Domestic Science. A very distinguished lady advocate and QC once told me that the only time she ever cried, at least in public, at her expensive private school was when her Victoria sandwich cake collapsed at her test in the third year. But that was back in the days when girls were taught cookery. Today's girls are weeping because they can't cook at all.

Vienna steak

This was once very popular in such places as the Lyons Corner Houses and other mass outlets. It is a hamburger of sorts, mixed with tomato purée and onions, and coated in bread-crumbs. (The French term *à la viennoise* refers to veal steaks which are egg-and-crumbed: **wiener schnitzel**, in fact.) Why Vienna steak has almost disappeared from Britain is un-known. But a Vienna sausage (or *wiener*) is a common North American term for a frankfurter (see **frankfurters**).

Viennese coffee

In Vienna, one of the most romantic cities in the world, there are innumerable coffee houses, which in fact serve food and alcohol as well as this special coffee, made of ground arabica coffee beans and dried figs. I first met this beverage in a won-derfully faded splendour called the Café Sperl in Wallner Gasse in the old city. The aged waiter – this was a quarter of a century ago – told me that when the Germans announced the *Anschluss* and annexed Austria, the then owner refused to serve German army officers and was arrested and never seen again. 'The Nazis didn't know how to drink coffee,' he said contemptuously, 'they put the sugar *in* it.' This was when I discovered that real Austrians put a lozenge of sugar loaf in their mouth and drink the coffee through it. Viennese coffee is often accompanied by slices of rich gateaux or little iced cakes.

Vin ordinaire

Literally 'ordinary wine', this is non-vintage red or white wine that you will find in carafes in little French restaurants of the cheaper kind. Though you can encounter some very poor wines, generally it is not to be sniffed at. As a near illiterate about wine, I may say that I rather enjoy the coarser wines of out-of-the-way French cafés and *estaminets*.

Vindaloo
There was a time back in the 1960s and '70s when young men were intrepid enough to order this curry, the hotter the better, as a show of rather ludicrous culinary *machismo*, as it was and is made with lots of chillies (see **chilli**). In fact a vindaloo is not neccessarily terribly hot at all and refers to a curry made with alcohol. (The word is a combination of the word *vin* meaning 'wine' and *aloo*, the Hindi word for 'potatoes'.)

The dish is of Goan and Sri Lankan origins and derived from the tastes of the quite large Portuguese merchant community who used spirits in their curries. Tamils, who have no religious objection to alcohol, or indeed **pork**, use whisky, and you can find both ingredients, forbidden to Muslims, in the pork *padre* curries of what was the former Ceylon.

Vinegar
The extraordinary affinity with fish and chips has made this acetic acid fermented from wine (and there are vinegars also fermented from malt and cider and other substances) a necessary member of any larder. In recent years some speciality vinegars have become fashionable, such as raspberry and balsamic, and other wine vinegars. The most common vinegars are the industrially produced spirit vinegar, and ones made from malt. Both are used extensively for pickling. But see **balsamic vinegar**.

Vitamins
A Dr Casimir Funk first identified the various categories of vitamins early in the twentieth century. He called them 'vital

amines' and showed that they were indeed vital to good health. One of the reasons why junk food is so harmful is that much of it has destroyed the vitamins necessary especially to children and young people.

In some cultures the diet precludes fundamental vitamins. The most common deficiency is that of vitamin C, found in, for instance, citrus fruits – hence the use of limes on board ships from the eighteenth century onwards to prevent scurvy. Many Asian people who emigrated to dreich British shores discovered that the lack of sunshine meant that their traditional diet did not provide them with sufficient vitamin D, and the bone disease rickets, long since banished from the British populace, was noted among the immigrant Asian community. This has been much alleviated by vitamin supplements. When I was a teacher in a school with a large number of Asian pupils, the local authority gave such children free vitamin supplements, just as they had done back in the 1940s and '50s with the free distribution of cod liver oil and orange juice.

It would be wise for every parent to find out about vitamins and to seek advice from their GP, any pharmacist or a local health food store. Incidentally, women who take the contraceptive pill are at considerable risk of vitamin deficiencies, as are women (especially young girls) during their menstrual period. To add another grim warning, the fad of **vegetarianism** has led to vitamin deficiencies which can be solved by supplements. Vegetarians should consult medical sources and act on the advice given.

Vitello tonnato

A strange and unique Italian summer dish much loved especially in the north of that country, this comprises slices of roast veal (though some cooks boil the veal), served cold in a sauce of tuna fish and anchovies, olive oil and capers, which is pounded as for a sort of mayonnaise. I ordered this in a Milan *ristorante* on my first fledgling trip to Italy because I recognized the word *vitello* and expected the usual veal escalope. Instead I got this unusual dish. Cold. It was a revelation, and I loved it immediately. Though a chilled white wine is very good to wash the repast down, so is – and I have already revealed that I do not like beer very much – a bottle of chilled lager.

Vodka

This spirit made from grain, or more usually, potatoes, is much favoured by women and young people as it is, as far as I can see, virtually tasteless. Thus the mixer – orange juice and Coca-Cola are especially popular – will have the flavour and the vodka the alcoholic kick. There are exceptions to this: such expensive and hard-to-come-by vodkas as the famed Moskovskaya and Stolichnaya brands are very good, especially with **caviar**.

Wafers

Thin unsweetened biscuits, used often for holding ice cream, in shapes such as fans or cones (also known as cornets). There is a luxurious version of these ice cream wafers which utilizes a light nougat covered in chocolate and was held, in my childhood, to be the height of luxury in the ice cream stakes. Wafer biscuits are also often covered in chocolate and sometimes have a toffee or cream filling.

But wafers also have a very important religious significance in that very thin unleavened rounds of the biscuit are used in the Eucharist to signify the body of Christ. Those who use unleavened bread for this purpose are called *azymites*, after the Greek word *azymous*, meaning 'unleavened, unfermented bread'. In the Roman Catholic Church the wafer actually becomes the body of Christ and the process is known as transubstantiation, as indeed does the wine become the blood of Christ. Though this is viewed with disbelief by non-Catholics, the doctrine is solemnly held by devout Catholics. In other Christian organizations the ceremony is regarded as symbolic. See **cannibalism**.

Waiters

Waiters in the UK are, unlike many of their counterparts in the mainland of Europe and even in the USA, largely underpaid, though a head waiter in a smart restaurant or a top hotel can earn a very large income indeed. The result is a culture of sullen and undertrained waiters and waitresses in many restaurants, especially if they are British-born. Waiting at table is seen by many Britons as a menial, and not a professional, job, while trained waiters elsewhere see it as a career. (The same holds true for bar staff in the UK.)

It is even worse for waitresses. (Whoever heard of a Head Waitress?) These women are usually grossly underpaid, and many of them are part time, often penniless young students. If the hospitality industry is to maximize its potential, it will have to increase the wages, and professional skills, of its workers. That being said, a good waiter in a restaurant with a good chef is a joy to watch and an extremely useful guide to your eating-out experience. And in the 1950s it was the eccentric billionaire Nubar Gulbenkian who said that the best dinner party was for two: 'myself – and a damn good head waiter'. In this he was not, well, alone. Some twenty centuries before Mr Gulbenkian's aphorism, the Roman general and epicure Lucullus, famed for his banquets, was asked by a friend who his dinner guests that night were to be. He replied: 'Lucullus will sup tonight with Lucullus' (see **Lucullan**).

Walnut

The crinkly inside kernel of the stone of the fruit of the walnut tree possesses a unique and very nutty taste and is used widely in cookery. It also produces an expensive oil which is highly prized by some. I may say I don't like walnuts myself. Nor do I enjoy the famous Waldorf salad, in which chopped walnuts are joined by chopped celery, apples and mayonnaise, though it is prominent in many American restaurants.

Wartime food

There is a legend that the diet of the years of the Second World War and the Austerity years following them produced a very healthy diet. This is not, in fact, exactly true. It was certainly healthier for the working-class family than the diet of the years preceding the conflict, but that would not be difficult: the pre-war eating habits of the working-class household were poor, and indeed in the Depression years the diet of the urban working class had descended to the levels of that of the Victorian slum-dweller, consisting of bread and margarine or dripping, jam, occasionally fried fish, and tea.

Much had improved by the outbreak of war in 1939, but the government was aware of the difficulties that had occurred during the Great War and set in process under the leadership of the new Minister of Food, Lord Woolton (see **Woolton pie**), and his adviser the biochemist Sir John Drummond, what was to become a national rationing programme for food. (Actually they had first been informed of what would constitute a healthy diet by the remarkable Scottish dietician Sir John Boyd Orr, who had earlier proved the efficacy of free school milk. Boyd Orr, famous throughout the entire world for his pioneering work, was held in distrust by the Establishment because of his left-wing radicalism.)

Food rationing did not really come into its own until mid-1940, but at its zenith in 1943 the diet was Spartan indeed: 1lb of meat was permitted to every adult per week, 2oz of butter, 3oz of cheese, one egg (which gave rise to dried egg being imported from the USA) and so on. There were points for luxury tinned foods such as fruits or sardines. Game and fish were unrationed but difficult to come by.

Bread was unrationed during the war, though after the war the introduction of bread rationing led to a public outcry that perhaps contributed to the defeat of the Labour government in 1951. (There seems to have been a puritanical ideology on the part of Labour on the question of rationing. We now know that there was little necessity for a strict interpretation of this policy and, in fact, war-torn mainland Europe amidst its ruins was eating considerably better than its British victor.)

Rationing was regarded by many as the greatest hardship of the war, and food became an obsession. Through the 'Dig For Victory' campaign, in which allotments, back gardens and public parks grew vegetables, there were adequate supplies of the more common vegetables (a *Punch* cartoon shows an upper-class lady in her garden with a caption that runs: 'I shall celebrate VE-Day by switching over to asparagus').

The diet was extremely monotonous, however, and attempts to import unfamiliar foods such as the infamous canned barracuda fish known as **snoek** were unsuccessful. Rationing itself was not as effective as it was said to be, although modern social historians have continued to repeat the propaganda of its efficacy. Take a look at the wartime William stories by Richmal Crompton and you will learn how far superior the diet of the better-off and the more rural population was. Country people, in particular, were deeply non-egalitarian: they hid much of their produce, bartered among themselves and, with access to game and poultry products unavailable to the mass of their fellow Britons, often had groaning tables of luxuries forgotten, even unknown, by town- and city-dwellers. The well-off could avail themselves of the black market. The myth of a Britain at war as an undivided people was a popular one, but it was a myth at that.

Yet during the war most Britons swallowed the myth, and the urban population was largely unaware of the discrepancies between the diets of the differing social groups. Much of this was due to the not inconsiderable talents of many of those at the Ministry of Food. The remarkable Marguerite Patten produced many ingenious recipes. George Orwell's first wife, Eileen, was an effective propagandist, especially in her scripts for the BBC *Home Front* programme, much assisted by the then popular novelist Lettice Cooper (whose *The New House* had been a bestseller in the late 1930s) and the effeminate Godfrey Winn.

Restaurants were badly hit because of the ruling that no more than 5 shillings could be spent per head on a meal, though some restaurants did manage, by fair means or foul, to present reasonably good food and wine. Ironically some of the finest chefs and restaurateurs were lost when the *Arandora Star*, the ship carrying foreign non-national internees, was torpedoed in the Atlantic on its way to Canada.

After the war there was an even greater shortage of food, and it could be said that British cookery has never really recovered from the years of rationing. (The situation was not helped by legislation limiting the amount of money that could be taken out of the country by British travellers: as late as the mid 1960s it was illegal for a British citizen to go abroad with more than £50, an injunction easily flouted by the rich but not by the average Brit.)

I remember sweet rations well myself, because as a small boy I did not enjoy sweets and was thus a highly prized family member. The truth is that if cooking skills had diminished after the Great War, they were almost lost after the second conflict. Sixty years on, despite the plethora of TV cookery programmes, household cookery is still pretty dire. But see **K rations**.

Water

Sure, I know that the human body is made up mainly of water; I just find it hard to believe. It is, of course, true all the same, as is the fact that almost all life forms require water as an essential nutrient.

Paradoxically, you might think, the communities that suffer from the greatest problem of finding drinkable water are not those of desert lands such as the northern Sahara, but those in areas in which the water is contaminated, for contaminated water is the greatest source of such catastrophic diseases as cholera or typhoid.

In fact water contamination was so widespread in the eighteenth and early nineteenth centuries that both these diseases, as well as many others, were rife in cities. The development of proper water supplies and sewerage systems was not due to philanthropy on the part of the ruling classes: the fact was that even the rich suffered along with the poor. Thus the growth of water and sewerage systems in the mid-nineteenth century.

Though water is necessary for life, many doctors will tell you that most people in today's Britain do not ingest enough liquids each day. At least 2 litres of liquids should be consumed daily.

For centuries, owing to water contamination, people took their liquids in the form of beer or wine. When readers are astonished that little children such as, for instance, David Copperfield in Dickens's novel, drank beer, they should know that this was the only safe way to obtain a liquid intake.

In my own native Glasgow the drinking water, which is taken from the lovely Loch Katrine, 60 miles from the city, is very soft and there really is no need to purchase the now ubiquitous bottled waters. Mind you, many newcomers to the west of Scotland find the water too soft, and southern English people complain that it doesn't make a good cup of tea. My Italian friend Aurelio Santonin has also claimed that it doesn't make for as good coffee as he can find in his country of origin. 'The water's too thin', he says. Nonetheless he drinks his Scottish water straight from the tap.

Watermelon

There was a 1970 movie titled *The Watermelon Man* in which Afro-American actor Godfrey Cambridge played the part of a white bigot who wakes up one morning to find himself turned into a negro. It was intended as a racially challenging comedy. Viewed in retrospect, it is astonishingly clichéd, and indeed racist in its own liberal way.

But the point is the title, for watermelons were held to be a fruit especially enjoyed by blacks in the south of the USA, who as has been noted above, have tended to possess a more varied, more imaginative and healthier cuisine than their poor white coevals, and watermelon is indeed often found in black community diets.

It is the largest kind of melon and does not have as much flavour or fragrance as its sisters, but its very high water content means that, when served chilled, it is one of the most refreshing fruits.

Waterzooi

As noted in the item on **carbonnade**, Belgian food is not, as some people imagine, boring at all, and this, the Belgian national dish, is stupendous and very showy when served in the great restaurants of the Grande Place in Brussels. A whole chicken is poached in white wine, and a sauce is made of a liaison of cream and egg yolks, which make a kind of cream soup. It is a spectacular dish, tricky to make until you have mastered it. It is served in soup plates, generally accompanied by boiled and parsleyed potatoes.

I had, of course, read about this speciality but I first met it in a Brussels restaurant when I visited my friend, the then European correspondent of a newspaper for which I worked, the veteran journalist Murray Ritchie. Murray was and is a noted curry addict, but he had taken to the remarkable array of world cuisines that Brussels can boast and dragged me out to savour the waterzooi: the *maître d'* carved it at the table with chafing dishes all around us. When the final serving was made, the other customers all applauded. The dish is, like many table displays such as the **flambé**, a sort of culinary showbiz.

Wedding cake

My friend John's late father, Tommy Nicholas, was a master baker with a national bakery company. He specialized in custom-made wedding cakes. The rich, fruit-laden cake (similar to that used for **Christmas cake**, though that mixture is more heavily laced with alcohol, spices, and treacle) is covered with **marzipan** and, over that, frosted icing. There are usually three or more tiers, supported by pillars. It is highly decorated. In Tommy's hands the wedding cake was truly a work of art, his tastes tending towards the Rococo.

Mr Nicholas will always be remembered for his ridiculous generosity: he made the wedding cakes for the sons and daughters of family and friends and lavished enough care and love on his art to fuel a successful marriage for ever.

Welsh rarebit

In the past this savoury was an extremely popular item in many restaurants, especially in the difficult days of post-war shortages and financial restraint. It is also sometimes known as Welsh rabbit. I can discern nothing Welsh about it. Slices of bread are coated in a mixture of grated cheese (a strong **cheddar** is common), milk, egg yolk and beer. Black pepper is added and sometimes paprika or a little cayenne pepper. The coated bread is then lightly toasted under the grill.

It was and is cheap and cheerful, savoury and filling, and I invariably end up making rarebits for my friends when I take them back to my residence after a long hard night down the pub.

Wensleydale

Though Britain has a great many fine cheeses (see **cheddar**), I mention this flaky, pale, parchment-coloured cheese from north Yorkshire because, with its salty and lightly tangy flavour (with a surprising honey aftertaste), it was once, and should still be, a regular accompaniment to apple pie.

Whale

You will, unwittingly, have tasted at least one of the products of this, the largest mammal on earth: its fat (blubber) is a major ingredient of most lipsticks. Many of you will also have tins of whale meat in your larder: it is commonly used for dog food. And you will have consumed the oil as well, because it is widely used in food manufacture, especially in prepared convenience foods.

But whale is enjoyed in Scandinavian countries and by the inhabitants of the Arctic areas. It was consumed by some Brits during the last war, and in medieval times salted whale meat called *craspois* was imported from France for consumption during Lent and meatless fast days.

Wheat

The history of wheat cultivation stretches back into prehistory and is largely confined to the West. China, for instance, did not see wheat until much later than did the European continent, America not at all until it was introduced by the Spanish *conquistadors* and their followers. Throughout the ancient world it possessed enormous symbolic powers. To this day the very image of a wheatsheaf signifies health (witness the perennial **Ovaltine** advertisement, though the sheaves of corn illustrated are actually of **barley**), fertility, harvest time and wealth.

Though this grain from what were once wild grasses has many varieties, and is cultivated throughout the world, there are two basic important varieties: hard, sometimes known as 'winter wheat', usually called durum, and used mainly for the manufacture of **pasta**; and soft, sown much earlier and used for bread, biscuits and other bakery foods. Ninety per cent of wheat grown is of the soft variety.

Whelk

As a child I used to see people in a famous Glasgow street market called The Barras (barrows) consuming these tiny carnivorous sea snails which they bought in huge brown paper bags. The customers were issued with a small steel pin that could winkle the meat from the shell. They looked like snotters. (This was in marked contrast to the bags of roast nuts from the Hot Chestnut Man. The aroma of the hot chestnuts permeated this massive site of stalls and their merchandise. I haven't seen roast chestnuts on sale in Britain in nearly fifty years, more's the pity.)

Whisky

This grain spirit can be made from barley, maize, rye or wheat. When Scottish and Irish immigrants first arrived in North America, they took with them their taste for their native spirit called, in the Gaelic tongue, *uisge beatha*: literally 'the water of life'. They also took their distilling skills. What they didn't have was barley, and they were therefore forced to utilize the American grains native to the continent. Thus in Canada there emerged rye whiskey. There is a very old Canadian folk song that brings together the refrain 'Whiskey and Gin, Oh, Whiskey and Gin', which at first seems an odd combination. It once had a larger meaning. The Scots drank their whiskey, and the French-speaking Québecois preferred gin. Both Scots and French fraternized freely, unlike the snooty English settlers, and the song was directed against both. Today two of the largest distillery companies in the

world, Seagrams and Hiram Walker's, are Canadian companies, owning large numbers of Scotch whisky distilleries in
Scotland.

In the USA both rye and bourbon are distilled. Bourbon
was named after a small county in Kentucky which had itself
been named after an aristocratic French family of settlers
there. There were once over 2,000 flourishing distilleries in
Kentucky, but now there are only a handful, and none at all in
the county that gave its name to this famous American potation. In fact, Scotch whisky has become much more popular
since the great experiment of Prohibition.

Other countries have tried to make their own versions of
Scotch, especially Japan, where the well-known Suntory brand
sells reasonably well to the natives, though even there sales of
Scotch have long overtaken those of the Japanese product. The
Japanese have long attempted to emulate Scotch, even going
to the extent of importing millions of barrels of the precious
Caledonian product and blending so much malt whisky with
their own grain spirit that it should indeed have produced a
passable blended whisky. It didn't and doesn't.

The mysteries of Scotch have defeated everybody, though
I once was told by a chemist in the whisky industry that it
might be possible to create a malt whisky using industrial
chemical methods. 'It would cost a fortune to make, though,'
he said ruefully, 'and there would hardly be much point.'

The subject of the manufacture of Scotch whisky (and Irish
whiskey, which is distilled three times, as against the Scotch
two) is too complex to describe in detail here. Those wishing
to find out more can glean any amount of information from
the thousands of books in print on the liquid.

A few things about Scotch, however. A single malt whisky
is not mixed with grain spirit, as is the case with blends. Malts
vary throughout Scotland, depending on many factors, such
as whether the kilns are coal- or peat-fired, what barleys are

used, the location of the distillery, the casks in which the spirit is stored, and the length of time it is held in bond. On this last point it must be noted that though some whiskies are casked for a great many years, this does not, as erroneously thought by many whisky connoisseurs, mean they are necessarily superior to those of a lesser age. I would maintain, for instance, as would a great many other writers and observers of Scotch, that more often than not a good fifteen-year-old malt is usually more to my taste than the same malt whisky aged for twenty-five years.

Then there is the question of the water supply source. For instance, there is the phenomenon of the legendary whiskies of the Scottish island of Islay (pronounced *ayelah*). There are seven distilleries on this tiny island, each with its own distinct character. The iodine-flavoured Laphraoig (pronounced *laf-froig*) uses the same water as the neighbouring distillery a few hundred yards away at Lagavulin. Its whisky also tastes strongly of iodine (from the seaweed of the nearby shores), yet there is no questioning the individual taste and character of each. Lagavulin distillery is at a slightly higher altitude, and the water does not go through as dense rock as at Laphraoig.

There is, in fact, no substitute for Scotch whisky. It is an intensely romantic industry, always impervious to the machinations of accountants and the like who infest the business and can never quite grasp that whisky is unique and beyond normal business methods. The following is going to sound ridiculous and as if I have just seen the fairies at the bottom of the garden. A considerable factor in the character of Scotch is, and all distillers will tell you this too, the air. For some reason this air, which affects the peat, the barley, the water, the landscape and the people who make it, can only be found in Scotland.

On the drinking of Scotch whisky, though: as noted before, the English habit of having a whisky and soda derives from the fact that English water is too hard to mix with their tipple. There was a fashion for whisky and Coca-Cola in the 1960s, much popularized by the emergent pop groups of that period. The now almost universal practice, taken from Americans, of putting ice cubes into even the most august of single malts is to be regarded with the utmost disdain. The subtleties of this most complicated of all the world's spirits are utterly lost. Today when I walk into virtually any bar I have to order my whisky with the curt words 'no ice'.

White bread

Bread using only white flour. There was, and still is, much snobbery concerning white bread, which is often made with over-refined flours. The snobbery comes from some middle-class people who associate white bread with the lower classes (though this is a reversal from what was held in previous years) and from some not very well-educated dieticians who underestimate the quality of good white bread.

Though not as nutritious as wholemeal flour, bread made with a good strong white flour is still good for you and, if made in the traditional manner, without too great a quick-yeast content (see **bread**), is very flavoursome. The modern practice of restaurateurs having their own bread baked on the premises has introduced a new market made up of customers who now know what bread can really taste like.

White pudding

There is, of course, a white pudding (in France called *boudin blanc*; see **black pudding**) which consists of finely minced white meat such as pork, veal or chicken and often oat or barley flours, spiced and peppered. It is rather bland.

But a speciality in north-east England, Northern Ireland and especially Scotland, where it is popular as a component of a fried breakfast, is a meatless white pudding, known usually as 'fruit pudding'. This consists of flour, spices and suet, and includes sultanas and raisins. It is sweet and fries wonderfully. I recommend it with bacon and eggs.

Whitebait

I first ate these fry of the herring family – the young of them, that is, and literally small fry – when I was invited to have lunch with the then journalist and now distinguished historian Michael (what else?) Fry. This was over a quarter of a century ago and we dined in what was then the best, and certainly the most expensive, restaurant in Glasgow, the Malmaison, which was situated in what had been a flagship for British Railways hotels, the Central Hotel. Michael is both one of the most charming of men when he wants to be, and one of the rudest. He even looks a little like Evelyn Waugh.

Michael ordered whitebait as a starter for us both. It was only then that I realized you ate the little fishes whole – bones, intestines and all. This did not put me off, and there are a number of other small fish in which nobody would question this. The small brislings that most Britons erroneously refer to as sardines (see **sardine**) come to mind.

Whiting

Once rather despised and said by some to be only for the cat (surely a very regal sort of cat), this delicate member of the **cod** family has been rediscovered by many fish restaurants, especially as it is relatively inexpensive. Whiting was thought to be a poor man's fish, though it was common enough. In my childhood, though, there were a great many fish you never saw on a fishmonger's slab and a great deal of caught fish were simply dumped, owing to the public's unfamiliarity with them.

There was indeed a time when many species of fish were unfashionable and held in contempt, at least in Britain. Indeed even today, despite the large variety of fish caught by the UK fishing fleet, there is still a reluctance to try out unfamiliar fish in Britain. A lot of people don't know what they're missing.

Wiener schnitzel

This is a speciality of Viennese cookery, a flattened-out slice of veal coated in egg and breadcrumbs and then lightly fried in butter. Probably Italian in origin (it is on almost all menus in Milan restaurants, where it is known as *scallope milanese*), it was brought to the Austrian court by the Hungarians, and the Turks of the Ottoman Empire are likely to have introduced it into Austria itself.

A variant, *schnitzel Holstein*, is the same dish topped with an egg, usually fried, though some, including myself, prefer the egg poached. In Austria a couple of little anchovies are laid across the egg, though most British cooks leave these out. Eaten with a salad or a few sauté potatoes, it makes a lovely dish.

Wild duck

Smaller than the domestic duck, and with a saltier taste, it is splendid when roasted, though is not as suitable for such dishes as the classic *caneton à l'orange*. Wild duck should be hung for at least two days. Once, when I ordered a wild duck for lunch in a rather chic Fifeshire restaurant, my god-daughter Clare, then aged ten, was distressed about my eating such a dear little bird, and I told her that wild ducks had a lovely life 'flyin' about and travellin' and seein' the world with all their pals 'not like those ducks you feed in the pond in the park'. She was satisfied with this until her father told her that we eat the ducks in the pond as well.

Wild rice

This is in fact not rice at all but an aquatic oat (*zizania aquatica*) that grows in North America in marshlands and riverbanks (and in the area of the Great Lakes). It is difficult to cultivate and grows best in the wild. The Iroquois called it *tuskaro*, and the Objibwa Native Americans named it *manomin*: both peoples lived in areas in which wild rice was widely grown, and it was a staple for them as it could grow where maize could not.

The stalks can rise to a height of 3 metres and end in a panicle of several small ears, which makes them look like tall branched candlesticks. Dark brown in colour when harvested, the rice turns a glorious purple when cooked. It is very expensive and is often combined with other, cheaper, rices. The American rite of the Thanksgiving dinner often has this delicious rice as a stuffing for **turkey**.

Wine

Rather to my gastronomic distress, I have never learned really to enjoy wine. I do have the occasional glass with a meal, but all who know about wine tell me that it is essential to good eating. What I do know is that it is often essential to good cooking.

There are those daft enough to be teetotal who even refuse to use alcohol in cooking. Alcohol in cookery is in fact 'burned' away and only the taste remains (though, like many cooks, I invariably add a little 'raw' wine at the very end of the cooking process in such dishes as daubes and Burgundian specialities such as **boeuf bourguignon** and **coq au vin**). Many teetotallers who are so through some irrational – and ignorant – religious belief that God punishes drinkers, think that man's fall in the garden of Eden was a result of imbibing wine. Actually the first biblical drunkard was Noah, whom God thought the very man to save all living creatures from the Flood. This tale is almost exactly replicated in the Babylonian text of the Gilgamesh epic, in which the captain of the Ark is Umapashtim. This Babylonian Noah (the Greek Noah was Deucalion, another great drinker of wine) gave the workmen who built his ark beer and wine 'as if it was river water' and then took them on board to save them from the Great Deluge, unlike Noah, who only took his own family. And to establish further the nonsense of faith-built total abstinence we can quote no less than Martin Luther: 'He who loves not women, wine, and song/Remains a fool his whole life long'.

These may be tales and legends, but the history of wine is so inextricably bound with legend that, for a start, while almost every culture claims to have been the first to invent wine, nobody knows where it arose. What is true is that the Greeks immortalized wine by having a special god, Dionysus, as its patron.

The wine of the Ancient Greeks was so sweet and thick that to take it neat would be rather like drinking jam; thus it was always mixed with water. Just when and where wines became fine wines and vintages were noted is unknown as well, but European gastronomy cannot do without wine. Though wine-drinking has declined on the continent of Europe – even, it is said, in France, where it is regarded as a sacrament even without religion – consumption has greatly increased in Britain. And it was Galileo who described wine as 'sunlight held in water', which is rather nice really.

Wishbone

Two bones that join at the collarbone of a fowl. Traditionally a girl and her swain will, on completion of eating the bird, take the bone with their little fingers, make a wish and pull it apart. Whoever gets the bone with the collar on it will find that their wish will come true. My advice to the swain is to ensure the girl gets the larger bone: even the most romantic of maidens rather likes her own way in small things.

Wood pigeon

Until recently British diners would never have dreamed of ordering pigeon, as they associated it with the pathetic little birds who strut around our city squares fouling the streets. Yet it was once a major element of rural diets, as the bird can be shot all year with impunity.

In Italy, however, even the smallest and most exotic birds are eaten, and in the Umbrian region, especially around Perugia, elaborate pigeon recipes abound. I had a wonderful stuffed roast pigeon, with a sauce made from red wine, garlic, sage and juniper berries, in a restaurant in a village a quarter of an hour's drive from Perugia itself. I cannot recall the name of the restaurant but remember that it was owned by a famous winemaker, Giorgio Lungarotti.

This was nearly twenty years ago, and on my return home I asked my friend the local Italian restaurateur Daniele Santini if he could give me something similar. His eyes glazed over at the memory of such dishes and said, 'but this is Scotland. Where can I get these pigeons?' That was in his old *ristorante*. Recently I ate in his new one, the Trattoria Gia in Glasgow's city centre. I had wood pigeon.

Woodruff

This old-fashioned herb was once used as an aromatic in pomanders and, in sachets, for use in lining drawers and wardrobes, rather as lavender once was. When partially dried, it exudes a lovely scent of new-mown hay. Today its use is mainly as a flavouring for wines, liqueurs and some German beers. The tree, which grows mainly in woodland, possesses a beautiful white blossom.

Woolton pie

So called because it was much promoted during the rationing days of the Second World War, when Lord Woolton was

Minister of Food, this was a pie in which the filling was meatless and consisted of mixed vegetables covered with a cheese pastry lid. It was regarded by the British public with horror.

Paradoxically such vegetable pies and tarts are now very fashionable. In fact, some smart restaurants proffer expensive flans for which the recipe is almost exactly that of this once despised item.

Worcestershire sauce

Pronounced 'wooster-shire', with the first two syllables as in P.G. Wodehouse's masterpiece of a character, Bertie Wooster (said to have been based on George Grossmith, a popular musical comedy star of the early twentieth century who also lived in the English county that gives this item its name), this is a thinnish proprietary brown sauce or condiment made from vinegar, molasses, tamarinds, anchovies, sugar, salt, shallots, garlic and spices. It is used widely in sauces and is essential with tomato juice, especially in a Bloody Mary. Its major manufacturer, by far, is the company Lea and Perrins – so much so that the firm's brand name has almost become a generic term for their product.

Xerophagy
This is the eating of dried foods, but is also used for the fasting process, whether voluntary or not, of a diet of bread and water, once much practised in prisons and monasteries. It is, in fact, a sustainable diet and the forced feeding of suffragettes was largely unnecessary and in essence punitive, for Mrs Pankhurst had permitted such a food regimen as part of their hunger strikes. The word itself derives from the Greek *xero* ('dry') and *phagein* ('to eat').

Xylitol
This fairly recent sugar substitute is used mainly in the UK.

Y

Yam

I first heard of this tuber, native to Africa, where there are hundreds of species, in R.M. Ballantyne's *Martin Rattler* when I was a child. (Ballantyne also wrote *Coral Island*. I doubt if any child in the last forty years has ever read either. Such adventure stories as Captain Maryatt's *Mr Midshipman Easy* or *Roderick Random* have also long since disappeared from bookshelves. True, the prose style would be unbelievably turgid to the modern boy or girl – the last time I attempted them, I found them so myself – but my generation learned a great many things about the world that, despite the internet, are no longer so easily vouchsafed to today's children.)

But to yams. They are ubiquitous in west African cookery, and in the south of that continent, and also now in Caribbean cookery. Although not of the same botanical genus as the **potato**, they are treated in much the same way. Though yams themselves are rather bland in flavour, they readily absorb the flavours of other ingredients and thus make a very useful filler in meat, poultry, vegetable and fish dishes.

Yang-hoe

A Korean version of steak tartare, which is seen throughout
other East Asian countries under many different names. In
yang-hoe the raw minced beef is usually mixed with sesame
oil, sesame seeds, ginger, garlic and sugar. It is topped with an
egg yolk and served with slivers of fresh peeled pears.

Yaout, yahourti

A Russian and Balkan name for **yoghurt**. In Greece the term
is *yiaorti*. In Egypt, the Sudan and Iraq yoghurt is known as
zabady.

Yeast

A living organism which reproduces itself in warm conditions
or with liquids: the natural enzymes convert it into alcohol
and carbon dioxide. In the case of baked goods the alcohol is
expelled and the carbon dioxide expands, causing the dough
to rise. It is prohibited for religious ceremonies at certain
points of the Jewish calendar and also in some Christian rites.

Let me put the record straight here concerning yeast. There
are some who believe that ingesting food that contains this
can cause infections such as the vaginal disorder thrush, a
serious and painful condition that can even be fatal. (There is
also a mouth and throat infection known by this name, often
seen in children. It has no relationship with the above condition.) The fact is that there are two different types of yeast.
The food yeast is physiological and causes no harm; the
other – the body one – is pathological and creates an immune
deficiency which can be very dangerous if untreated.

Yoghurt

I find this milk product so boring that I am almost loath
to write about it. I refer, of course, to those little tubs of
(usually) flavoured yoghurts, often with added fruits such as

raspberries of which children and women consume so much. In Britain it was not always so. It was in the 1960s that it became fashionable in the middle-class diet, and in the 1970s that it became ubiquitous for weans and wimmin of all social classes.

Considering that yoghurt has been made for centuries, it was fairly late on that the culture that produces this milk product was identified in the early twentieth century, by Professor Metchnikoff at the Pasteur Institute in Paris. Notwithstanding all I have said above, the yoghurts of the Balkans (Bulgaria is for some reason the world's major yoghurt centre: the product is said to be responsible for the remarkable longevity of the Bulgarians) are indeed very good and are used throughout central European cookery and beyond.

Incidentally, if you are addicted to yoghurt it is very easy to make it yourself by heating a pint of milk and adding a small carton of natural yoghurt. Other than for its use in cooking I would not have it in the house myself.

Yule log

See **Swiss roll**. This sponge cake, usually permeated with cocoa powder, is covered in chocolate icing, combed with a fork to simulate bark, lightly dusted with caster sugar (for snow) and then decorated with a couple of holly sprigs and their berries. It is a Christmas dessert and has its origins in the French Christmas treat *bûche de Noël*. (The original log for Yule – the Scandinavian Christmas feast – was a block of wood cut from a felled tree and dragged ceremoniously to the house to be lit and to heat the house during the festivities.)

Z

Zabaglione

As a very young man in the early 1960s in the pre-Swinging London, I was taken by Martin O'Neil, whose advertising agency eventually became global, to a famous Italian restaurant called Sardelli's in the then unfashionable district of Islington to celebrate my appointment as his first illustrator. Martin was, despite being a raw Ulsterman, already a connoisseur of food, having been taught by his lovely wife, Oxford graduate Gwen. He ordered all the food, as I was then largely unfamiliar with Italian cuisine. At the conclusion of the meal he demanded this foamy concoction of egg yolks, sugar and **marsala** wine, and I was enchanted then – as I still am to this day.

A tale to tell here. In 1997 a Scottish procurator fiscal tried to prosecute a Glasgow Italian restaurateur because he had served this mildly alcoholic dessert to under-age children who were dining with their parents (who were Italian). When it was discovered that the Italian couple, both academics at Glasgow University, habitually gave their little girls wine and water with their meals, there was a move to have the children taken into care. It was only by the intervention of the Scottish consul for Italy, the Glasgow lawyer Osvaldo Franchi (my lawyer, in fact), and my own newspaper column expressing incredulity, that the charges were dropped.

Zakuska
This is the term for the Russian version of **hors d'œuvres**. The word gives rise to the Russian for the open table, *zakuski*.

Zambucca (also sambuca)
This sweet Italian liqueur spirit, flavoured from the unlikely herb dogweed, is served in small thick glasses. A coffee bean is put into the glass and the liqueur is then set alight. The first time I encountered this was at a celebration of my god-daughter Clare's twenty-first birthday. I had no knowledge of the flame, which in sunshine is virtually invisible. It nearly did for my moustache.

Zamia
An edible starch from the pith of the fruit of the west African palm tree. It makes a nutritious porridge.

Zampone
This speciality of the Emilia-Romagna region of Italy consists of a spiced sausage meat (oddly not unlike the Shetland *sassermaet*), which is inserted into a boned pig's trotter and boiled. It is served with **zabaglione** and fried potatoes. I know this because I had it in a *ristorante* in Rimini when I attended a festival of Federico Fellini's films (Fellini was a native of this beautiful city), and it was suggested by my host, Danila Donati, who had been Fellini's art director on his wonderful film *Amarcord* (the title means 'I remember'). I remember the film itself because it was not popular with critics at the time but has now become, rightly, something of a cult movie.

And this extraordinary dish should well be a wee cult in its own right.

Zanf
An Arab holder for coffee cups. Arabs drink their coffee in goblets, and as the coffee is served very hot you will be offered the ubiquitous coffee in these often elaborately designed holders, sometimes made of precious metals.

Zest
The outer peel of citrus fruits, usually oranges and lemons. (The inside pith is not used.) The zest is used in both savoury and dessert dishes. Usually grated, it lends itself to so many dishes that I cannot enumerate them. You will just have to read all of this book to discover what I mean. It is difficult to grate fresh fruit, though. I get minions such as girlfriends to do it for me. As if.

Zinc
A term for the small and basic bar that once abounded in working-class neighbourhoods in the industrial areas of France, so called because they invariably had a bar top made of the washable zinc. There are today few of them about (rather like old-fashioned pubs in Britain, or taverns in North America). They sold rough red wine, **marc**, cheap cognac and occasionally bread and sausage or such. Simenon had his Maigret forever dropping into zincs.

Zingara, à la
This is a French term for food cooked in gypsy style. Until the German Nazis took to the genocide of European gypsies the Romanies were regarded as rather romantic pests. The problem for the Nazis with gypsies was twofold: 1) they were nomadic and anarchic; 2) they were irretrievably Slavic and thus of

the *untermenschen*. What made it worse in the eyes of the appallingly ill-educated Heinrich Himmler was that for him legend had it that the Romanies are of Indian and Eastern origin. In this he was unwittingly correct: the Romany language is also known as *gadgery*, a corruption of the Indian language Gujerati. In France the gypsies called themselves *gutanes*, later *gitanes*, which became the name of a popular brand of French *caporal* cigarettes.

Let us start this again: French gypsies had an effect on French cuisine, bringing recipes from such diverse countries as Hungary, Poland, Czechoslovakia, Italy and Spain.

Zucchini

The reason why I have included this baby marrow in its Italian name is that there are a huge number of recipes involving *zucchini* (see also **courgette**) in Italian cuisine. Italians like them dipped in batter, then deep-fried. You will find these *zucchini fritti* in every trattoria in Italy, and often stewed courgettes, or courgettes in a sweet and sour sauce (*agrodolce*) or stuffed like green peppers. This vegetable is now much more common in the UK than it was back when Elizabeth David quite rightly bemoaned its absence from British shops, but we still do not make as much use of it as we should.

Zuppa inglese

The Italian version of **trifle**. It is made with a macaroon (**amaretti**) base and usually **marsala** wine, then richly decorated. When I visited the great fish and chip festival in the Tuscan town of Barga (from where the majority of Scots-Italians hail), the trifle was called – what else? – *zuppa scozzese*.

Zwiebelrostbraten

In Vienna you will find this on every Sunday lunch menu, from the smart restaurants in the Heldenplatz to the little cafés of the Prater. It is a dish of fried steak and onions, usually served with sauté potatoes and gherkins. In the gypsy restaurants of Vienna a Hungarian recipe is made with a sour cream sauce, highly laced with hot **paprika**.

Zymurgy
The name for the technological chemical science of the manufacture of wine, beer and spirits: anything to do with alcohol fermentation.

Zythum
This was the name for the beer brewed by the Ancient Egyptians, much commended by the Greek historian Diodorus. There is now a brand of Egyptian lager beer manufactured in Alexandria which goes by this name. Its label has the purported head of Alexander the Great.